I0112422

Experiencing Citizenship

Concepts and Models
for Service-Learning
in **Political Science**

Richard M. Battistoni and William E. Hudson, volume editors

Edward Zlotkowski, series editor

Routledge
Taylor & Francis Group
NEW YORK AND LONDON

Experiencing Citizenship: Concepts and Models for Service-Learning in Political Science

First published in 1997 by American Association for Higher Education and in 2006 by Stylus Publishing, LLC.

Published 2023 by Routledge
605 Third Avenue, New York, NY 10017
4 Park Square, Milton Park, Abingdon, Oxon OX14 4RN

Routledge is an imprint of the Taylor & Francis Group, an informa business

© 1997 by Taylor & Francis
© 2006 by Taylor & Francis

All rights reserved. No part of this book may be reprinted or reproduced or utilised in any form or by any electronic, mechanical, or other means, now known or hereafter invented, including photocopying and recording, or in any information storage or retrieval system, without permission in writing from the publishers.

Notice:
Product or corporate names may be trademarks or registered trademarks and are used only for identification and explanation without intent to infringe.

ISBN 13: 978-1-56377-007-4 (pbk)
ISBN 13: 978-1-00-344471-8 (ebk)

DOI: 10.4324/9781003444718

Contents

Part 3: The Discipline and Beyond

Appendix

Foreword

by Edward Zlotkowski

The following volume, *Experiencing Citizenship: Concepts and Models for Service-Learning in Political Science,* represents the second in a series of monographs on service-learning and the individual academic disciplines. Ever since the early 1990s, educators interested in reconnecting higher education not only with neighboring communities but also with the American tradition of education for service have recognized the critical importance of winning faculty support for this work. Faculty, however, tend to define themselves and their responsibilities largely in terms of the academic disciplines/interdisciplinary areas in which they have been trained. Hence, the logic of the present series.

The idea for this series first surfaced approximately three years ago at a meeting convened by Campus Compact to explore the feasibility of developing a national network of service-learning educators. At that meeting, it quickly became clear that some of those assembled saw the primary value of such a network in its ability to provide concrete resources to faculty working in or wishing to explore service-learning. Out of that meeting there developed, under the auspices of Campus Compact, a new national group of educators called the Invisible College, and it was within the Invisible College that the monograph project was first conceived. Indeed, a review of both the editors and contributors responsible for many of the volumes in this series would reveal significant representation by faculty associated with the Invisible College.

If Campus Compact helped supply the initial financial backing and impulse for the Invisible College and for this series, it was the American Association for Higher Education (AAHE) that made completion of the project feasible. Thanks to its reputation for innovative work, AAHE was not only able to obtain the funding needed to support the project up through actual publication, it was also able to assist in attracting many of the teacher-scholars who participated as writers and editors.

Three individuals in particular deserve to be singled out for their contributions. Sandra Enos, Campus Compact project director for Integrating Service and Academic Study, has been shepherd to the Invisible College project. John Wallace, professor of philosophy at the University of Minnesota, has been the driving force behind the creation of the Invisible College. Without his vision and faith in the possibility of such an undertaking, assembling the human resources needed for this series would have been very difficult. Third, AAHE's endorsement — and all that followed in its wake

— was due largely to AAHE vice president Lou Albert. Lou's enthusiasm for the monograph project and his determination to see it adequately supported have been critical to its success. It is to Sandra, John, and Lou that the monograph series as a whole must be dedicated.

Other individuals to whom the series owes a special note of thanks include Matt Bliss, who, as my graduate assistant, helped set up many of the communications mechanisms that got the project going, and Jeannette MacInnes, coordinator of student programs at the Bentley Service-Learning Project, who has served as a reliable source of both practical and moral support.

The Rationale Behind the Series

A few words should be said at this point about the makeup of both the general series and the individual volumes. Although political science may seem a natural choice of disciplines with which to link service-learning, being intrinsically concerned with questions of policy and civic participation, "natural fit" has not, in fact, been a determinant factor in deciding which disciplines/interdisciplinary areas the series should include. Far more important have been considerations related to the overall range of disciplines represented. Since experience has shown that there is probably no disciplinary area — from architecture to zoology — where service-learning cannot be fruitfully employed to strengthen students' abilities to become active learners as well as responsible citizens, a primary goal in putting the series together has been to demonstrate this fact. Thus, some rather natural choices for inclusion — disciplines such as anthropology, geography, and religious studies — have been passed over in favor of other, sometimes less obvious selections from the business disciplines and natural sciences as well as several important interdisciplinary areas. Should this first series of volumes prove useful and well received, we can then consider filling in the many gaps we have left this first time around.

If a concern for variety has helped shape the series as a whole, a concern for legitimacy has been central to the design of the individual volumes. To this end, each volume has been both written by and aimed primarily at academics working in a particular disciplinary/interdisciplinary area. Many individual volumes have, in fact, been produced with the encouragement and active support of relevant discipline-specific national societies. For this volume on political science, we owe thanks to Sheilah Mann, director for education and professional development at the American Political Science Association.

Furthermore, each volume has been designed to include its own appropriate theoretical, pedagogical, and bibliographical material. Especially with regard to theoretical and bibliographical material, this design has resulted in considerable variation both in quantity and in level of discourse. Thus, for example, a volume such as Accounting contains more introductory and less bibliographical material than does Composition — simply because there is less written on and less familiarity with service-learning in accounting. However, no volume is meant to provide an extended introduction to service-learning as a *generic concept.* For material of this nature, the reader is referred to such texts as Kendall's *Combining Service and Learning: A Resource Book for Community and Public Service* (NSIEE, 1990) and Jacoby's *Service-Learning in Higher Education* (Jossey-Bass, 1996).

I would like to conclude this foreword with a note of special thanks to Rick Battistoni and Bill Hudson, the coeditors of the Political Science monograph. Not only have they demonstrated great skill and resourcefulness in putting it together, they have also maintained throughout the entire process a welcome flexibility and patience. I would also like to acknowledge the generous assistance of Craig Rimmerman of Hobart and William Smith Colleges, who provided valuable feedback on the manuscript.

February 1997

Introduction

by Richard M. Battistoni and William E. Hudson

This monograph stands as one of several volumes in a series connecting service-learning to individual academic disciplines in higher education. When this monograph series was initiated in 1994, those of us designing it sought to provide resources for faculty members interested in service-learning in particular disciplines. We wanted to begin building a body of shared experience and knowledge that would link particular disciplines to the theory and practice of service-learning. The essays contained in this volume are the beginning of such a body of shared knowledge in political science.

Over the past decade, service-learning has assumed a position of prominence on many college campuses. Originally understood in the 1980s as student-initiated and extracurricular, service is being rapidly integrated into the curriculum and institutional fabric of a growing number of colleges and universities. Those of us who have been involved in the "service-learning movement" believe that we are at a point where our service-learning experiences may be outstripping our understanding of what constitutes good practice. These essays represent the efforts of a diverse group of political scientists who are developing that understanding through their practice and reflection. Borrowing from John Dewey, whose philosophy inspires many of the current practitioners in the field, the essays that follow subject "the discipline of experience . . . to the tests of intelligent development and direction" (1938: 90).

It is fitting for political scientists to be among the first discipline-based groups of educators to make such a contribution to the service-learning field. Since its founding at the turn of the century as a distinct academic discipline, under the auspices of the American Political Science Association (APSA), political science has maintained as one of its prime objectives the linkage between "real-world" experience and theoretical understanding. From the beginning, political scientists have argued that direct experience could enhance both our specific knowledge of governmental institutions and political behavior and our general understanding of what it means to be a citizen in a pluralistic, democratic society. We hope that the contributions contained in this volume will serve to reconnect political science to its original foundations, by taking us through the logistics of integrating service into particular political science classes and beyond, to a richer theoretical understanding of the stakes involved, both for our academic colleagues inside and outside the discipline and for our democracy.

The volume begins with four essays that develop a theoretical framework for understanding service-learning as a mode of civic education, as well as of teaching politics. Jean Bethke Elshtain's "The Decline of Democratic Faith" puts service-learning in the larger context of a growing distrust and isolation in American public life. Like Robert Putnam's oft-cited work on America's declining social capital, Elshtain's essay documents the "unraveling of the institutions of civil society" (see p. 12) and the concurrent deterioration in the conditions necessary for a vibrant democratic polity. From the perspective of a political theorist, Elshtain puts our efforts to do service-learning in political science into an appropriate socio-historical context.

In "Teaching/Theorizing/Practicing Democracy," Meta Mendel-Reyes draws upon her own experiences as a labor and community organizer to ground service-learning in a theory of participatory democracy, one that enhances both the content and the pedagogy of political science. She then applies this theory to courses she is currently teaching through the Democracy Project at Swarthmore College. Similarly, Harry Boyte and James Farr take lessons from the Civilian Conservation Corps and the civil rights movement to suggest a new way to view both service-learning and citizenship; namely, as "public work." Drawing from their own experiences in Project Public Life and the Center for Democracy and Citizenship at the University of Minnesota, Boyte and Farr develop a rich framework for understanding service-learning as citizen education: "education in and for public work" (see p. 47).

Finally, Part 1 concludes with an essay by Karen Zivi that raises serious questions for political scientists attempting to bring civic lessons into the service-learning classroom. From the perspective of a graduate teaching assistant attempting to adapt an existing introductory course as a service-learning section, Zivi brings us back from theories of democracy and citizenship to general issues of teaching and pedagogy in service-learning, as a precursor to the specific course narratives that appear in Part 2.

Part 2 provides the practical how-to guidance on introducing service-learning into a political science course. The authors in this section present case studies of their own experiences combining service and learning in their courses. They depict their experiences in different types of courses taught at a variety of institutions. We have included accounts from large research universities, such as the University of Michigan and Rutgers; liberal arts colleges, such as Hobart and William Smith; and a community college, Glendale Community College (CA). While few readers will be surprised that service-learning is being practiced in many types of institutions, some may find remarkable the many different kinds of courses represented in this section. Not only have our political science colleagues tried service-learning in courses usually associated with civic education, such as political theory,

American government, or public policy; this section also offers examples of the use of service-learning in courses such as research methods, women and politics, or Latin American politics where most of us would not necessarily expect a community service component. No matter what one teaches or where, we think this section will provide insights into how any political scientist might make use of service-learning.

While most practitioners in this section remain enthusiastic proponents of service-learning, one should not expect to find here only reports of unbridled success. All of these chapters provide balanced assessments of the service-learning experience. Some raise difficult and skeptical questions about the value or possibility of service-learning in some contexts. Cynthia Daniels, for example, discusses the difficult issues of confidentiality and long-term relationship building with community-based organizations in the context of courses in the area of gender and politics. Mona Field questions whether the demands on the lives of her Glendale Community College students can allow for the sometimes burdensome requirement of community service as a part of coursework. As a recipient of a federal Learn and Serve America grant, she has experienced further frustration from the grant's restrictions on political activity — precisely those sorts of experiences that might be most valuable for learning in her political science classes. Grant or other, institutional restrictions on the types of service activities may be a significant barrier to combining service and learning in many types of political science classes. Bob Trudeau found that, although he continues to believe that the rationale for including community service as a part of this Latin American politics class at Providence College was sound, getting students to make the not-so-obvious intellectual connections was a bigger challenge than he expected. His account emphasizes the need for in-class reflection explicitly connecting the service experience to the learning goals of the course. While this latter point seems understandable in Latin American politics, it is echoed even in the accounts where the service–civic education link might seem more obvious. Greg Markus finds making time for explicit reflection relating student service to course readings and lectures imperative in his American government class; one of us (Hudson) found the same in American public policy. Yet, such in-class reflection, while essential for truly integrating service into the class, involves trade-offs against other possible uses of class time.

Markus makes an additional point, based on his experience, that we will expand upon later in this essay: Service-learning in his course has led him to rethink his students' role in designing course goals, particularly the service experience. While that point is only implicit in some of these essays, all suggest that one practical consequence of opting to introduce a service component is a need to rethink how and why one teaches what one does in a particular course. While these essays suggest the broad value of service-learning in a wide array of possible courses, they suggest also a common impact on forcing changes in the goals and objectives of a course. No matter what course one teaches, once service-learning is introduced not only *how* but also *what* one teaches are affected. Service-learning seems to be not simply an add-on that enhances whatever goals one has for a course but also an epistemological reorientation that requires adjustments in all aspects of a course.

The essays in Part 3 take off from the theory and practice of our discipline-based courses to examine more general concerns. First, Sheilah Mann and Stephen Frantzich provide a history of teaching political science through internships and other direct public-service experiences. They trace the development of experiential education in political science back to the origins of the APSA, and then follow that development through to the growth of formal undergraduate and graduate internship programs after World War II. Their historical analysis of the growth of political science internships offers a number of concrete suggestions and insights for those wishing to incorporate service-learning into political science curricula. In particular, Mann and Frantzich emphasize the need to fashion service-learning initiatives to the particular mission and structure of each college department and the agencies with which the students will work. Ed Schwerin and Richard Couto follow with pieces that connect the service-learning efforts of political scientists to concepts, respectively, of empowerment and social transformation (Schwerin) and civic leadership (Couto) that can be developed into a service-learning pedagogy that extends beyond political science departments in the university.

Finally, in his Afterword to the entire volume, Benjamin Barber works to connect our individual colleagues' efforts to incorporate service-learning in their own classes to the origins of the discipline of political science as a whole and its concerns with citizen education. In tying our particular course narratives to the broader goal of civic education and in providing us with data from a national study that suggests that such teaching for better citizenship through service-learning actually works, Barber attempts to restore to our profession the civic mission that once defined and united all political scientists.

The richness of this volume lies in its variety. Authors represented include theorists as well as methodologists, Americanists as well as comparativists, activist-scholars as well as "pure" researchers. The courses represented in Part 2 and in the Appendix run the entire gamut of courses most political science departments offer. As such, there is something in this volume for almost anyone who finds herself or himself teaching about politics on a college or university campus.

But perhaps more important, these separate essays suggest the centrality of connecting service-learning to civic education. Each of our colleagues' essays recognizes that service-learning in a democracy — whatever its particular connection to courses or the curriculum — must be seen as a crucial aspect of civic responsibility: a model of the relationship between rights-bearing citizens and the many communities to which they belong. To be a citizen is not merely to possess a knowledge of government and its workings or to have legal rights; it is to take responsibility, to see ourselves and our interests as flourishing only as our communities flourish. Whether the language we prefer in describing our work is that of enhancing community involvement, political activism, citizen participation, public work, or social capital, we political scientists are claiming our pivotal role as civic educators, as "public intellectuals," to use a phrase from an earlier age.

To claim a role as civic educators means to move beyond the confines of our individual political science classes, departments, and curricula. It leads us to examine the place of our educational institutions in the larger public world. This requires that we pay greater attention to two matters that are only hinted at by many of the essays in this volume and by service-learning programs in general: the pedagogy and epistemology of higher learning and the nature of our campus-community partnerships.

The case for a more democratic pedagogy has been made before but is worth reiterating here. Democracy demands equal participation and voice by all citizens. In contrast to this ideal, even with all of the reforms of the past generation, the college classroom often mirrors hierarchy: what Paulo Freire termed the "banking model of education" — the knowledgeable teacher "depositing" information into the minds of passive student–ATM machines (see Freire 1970; hooks 1994). Moreover, in most classrooms, even those with experiential components, students do their work and are judged as individuals. A citizen education model for service-learning that does not challenge this traditional pedagogy is not modeling what it wants students to learn about democratic public life. More important, it may not contribute to student learning in ways those engaged in service-learning intend. Long ago, Dewey argued that any educational regimen consisting of "authorities at the upper end handing down to the receivers at the lower end what they must accept" was an education "fit to subvert, pervert, and destroy the foundations of democratic society" (1916: 133). The creation of a democratic classroom — in political science or anywhere else — is not an automatic consequence of service-learning; it involves much greater time and effort in coordinating and structuring activities and class discussions, and much more attention to "process," than does the "traditional" classroom. Additionally, even when successful, individual faculty or departmental efforts to create democratic service-learning classes may cause students pain and cognitive dissonance, especially if a more democratic pedagogy conflicts with the school's institutional or academic culture. Moreover, if we fail to confront and transform the epistemological assumptions that traditionally inform academic life, our efforts at service-learning may do little to advance democratic civic engagement (see Liu 1995).

If, as political scientists, we are concerned about the impact of service-learning on engaged citizenship, we must pay attention to our relationships with the larger community, as well as the structure of individual classes or the curriculum as a whole. As the Boyte and Farr and Mendel-Reyes essays in Part 1 of this volume strongly attest, if students are to think about citizenship as being actively involved in a committed relationship with others in the public realm, then the campus as a whole — not just the service-learning program — needs to mirror the values of neighborly civic responsibility. This may mean that, in addition to doing collaborative teaching and research with our community partners, we work toward making our institution of higher education a better "citizen" in the larger community. Much of the disconnect between town and gown that students often feel comes not from themselves or from the larger community but from the apathetic citizenship of the university or college, which is not engaged in the life of the surrounding neighborhoods. Here at Providence College, we have found that the more our students get involved in the community as part of their academic curriculum, the more the "explicit" message of our campus program — that of the connection of service to civic engagement — pushes an "implicit" message on the college itself to be a better institutional citizen (in return for the community's role in helping to educate our students). For example, we have been asked by our community partners to provide space for a community garden and for community education classes — which we have done — and are being asked to participate actively in neighborhood plans for housing and economic development. As we work with low-income youth in a variety of projects, we are being asked whether Providence College will be an inviting place for them when they graduate from high school. As our community partners ask us to be better institutional citizens, we ask them to participate more fully in the education of our students, by coming into the classroom as advisers and "co-faculty." This mutual relationship between campus and community not only models democratic citizenship and "neighborliness"; we have found that it also makes it easier for our students to connect their actions to those of citizens in the larger urban community, to join in common cause, and to learn about their neighbors and the possible solutions to their concerns.

Service-learning in political science, then, will raise questions that go beyond improving learning in our particular subject. While these essays provide many examples of how and why service-learning helps students learn more about politics, they also imply how service-learning transforms higher education. Service-learning renews political science's commitment to civic education and, thus, moves our students from being subjects to citizens. These new student citizens will demand a more active role in directing their own learning. As teachers and fellow learners, we must learn how our classrooms and institutions can become arenas where this happens. It is our hope that the essays in this volume will help to point the way.

References

Dewey, John. (1916). *Democracy and Education*. New York: MacMillan.

——————. (1938). *Experience and Education*. New York: MacMillan.

Freire, Paulo. (1970). *Pedagogy of the Oppressed*. New York: Continuum.

hooks, bell. (1994). *Teaching to Transgress: Education as the Practice of Freedom*. New York: Routledge.

Liu, Goodwin. (1995). "Knowledge, Foundations, and Discourse: Philosophical Support for Service-Learning." *Michigan Journal of Community Service Learning* 2:5-18.

The Decline of Democratic Faith

by Jean Bethke Elshtain

Democracy is on trial in America. Experts and ordinary citizens lament the growth of a culture of mistrust, cynicism, and scandal. Although a dwindling band of pundits and apologists insist that Americans are suffering the pangs of dislocation en route to salutary change, even progress, such reassurances ring increasingly hollow. By any standard of objective evidence, those who point to the growth of corrosive forms of isolation, boredom, and despair . . . to declining levels of involvement in politics — from simple acts like the vote to more demanding participation in political parties and local, civic associations . . . to the overall weakening, in other words, of that world known as democratic civil society . . . have the better case.

Social scientists who have researched the sharp decline in participation argue that the evidence points to nothing less than a crisis in "social capital formation," the forging of bonds of social and political trust and competence. The pernicious effects of rising mistrust, privatization, and anomie are many. For example, there is empirical support for the popularly held view that where neighborhoods are intact, drug and alcohol abuse, crime, and truancy among the young diminish. Because neighborhoods are less and less likely to be intact, all forms of socially destructive behavior are on the rise. Americans at the end of the 20th century suffer from the effects of a dramatic decline in the formation of social bonds, networks, and trust coupled with a diminution in investment in children. Children, in particular, have borne the brunt of negative social trends. All one need do is look at any American newspaper any day of the week to learn about the devastating effects on the young. Family breakdown generates unparented children who attend schools that increasingly resemble detention homes rather than centers of enduring training, discipline, and education and contributes to out-of-wedlock births and violence at unprecedented levels.

Why is this such a worry? Because, given our tendency to hunker down into bristling "identity groups" that claim to have nothing to say to one another, these trends point to a deterioration of the web of mediating institutions, vibrant informal and formal civic associations that democratic theorists historically either have taken for granted as a backdrop or, like Alexis de Tocqueville, have articulated explicitly in exploring the relationship between democracy and the everyday actions and spirit of a people. Democracy requires laws, constitutions, and authoritative institutions, but also depends on democratic dispositions. These include a preparedness to work with others for shared ends; a combination of often strong convictions coupled with a readiness to compromise in the recognition that one can't always get everything one wants; a sense of individuality and a commitment to civic goods that are not the possession of one person or of one small group alone. The world that nourished and sustained such democratic dispositions was a thickly interwoven social fabric — the web of mediating institutions already noted. Tocqueville saw Americans as civically engaged, arguing that "Americans of all ages, all conditions, and all dispositions constantly form associations." From this associational enthusiasm, currents of social trust and helpfulness flowed; indeed, such social trust no doubt helped to account for the enthusiasm for joining and helping. Other famous visitors to our shores spoke of the "active beneficence" that characterized the American public.

But this public spiritedness is in jeopardy. Our social fabric is frayed. Our trust in our neighbors is low. We don't join as much. We give less money, as an overall percentage of our gross national product, to charity. Where once rough comity pertained, now we see "in your face" and "you just don't get it." Perhaps a few words about the trust data are in order. The question "Do you believe most people can be trusted, or can you not be too careful?" was first posed in 1960 in a famous Civic Culture study conducted by Gabriel Almond and Sydney Verba. Since 1971, it has been repeated yearly. In 1960, trust stood at nearly 60 percent. Social trust waned, with some up-and-down fluctuations, throughout the 1960s and 1970s; did a bit of bouncing up in the mid-1980s; but now stands at *an all-time low* — 37.5 percent. When even mainstream social scientists begin to get alarmed, we should perhaps pay attention. The general, widely shared consensus now is that overall social trust is far too low to sustain consensual norms, to generate robust communal action, and to build workable coalitions. This is not good news.

Actually, the ever-prescient Tocqueville, in *Democracy in America*, offered foreboding thoughts along these lines. He warned of a world different from the robust democracy he surveyed. He urged Americans to take to heart a possible corruption of their way of life. In his worst-case scenario, narrowly self-involved individualists, disarticulated from the saving constraints and nurture of overlapping associations of social life, would require more and more controls "from above" to muffle at least somewhat the disintegrative effects of egoism. To this end, civic spaces between citizens and the state needed to be secured and nourished. Only many small-scale civic bodies would enable citizens to cultivate democratic virtues and to play an active role in the democratic community. These civic bodies were in and of the community but were not governmentally derived — not the creatures of the state, so to speak. Tocqueville's fears were not that anarchy would result should this world of associational life weaken but, rather, that new forms of domination might arise. All social webs that once held persons intact having disintegrated, the individual would find himself or herself isolated and impotent, exposed and unprotected. Into this power vacuum would move a centralized, top-heavy state or other centralized and organized forces that would push social life to the lowest common denominator.

A recent *New York Times* article on the 1994 campaign reported that "U.S. Voters Focus on Selves . . ." and brings into question the long-range effects of such a focus on the legitimacy and sustainability of liberal democratic institutions. The *Times* noted a "turn inward" and the lack of any "clear direction in the public's political thinking other than frustration with the current system and an eager responsiveness to alternative political solutions and appeals" (1994: A21). Based on a Times-Mirror survey, the article included, among manifestations of voter frustration, a growing disidentification with either of the major parties and massive political rootlessness among the young tethered to high rates of pessimism about the future. Most striking was a significant decline in "public support for social welfare programs," although the level of social tolerance for minorities and homosexuals was high so long as one did not have to bear the burden of financial support or direct "hands-on" involvement in the issue (Times-Mirror 1994: 21).

I want to speculate, briefly, on other trends that are traceable directly to the collapse of America's social ecology or, alternatively, that helped to bring about the negative developments reported in the Times-Mirror survey. One is the tendency to remove political disputation from the political arena into the courts. Over the past four decades, Americans have witnessed a tendency to derail public debate by judicial fiat. The second is the emergence of a new form of plebiscitary democracy that reduces voters and legislators alike to passive (albeit angry) consumers and instruments. It is not overstating the case to speak of a "spiral of delegitimization" that has its origins in widespread cynicism about government and politics, the disintegration of civil society, a pervasive sense of powerlessness, and other cultural phenomena.

Political scientist James Q. Wilson argues that one reason Americans are more cynical and less trusting than they used to be is that government has taken on more and more issues that it is ill-equipped to handle well — volatile moral questions such as abortion and "family values," for example, or some aspects of race relations that treat "blacks" and "whites" as though they were homogeneous interest groups, rather than collectivities themselves divided by regional, religious, class, and other lines. These "wedge issues," as political strategists call them, were generated in part by federal courts that made decisions in the 1960s and 1970s on a whole range of cultural questions without due consideration of how public support for juridically mandated outcomes might be generated. Such juridical moves not only froze out citizen debate but deepened a juridical model of politics, first pushed by liberal activists but now embraced by their conservative counterparts. Juridical politics is "winner take all" built on an adversarial model. This model, in turn, spurs "direct mail" and other mass-membership organizations whose primary goal is to give no quarter in any matter of direct interest to them and to them alone. By guaranteeing that the forces on either side of such issues as abortion, or certain highly controversial mandated "remedies" to enforce racial or gender equity, need never debate directly with each other through deliberate processes and legislatures, the courts deepened citizen frustration and fueled a politics of resentment.

This politics of resentment, in turn, tends to reduce legislators to passive instruments of single-issue lobbies and media overkill, thereby deepening the social mistrust that helps to give rise to such efforts in the first place. If one were to revisit the most controversial and divisive issues of the past three or four decades, one would probably discover a dynamic not unlike the one I here describe. At present, aggrieved citizens say, in effect, "Let's take things back" — through direct, rather than representative democracy. Indeed, the Times-Mirror survey I cited above concluded that the "Ross Perot phenomenon" that speaks to widespread voter anger and resentment went deeper and was more persistent than experts believed. The director of surveys for Times-Mirror professes shock at the Perot phenomenon even as the Democratic Party is "depleted and dispirited" and the Republican Party is divided on social tolerance issues (New York Times 1994: A21). It comes down to this: Judicial fiat displaces institutions of constitutional democracy by radically expanding its own mandate into the realm of democratic debate and compromise where things can be worked out in a rough-and-ready way. In turn, the proclaimed solution to expanded juridical power, plebiscitary or direct democracy, poses a threat of another (albeit related) sort by promoting the illusion that the unmediated "will of the people" will have final say on all issues. Although we are nowhere close to an *official* plebiscitary system, the trend is disturbing. And the emergence of a sour populism only feeds the conviction that we cannot talk to one another. Paradoxically, in the name of multiculturalism, we seem to be heading toward competing *monoculturalisms*, with each group playing what political scientists call a "zero-sum game": I win; you lose. Or, my group is vindicated; yours is reviled.

The tale here gestured toward is a story of the unraveling of the institutions of civil society, hence the dramatic upsurge in all forms of social mistrust and generalized fearfulness and cynicism, to the current crisis of governing I have called a "spiral of delegitimization." Recent studies show that Americans, without regard for race, "cite the same social problems: crime, poor education, imperiled sanctity of home and family" (Seib and Davidson 1994: A-1, 6). Not only does this challenge the racial monocultural insistence that blacks and whites are entirely separable groups with competing interests as well as identities, it shows that, if anything, black Americans are more insistent that their society faces a crisis in values, beginning with the family, than white respondents overall. But there is less agreement on why things have gone wrong and what can be done to put them right. "More economic opportunity" is noted, vaguely but persistently, as a goal for blacks, who also express almost no confidence in American legal institutions or politics, yet want "government" to create jobs and opportunities. Whites see a smaller role for government. But, not surprisingly, given recent developments, neither whites nor blacks express confidence in the institutions of liberal democratic society. Both groups, in other words, seem ripe for Perot-type "direct democracy" efforts, and both seem equally susceptible to the distortion of democratic debate in the hands of media scandal mongers and unscrupulous demagogues. This is a situation begging for a true democratic debate, courageous leadership, wise legislation, and the rebuilding of a sturdy civil society of which NGOs are a central and indispensable feature.

In the wake of this complex decline in our democratic faith, service-learning offers a promise of renewal. Service-learning, when practiced in the ways discussed by other contributions to this volume, can work in three different ways toward counteracting the forces of democratic deterioration. First, service-learning is a pedagogy that addresses directly the formation of the democratic dispositions that citizens need. Many times, community service activities, in themselves, teach students something about the need to work for shared ends, cultivate a readiness to compromise, and help form an understanding of the collective nature of civic goods. When these activities are combined with the academic learning in a political science class, the understanding derived from the community experiences can be connected to the theoretical arguments in support of democratic values, turning the classroom into a school for democratic citizenship.

Second, service-learning places students in direct contact with the kinds of civic associations and civic spaces that Tocqueville and, more recently, Robert Putnam discuss as central to vibrant democratic life. In an America in which such associational life is weakening, students who have not had deep contacts with small-scale civic bodies can perform service with voluntary not-for-profit associations in such a way that they are led to reflect on their significance in American democracy.

Finally, service-learning, to the extent that it involves people working together across ethnic, racial, or class lines, can help to break down the competing monoculturalisms of which I spoke earlier in this essay. Service in the larger community allows, and often requires, students from diverse backgrounds and experiences to work on common projects or to reach common goals. Service-learning offers one of the more effective vehicles for concretely and meaningfully engaging issues concerning diversity and democracy.

Still, the promise contained in service-learning will be difficult to realize. The sociologist Robert Bellah reports that Americans today brighten to tales of community, especially if the talk is soothing and doesn't appear to demand very much from them. Yet when the discussion turns to institutions and the need to sustain and to support authoritative civic institutions, attention withers and a certain sourness arises. This bodes ill for liberal democratic society, a political regime that requires robust yet resilient institutions that embody and reflect, yet mediate and shape, the urgencies of democratic passions and interests. As our mediating institutions, from the PTA to political parties, disappear or are stripped of legitimacy, a political wilderness spreads. People roam the prairie fixing on objects or policies or persons to excoriate or to celebrate, at least for a time, until some other enthusiasm or scandal sweeps over them. If we have lost the sturdiness and patience necessary to sustain civil society over the long haul, liberal democracy itself — as a system, a social world, and a culture — is in trouble.

References

The New York Times. (September 21, 1994). "The People, the Press, and Politics: The Political Landscape," p. A21.

Seib, Gerald F., and Joe Davidson. (September 29, 1994). "Whites, Blacks Agree on Problems; the Issue Is How to Solve Them." The Wall Street Journal, pp. A-1, 6.

Teaching/Theorizing/Practicing Democracy: An Activist's Perspective on Service-Learning in Political Science

by Meta Mendel-Reyes

The scene: a hotel lobby at the American Political Science Association convention.

The players: two political scientists who were in graduate school together at the University meeting for the first time since receiving their Ph.D.'s many years ago.

The time: the present.

Political Scientist #1: "Well, well, it's been a long time. How are you?"

Political Scientist #2: "Great! Are you still at . . . College?"

#1: "Yes, I am. Say, I saw your book in the catalogue. Way to go!"

#2: "Thanks. But you must have a book out by now?"

#1: "Well, I've been working on it. But what I'm really excited about is the course I'm teaching in service-learning."

#2: "I think I might have heard of that . . . internships or something? But I thought you had a tenure-track position, in American politics."

#1: "I do. The students learn about democracy in practice through their experiences with community organizations."

#2 *(looking around):* "Isn't that a little flaky?"

#1: "No, it's actually the most exciting and challenging teaching I've ever. . . ."

#2 *(walking off):* "Oh, there's . . . you know, he wrote. . . . It's been great talking."

The Education of a Teacher/Theorist/Activist

The scenario is based on a true story; only the names have been removed to protect those guilty of introducing a suspect pedagogy into political science. Of course, the "plot" could have taken a different turn; many of us who teach these courses have gotten positive as well as negative reactions from our colleagues, especially now that service-learning has become more publicized within political science. However, I suspect that I am not the only political scientist who is hesitant to "come out" as a practitioner of service-learning, in a profession that rewards published research above teaching of any kind, and that is especially suspicious of a pedagogy that seems to substitute experience for "science."

My commitment to service-learning reflects my own political education, which occurred in the fields as well as in the classroom. In 1974, shortly after earning an M.A. from the University of California at Berkeley, I left graduate school, frustrated by the distance between the study and practice of politics. For the next four years, I worked as a volunteer labor organizer with the United Farm Workers (UFW), led by Cesar Chavez; after that, I became a rank-and-file steward with the Communications Workers of America (CWA), then a field representative for two locals of the Service Employees International Union (SEIU). As a labor and community organizer for almost 15 years, my teachers were farm workers, telephone operators, secretaries, mechanics, and laborers, who showed me how democracy works, and doesn't work, in practice.

From them, I learned that the formal political equality offered by the American political system masks tremendous gaps in the social and economic resources needed to participate effectively in politics. Because the poor and people of color are less able to influence decisions, the political process tends to widen, rather than narrow, the gap between the haves and have-nots. Yet, despite the tremendous odds against them, communities of poor people and people of color are seeking to empower themselves, and often succeeding, to a limited extent, in the fields, factories, and neighborhoods. Why don't these local examples add up to a national movement for greater democracy? In 1988, I returned to Berkeley to try to figure out why, hoping to combine eventually my roles as political theorist, teacher, and activist.

To many in my profession, these roles appear to be mutually exclusive. By way of illustration, the conventional format of the curriculum vitae contains no category for "Activism"; a career as a political scientist is assumed to be encompassed by the listing of degrees, publications, teaching, and research appointments. (I've tried to get around this by reducing my 15 years as an organizer to a single paragraph labeled "Related Work Experience.") The cv reflects a long tradition in which political science occurs far away from the public sphere, which compromises the necessary detachment, objectivity, and disinterestedness.

Since Plato, students of politics have felt threatened by its actual presence, as exemplified by Plato's account of Socrates, who was put to death for engaging in what could be considered a form of service-learning.[1] In defending his unusual approach to education in the marketplace, Socrates claimed to benefit the community by acting as a gadfly to the state. Instead of lecturing, Socrates entered into dialogue with any willing Athenian, whether a wealthy man or a slave. By opening their eyes to ignorance and corruption, including their own, Socrates made it possible for his listeners to discover "the Good" for themselves, and to hold their leaders accountable to this higher standard. But, according to Plato in the "The Apology," Socrates's fellow citizens, egged on by nervous leaders, rejected his "service," condemning him to a traitor's death.

Although Plato himself avoided Socrates's fate, his own foray into activism, as adviser to a tyrant, was similarly disastrous. Once ransomed from a Sicilian jail by his friends, Plato retreated to his Academy, where scholars could be safe but also isolated in what was essentially the first "department of political science." In *The Republic*, Plato has Socrates voice the only circumstances under which he would reenter politics: as a "philosopher-king," independent of selfish tyrants and fickle masses.[2]

Today, the academy's claim to disinterestedness disguises the actual role played by most political scientists in articulating and helping to sustain conventional relations of power. Neither philosopher-kings nor gadflies, on the rare occasions when members of the profession participate directly in politics, they are likely to spend a sabbatical as an analyst with the State Department or join one of the many think tanks "inside the beltway." A true gadfly would have little chance of employment or tenure (particularly if she emulated Socrates's famous refusal to "publish").

For me, however, scholarship, teaching, and activism have always been linked — through the concept of education. As a labor and community organizer, I was also an educator; my task was to teach people to no longer need teachers, to organize people to become their own organizers. Sometimes, this education took place in formal settings. The UFW, for instance, held training sessions for farm workers in workplace democracy, on topics from organizing an election for union representation to how to run a meeting. Without reading "The Apology," Cesar Chavez had developed a pedagogy designed to help people to teach themselves.

I remember particularly one of the earliest training sessions, when Cesar led us through a simulated meeting. Farm workers and volunteer organizers played various roles, including the ranch committee trying to preside over a more or less attentive audience of workers and their families. I was assigned to be a baby whose crying was a constant distraction. Cesar himself played a young man more interested in girls than grievances; I'll never forget how he strutted at the back of the hall, combing his hair elaborately, an image of self-absorption diametrically opposed to the quiet, modest leader whom we loved. After a free-wheeling discussion about running a meeting, Cesar "punished" the most disruptive characters by making us play the ranch committee and letting others have the fun of disrupting us.

However, our most important education occurred in the field, literally, where we learned about democracy by doing it. Although I did not realize it until much later, we were actually engaged in popular education, a pedagogy designed to empower adults, based on the principle that people can and should take responsibility for their own learning, just as they are both capable of and responsible for self-rule. Popular education, most closely associated with the work of educators Paulo Freire and Ira Shor, occurs through dialogue between teacher and students, rather than the hierarchical transmission of knowledge that characterizes conventional teaching. By encouraging them to reflect upon their own experiences, the popular educator helps the learners to become aware simultaneously of their personal disempowerment and their collective capacity to empower themselves in education and in politics. Through a "spiral" of action and reflection, people learn how to transform themselves and their society. Popular education, credited with contributing to democratization in places such as Brazil and South Africa, also played a key role in the early days of the civil rights movement in the United States. As an organizer with the UFW, I saw how popular education methods could help to empower migrant farm workers to fight against some of the harshest working conditions in this country.[3]

At the beginning, our learning curve was shaped by urgency — failure could mean a worker fired for union organizing, an election lost — so we constantly tested theory against practice, reporting and analyzing the day's experiences in late-night meetings, seven days a week. Later on, when we stopped listening to the people, they paid the price. During the pivotal campaign to represent workers for the largest grape company in California, overconfident organizers paid no attention to daily reports of fear and uncertainty. Following the overwhelming defeat, the strongest UFW supporters were fired from their jobs, and the stunned union began the retreat from participatory democracy that characterized the great popular movements of the 1960s and early 1970s.

After my return to graduate school, I wrote a dissertation and then a book, *Reclaiming Democracy: The Sixties in Politics and Memory* (Routledge, 1995), which explored one aspect of this history: the irony that the collective memory of the 1960s (of the civil rights movement, the New Left, and the early stages of the women's liberation movement) discourages a more participatory politics today. Democratic theorists, from Tocqueville to Putnam, have argued that the health of democracy depends on the education of citizens through participation in voluntary associations and local communities.[4] During a period of declining confidence in the ability or willingness of national government to solve pressing economic and social problems, many activists and scholars have called for the revitalization of such participatory politics. Yet, most Americans seem to have given up on collective action, even the poor and the powerless, who would have the most to gain.

Teaching democracy in political science in the 1990s, therefore, takes place in the context of twin crises in politics and education. Our political crisis is defined by the gap between the theory and practice of democracy, between the ideal of the rule of the people and the reality of the "rule by a few supposedly in the interests of the many," as the political theorist Hannah Arendt put it.[5] The phrases made famous by America's greatest teacher of democracy, Abraham Lincoln, must be rewritten: "this government of all the people [in only the vaguest sense], by [only a few of] the people, and for [a few of] the people."

However, the elite theorists of democracy, whose views still dominate the profession of political science, argue that minimal popular participation is actually good for democracy, because the masses are ignorant or fanatical or both.[6] But this claim rings hollow in the United States, where such problems as poverty, racism, homelessness, inadequate education, lack of access to health care, unemployment, and environmental pollution have become daily realities for many people. How can democracy be said to work when one in four children (and every other black child) is poor? The "people," whom the government is supposedly of, by, and for, has been rent by income, race, ethnicity, sexual orientation, region, and many other differences, into shards of rich, poor, blacks, whites, Asians, Latinos, men, women, heterosexuals, bisexuals, and gays, southerners, westerners, among many others. More and more Americans have turned away from political participation, even as politics becomes more urgent. The ascendance of the Republican party makes it even less likely that the national government will act on behalf of local, especially urban, communities.

The crisis in higher education takes the form of a gap between a vague ideal of the quest for knowledge for both its own sake and for the common good, and the pressing reality that colleges and universities have become increasingly exclusive, fragmented, and driven by the bottom line. Competing with other disciplines for pieces of a shrinking pie, most departments of political science give lip service, at best, to citizenship education; now and then, a professor may issue an eloquent call for teaching the skills of democracy at the secondary or elementary level. But the public schools are even more strapped for money and vision; finding enough chairs for students to sit on inevitably becomes a higher priority than training them to be citizens. In practice, if not in theory, the effect of K-12 education is to separate the future citizenry into elite and mass, and to divide the latter into skilled and unskilled workers, and the unemployed. The possibility of occasional mobility among these categories does not alter the fact that economic security and active citizenship have become the privileges of a few rather than the rights of all.

Despite the Quaker tradition of social responsibility featured so proudly in the admissions brochure, the chief function of the prestigious liberal arts college where I teach is to reproduce a small segment of the nation's elite. My students enjoy listening to my activist stories, but most of them are as skeptical about education as they are about politics. To me, they seem to be as disillusioned as my college generation (1968-72), but much less likely to feel the need or the capacity to bridge the gap between democratic ideals and undemocratic reality. Above all, they are skeptical about their ability to make a difference. This is expressed in part as resentment toward the '60s generation, which, as contemporary leaders constantly remind them, did drugs and slept around and called that politics. Many '90s students resent what they feel is hypocritical nagging by their real or generational "parents," who enjoyed the fruits of "selling out" while leaving their children with poorer prospects for job security and quality of life. The relative few who do, or plan to, participate in politics envision themselves as powerful policymakers or crusading lawyers, that is, as specialized, 20th-century versions of philosopher-kings.

The reality is that their B.A.'s in political science from a highly ranked college will probably enable them to get into good law or public policy schools, where they'll be recruited by corporate law firms or governmental bureaucracies. Most of them will become what Plato might have called "philosopher middle-managers." Those who are inspired to emulate the careers of their professors of political science are in for a greater shock when they discover, upon receiving their Ph.D.'s, that their mentors are occupying nearly all of the tenure-track jobs. Still, nearly all of our graduates are likely to remain in the upper-middle-class stratum occupied by their parents, even if their actual standard of living is lower. Of course, some of my students will enter directly into politics, a few as candidates, most as aides or consultants. A few will even become community organizers, as I did, continuing their democratic education by working for a democracy that does not yet exist.

The Democracy Project

In the Department of Political Science at Swarthmore College, service-learning is a central feature of the Democracy Project, which is designed to deepen students' understanding of and commitment to democratic citizenship in a multicultural society, through participation in community action. As professor of democratic theory and practice, to my knowledge the only such position in the country, I direct the project and teach the three core courses; my secondary teaching responsibilities are in more familiar subfields, political theory and American politics.

The three linked core courses — Democratic Theory and Practice, Multicultural Politics, and Community Politics: The Internship Seminar — all involve what we call community-based learning; in the seminar, students engage in public service internships as part of the coursework, while the other two courses include a class community service activity. From my perspective as activist as well as professor, community-based learning gives me the opportunity to offer my students a taste of both my political educations.

The substitution of the word "community" for "service" seems to better describe our relationship to communities that are empowering themselves. To us, "service-learning" implies that the exchange goes in one direction only, that students service and learn about communities, but not the other way around. Instead, the goal of the Democracy Project is to establish relationships based not on charity but on a mutual partnership in the struggle for justice. The activist/educator Nadinne Cruz taught me an aboriginal saying that captures the spirit of the project: "If you've come to help me, no thank you; but if your liberation is bound up with mine, then come let us work together." Of course, liberation has different meanings to a privileged student at a Swarthmore College, ranked consistently as one of the top three liberal arts colleges in the country, and to a poor child attending a school in the nearby city of Chester, which has the worst public school system in the state. Yet, all of us have a stake in bridging the deepening chasms among us; and the first step toward doing so is the realization that even the most disadvantaged community has much to teach and to share.

Democratic Theory and Practice explores the relationship between theories of democracy and the ways in which democracy is practiced in the United States, focusing on efforts to bring about a more participatory theory and practice of democracy. Today, nearly everyone agrees that political power belongs in the hands of the people. But this consensus is deceptive: Democracy in the United States raises a host of complex questions, both practical and theoretical, which this course seeks to answer.

What explains the gap between the nearly universal commitment to democracy and the fact that most people barely participate in ruling themselves? Can people wield power effectively in large nations governed by complex bureaucracies? Is democracy simply about the institutions of government? Power is surely also exercised, for example, in the economy, families, and educational institutions. What does democracy entail in these contexts? Can political democracy occur in a country in which there are tremendous economic and social inequalities? Does democracy require absolute equality? And what does it mean for "the people" to "have" power, anyway? Must political decisions be made by consensus to be considered truly democratic? When and how do political movements arise, in which people attempt to empower themselves and to reclaim democracy?

Following an introduction to the range of definitions of democracy, this course alternates between case studies of democracy in practice and works of democratic theory. A case study of the civil rights movement in a small town on the coast of Georgia illustrates the contrast between the classical participatory and representative theories of democracy. Later units focus on the Civil War, as the greatest historical example of the American struggle to reconcile the treatment of racial minorities with democratic principles; on efforts to organize Appalachian miners, as an instance of the conflict between democracy and economic inequality; and on environmental politics in Montana, which illuminates the tension between democracy and community.

In line with the dual focus on theory and practice, the course features a weeklong simulation, "Swattown" ("Swat" is a nickname for Swarthmore), about a crisis in a local high school that culminates in a town meeting. Student teams play the roles of the school board, the parent-teacher association, the student council, and a radical student group (called SWAT, for "Students With Attitude and Time"); the students are graded, as individuals and as members of their teams, on the basis of their effort to achieve a realistic and democratic outcome. The course assignments also include a theory-in-practice report on an activist experience during the semester.

Multicultural Politics investigates the ways in which racial, ethnic, and cultural diversity has shaped the American past and present. Is the United States a melting pot, a mosaic, or a battleground of racial, ethnic, and cultural differences? To many people, nostalgia for an America composed of united, assimilated, successful immigrants contrasts with widespread anxiety about a nation increasingly divided between citizens and newcomers, whites and people of color, rich and poor, the "normal" and the deviant, the powerful and the powerless.

This course begins with the historical experiences of Native Americans, African Americans, Latinos, Asian Americans, European immigrants, and gays and lesbians, focusing on the political and economic subordination of these minorities, but also on their efforts to empower themselves. Next, students explore specific attempts of community activists and popular movements to practice democratic, egalitarian, multicultural politics today. Lastly, they turn to contemporary issues, including immigration, poverty, environmental racism, and affirmative action, which illuminate the complex relationships among race, ethnicity, gender, class, religion, sexual preference, and other differences.

The class materials include fiction and memoirs by members of racial, ethnic, and cultural minorities who have often been ignored or silenced, in addition to works of social science, history, and journalism and videos, all expressing a wide variety of political perspectives. Students also draw on their own experiences and family histories, engage in dialogues with community activists and other presenters, and participate in a class project off-campus.

The heart of the Democracy Project is Community Politics: The Internship Seminar, which explores democratic and multicultural political practice in American communities through semester-long internships of at least five hours per week with local service and advocacy organizations. How do disempowered communities organize themselves to take collective action? How can individual activists, from inside and outside the community, help to achieve democratic and multicultural political change? Students explore these questions by integrating reflection and experience, primarily through their internships, but also through dialogues with local activists, readings, journals and other writing assignments, community building within the class, and group exercises that connect theory and practice.

In trying to answer these basic questions of the course, students encounter many others. Is it possible to achieve significant political change at the local level when critical decisions are made at the national and even international levels? How can communities have an impact on large, bureaucratic nation-states and on multinational corporations? What role, if any, should outsiders play in community politics? How should an activist work with people who are different in terms of education, race, income, gender, etc.? Can people from one group understand, judge, or work politically with other groups? What is the relationship between community service and community action? What type of knowledge and education is appropriate to community politics? Does providing direct service to people undercut their political empowerment? Should community organizations be democratic in structure? Are there times when too much internal democracy makes it harder to achieve democratic political change? What is democratic leadership? How do activists sustain their work without burning out? How do community organizations sustain themselves?

The full syllabi of the three Democracy Project core courses are reproduced at the end of this chapter. The rest of this essay highlights the pedagogical features related to community-based learning that reflect my activist perspective on education for democracy.

In the Internship Seminar, democracy informs the structure as well as the content of the course. The students choose from among a group of potential placements with advocacy and service organizations, which are answering the questions about community empowerment in practice. These organizations include the Chester Community Improvement Project, which rehabilitates abandoned housing and sells it to first-time buyers as a way of increasing the number of people with a stake in the future of Chester, an economically depressed Northeastern city, Chester Residents Concerned for Quality Living (CRCQL), a group of neighbors who have banded together to fight pollution from a waste incinerator built, literally, across the street; and Asian Americans United, which runs a youth leadership program for the diverse and growing Asian community of Philadelphia. At the beginning of each internship, the student, his or her supervisor from the host organization, and I sign off on a "community involvement agreement," which spells out each of our expectations and responsibilities.

Each weekly, three-hour session of this course is divided into three parts, following a meal, which we take turns in preparing. While eating, we do "excitement sharing," in which each person shares a highlight from her or his internship. This is also the time to ask for the class's help, later on during the session, on a problem that came up during the week. After we eat, there is usually a dialogue with a community presenter, such as an organizer for the homeless or the supervisor of the children's program at a shelter for battered women; students are also encouraged to invite someone from their host organization to present. In keeping with the spirit of partnership with the community, the presenters share in the design of their segments of the course, and are compensated for their contributions. Zulene Mayfield, of CRCQL, for instance, led a lively discussion about how outsiders should approach volunteering in communities very different from their own. Zulene told the students not to hold back their ideas because they were afraid of insulting her largely poor and black group, but instead to "bring your brains!"

Next, one student each week will make a presentation about his or her internship. I encourage the students to think of this assignment not so much as a conventional report but as a teaching moment, an opportunity to convey something of their experience, perhaps through an exercise or by leading a discussion on an issue in democratic or multicultural politics. For example, one intern asked for guidance because he had been asked to take sides on a split within the leadership of the organization; the ensuing conversation ranged from the qualities of an effective leader to the role an outsider should play, if any, in the internal structure of a community group.

In the last section of the course, we consider a question raised by the readings for the week; if no community presenter is scheduled for the week, I may lead an interactive exercise related to the week's topic, such as a "quick decision" game, which highlights the need for leadership in the decision-making process. Often, this discussion has already begun during the community or internship presentation. The exercise, too, may grow out of an earlier segment of the class, such as a role play intended to help an intern work on her difficult relationship with a particularly aggressive child in the shelter. Several of us played children, while others took turns playing her role; I played a child with a very short attention span, whose running around the room and banging on furniture brought giggles and laughter. Like this one, the exercises teach more than one lesson — in this case, that a teacher's authority doesn't preclude humor or play (and that education can be fun!). As in this example, the class schedule is flexible and responsive to the needs and preferences of the students, another way in which the subject matter of democracy is incorporated into the format of the course.

The Internship Seminar is also designed to build community within the classroom as a way of studying community building outside of it. The shared meal, for example, helps to create an atmosphere that is more relaxed and cooperative than the typical classroom; it also demonstrates subtly that community doesn't just happen, but must be built through ritual and effort. The students are very enthusiastic about this aspect of the course, and I am too, since they are nearly always better cooks than I (which is not saying much). They take their responsibilities very seriously, arriving early, cooking more, and more elaborately, than is really necessary. Even the occasional lapses are lessons in community building. Once, a student forgot about cooking dessert until the last minute and ended up serving raw cookie dough; we nibbled politely, but he got the message. Often, the students prepare a traditional meal, such as the wonderful, spicy chicken and vegetable dish from Botswana.

Community building also involves learning how to work together despite differences, one of the most difficult lessons in the classroom and politics. Although they share an interest in community service, the 12 or so students who compose the seminar come from a range of racial, ethnic, and class backgrounds. Like many of their elders, they associate "community" with harmony and resist the idea that democratic deliberation does not prevent or eliminate conflict but offers, at best, a way to achieve temporary resolutions. In typical classrooms, students shy away from heated conflict, unless it takes the accepted, but not painless, forms of competitive criticism or one-upmanship, which are all too often modeled by the faculty. The resistance to conflict goes much deeper than the oft-noted pressure for "political correctness"; regardless of their political orientation, students seem genuinely to believe that truth and democracy necessarily produce consensus.

The syllabus is also structured to give the students the chance to work on specific tensions, through the dialogues with community presenters, the readings, and exercises about situations in our internships, such as confronting our own or others' prejudice. During a period when tensions between Jews and blacks were in the news, we watched a video, went on a field trip, and participated in a "thoughts" exercise about this issue. I also invoke Martin Luther King's phrase "creative tension," which he uses in "Letter From a Birmingham Jail" to describe Socrates's commitment to growth through challenge. Education, whether in the classroom, in the marketplace, or at the segregated lunch counter, causes tension because the "student" is simultaneously learning and "unlearning." Questioning one's previously held beliefs, in the inferiority of a race, for example, is liberating but also stressful. I also point out that not every tension is creative, which means that democratic deliberation must be structured to promote respect as well as the open expression of ideas and disagreements.

In the classroom, for example, we alternate the role of "vibeswatcher," the person responsible for paying attention to the "vibes" of the group. The vibeswatcher has the authority to jump in and call the group's attention not to discomfort by itself but to a range of feelings or behaviors that seem to interfere with learning, such as personal attacks, going off on a tangent, even simple boredom. Her or his interventions are questions rather than commands; the class must stop and pay attention to group dynamics, even if we decide quickly to continue in the same way. Although vibes watching does sometimes slow down or distract us, the overall effect is that each member of the class becomes more aware and feels more responsible for the group as a whole. Moreover, the interventions often turn out to be the most exciting teaching moments, especially when a student challenges something I have done.

Finally, it should be noted that my approach to teaching democracy through community-based learning could not have been undertaken without the support I have received from the Department of Political Science at Swarthmore College. My position in democratic theory and practice represents the department's commitment to the importance of democracy as a subject matter, and to the philosophy that democratic theory should be taught in relation to practice. Instead of being marginalized in the way that service-learning so often is, these courses are eligible for the honors program, and are taught by a tenure-track professor. Moreover, the criteria for tenure include evaluation of my community-based pedagogy by professionals in the field, including local activists, as part of the teaching section of the review process.

I do not mean to suggest that there are no problems. Without support staff, I am solely responsible for setting up, monitoring, and evaluating the internships: The course release that I receive for these activities does not cover fully the time required. Planning is difficult because I do not yet have a solid budget, which is especially needed for compensating the presenters from the community. And, until I actually go through the tenure process, the possibility remains that service-learning will weigh very little compared with conventional standards for teaching and, especially, research. But, the Democracy Project is still evolving, and even with the uncertainty, my situation is very different from that captured in the dialogue at the beginning of this essay.

Community-based learning allows me to be who I am — a teacher/theorist/activist for democracy.

Notes

1. Recounted in Plato's "The Apology," in *The Last Days of Socrates* (New York: Penguin, 1959).

2. Plato, *The Republic*, translated by F. Cornford (London: Oxford University Press, 1945), VI, 496 D. See Sheldon Wolin, *Politics and Vision: Continuity and Innovation in Western Political Thought* (Boston: Little, Brown, 1960), ch. 2.

3. See Paulo Freire, *Pedagogy of the Oppressed* (New York: Herder and Herder, 1972); Ira Shor, *Critical Teaching and Everyday Life* (Chicago: University of Chicago Press, 1987).

4. Alexis de Tocqueville, *Democracy in America*, translated by George Lawrence, edited by J.P. Mayer (New York: Harper & Row, 1988), originally published 1838; Benjamin Barber, *An Aristocracy of Everyone: The Politics of Education and the Future of America* (New York: Ballantine Books, 1992).

5. Hannah Arendt, *On Revolution* (New York: Penguin Books, 1987), 269.

6. See Joseph A. Schumpeter, *Capitalism, Socialism, and Democracy*, 3d ed. (New York: Harper Torchbooks, 1976). As an example of the influence of the elite theory of democracy on political science, see Bernard R. Berelson, Paul F. Lazarsfeld, and William N. McPhee, *Voting* (Chicago: University of Chicago Press, 1954).

Political Science 19 DEMOCRATIC THEORY AND PRACTICE

Spring 1995, Th 11:20 am - 12:35 pm, Trotter 128.
Professor Meta Mendel-Reyes, nimendel 1, x8O98, Trotter 8.
Office hours: Tuesday 1:30-3:30 (sign-up or drop-in), Wednesday 3-5 (by appt. only); student lunch: Thursday 11:45-1245.

"In the case of a word like democracy, not only is there no agreed definition, but the attempt to make one is resisted from all sides. It is almost universally felt that when we call a country democratic we are praising it; consequently the defenders of every kind of regime claim that it is a democracy, and fear that they might have to stop using the word if it were tied down to one meaning." - George Orwell, "Politics and the English Language"

"What we call today democracy is a form of government where the few rule, at least supposedly. in the interests of the many." - Hannah Arendt, On Revolution

The root meaning of the word democracy is "rule of the people." This seems like a simple, straightforward idea. Today, nearly everyone agrees that political power belongs in the hands of the people. But the appearance is deceptive: democracy in the United States raises a host of complex questions, both practical and theoretical. What explains the gap between the nearly universal commitment to democracy, and the fact that most people barely participate in ruling themselves? Can people wield power effectively in a large, bureaucratic, nation-state? Is democracy simply about the institutions of government? Power is surely also exercised, for example, in the economy, families, and educational institutions. What does democracy entail in these contexts? Can political democracy occur in a country in which there are tremendous economic and social equalities? Does democracy require absolute equality? And what does it mean for "the people" to "have" power, anyway? Must political decisions be made by consensus to be considered truly democratic? When and how do political movements arise, in which people attempt to empower themselves and to reclaim democracy?

In this class we will explore these and other questions by comparing a wide range of democratic political theory to the practice of American politics. Because the questions are big and difficult, we can pursue them only in a preliminary way. The aim of our work together is not to reach definitive conclusions, but to challenge your preconceptions, raise some basic problems, introduce you to some of the most important attempts at answers, and to give you opportunities to engage in the activity of theorizing about democracy, which is, in my experience, essential yet often missing from democratic practice.

Course Format and Assignments:

This class emphasizes discussion and brief lectures, but there will also be classroom exercises, videos, one or more outside speakers, and a theory in practice experience which will take place in the community. Your participation is indispensable, because the most important political thinking occurs in public discourse about common problems or divisive differences. Although a classroom has different purposes and standards from those of a town meeting or a campaign debate, this course should still be a forum for genuinely political conversation.

Together, we will try to create a class environment in which we all try to express our views AND to listen to the views of others. This requires a degree of courage and trust; it is sometimes very hard to take a different stand on a controversial or sensitive issue, or to open ourselves to a very different viewpoint. But if we can't do it in the class, how will we ever be able to do so in public life?

Class participation is a large percentage of the final grade: 25%. You will be graded on your daily participation in class discussion, and in other class activities, including helping to lead discussion, a debate, and a town meeting. On the first day, I will collect information about the kind of class participation that helps each of you learn the best (small group discussion, large group discussion, debate, lecture), and I will try to accommodate you as much as possible. There is no midterm or final, so your participation in class will be the only way to demonstrate your overall knowledge of the subject matter of this course. So, I expect you to come to class each day, having read the materials and thought carefully about them. I will let you know what your class participation grade is at mid-semester.

There will be several, very short writing assignments (25% of the grade), which will ask you to do different kinds of written work appropriate to democratic theory or practice, including a theory in practice report. There will be an essay grade (50%), based on one 5-7 page essay and one 10- 1 2 page essay. Writing about and doing political theory will likely be new to many of you, and challenging to all of us. In the first paper, you will critically analyze political theories about an issue raised in the first part of the course. The second paper will give you an opportunity to theorize politically yourself about a problem in democratic theory and practice, in light of texts from the last part of the course. NOTE that no late papers will be accepted, and all assignments must be completed to pass the course.

Additional information about assignments will be given in class. The assignments are indicated in the course outline below (subject to change). There will be a folder for this class on the classes server, which includes a folder for you to talk with each other about democratic theory and practice, and the class. Another internal folder will contain this syllabus and all assignments, reading and discussion guides, the video dates, and all changes and updates, etc. (this is an experiment - I want to be able to communicate with you more efficiently, and conserve paper - You may also submit written work to me electronically). The video classroom has been reserved for Wednesdays 4-1 1 (to make it easier for everyone to see the films, we will schedule two showings); a schedule will be posted in the class folder. IMPORTANT: please get in the habit of checking the classes server the day after each class, and checking email from time to time.

Readings: The following required books are available for purchase in the bookstore; they are also on reserve in McCabe library. Readings marked with an asterisk are in Green, ed., Democracy; readings marked with a @ will be distributed.

> John Gaventa, Power and Powerlessness: Quiescence and Rebellion in an Appalachian Vale
> Phillip Green, ed., Democracy: Key Concepts in Critical Theory
> Melissa F. Greene, Praying for Sheetrock
> Daniel C. Kemmis, Communiiy and The Politics of Place
> Abraham Lincoln, ed. and introduced by Cuomo and Holzer, Lincoln on Democracy
> James Miller, "Democracy Is In the Streets": From Port Huron to the Sieae of Chica2o

Course Outline and Schedule of Assignments:

T 1/17   Introduction

A.   **What is democracy?**

Th 1/19   Green, Williams (intro & selection I)* Personal experience in democracy due (1/2 page)

B.   **Democratic theory and practice 1: the civil rights movement**

T 1/24   Greene, Prayin@ for Sheetrock, Parts One and Two
Th 1/26   Greene, Part Three

C.   **The classical theory of democracy**

T 1/31   Rousseau, Mill, Tocqueville (sels. 2-4)* Abstract due (I page)

D.   **Representative democracy**

Th 2/2   Madison, Mill, Dahl (5-7)*

E.   **Democratic theory and practice III: Lincoln, slavery, the Civil War**

T 2/7   Lincoln, tba
Th 2/9   Lincoln, tba
          Class debate: Lincoln-Douglass
          Debate statement due (I page)
T 2/14   Lincoln, tba Happy Valentine's Day!
Th 2/16   King, "Letter From a Bim-lingham Jail"*
          Theory in practice proposal due

F.   **Inequality and democracy**

T 2/21   Freidman, Macpherson, Parenti, Green (17-20)*
Th 2/23   Bowles & Gintis, Elkin, Parenti, Phillips (21-24)*

G.   **Democratic theory and practice IV: Appalachian miners**

T 2/28   Gaventa, Power and Powerlessness, Part I (I. I- 1.3), Part 11 (all)
Th 3/2   Gaventa, 5, 6 (intro, 6.3), 7 (intro, 7.4, 7.5), Part IV (all), 10

BREAK   Be sure to theorize and practice democracy regularly!

H.   **Democratic elitism**

T 3/14   Michels, Weber, Schumpeter, Berelson, Crozieet al, Dahl (8-13)*
Th 3/16   Dewey, Bachrach, Prewitt & Stone (14-16)*

I.   **Democratic theory and practice V: SDS during the Sixties**

T 3/21   Miller "Democracy Is In the Streets", tba
Th 3/23   Miller, tba
            First essay due

J.   **Action**

T 3/28   Luxembourg, Arendt, Carter, Walzer (25-28)*

K.   **Participation and Representation**

Th 3/30   Gould, Green, Barber (29-30)*
            Theory in practice report due

L.   **Community and Democracy**

T 4/4   Kemmis, Community and the Politics of Place, Chs. One-Five
Th 4/6   Kemmis, Chs. Six-Eight

M.   **Town meeting**

T 4/11   no readings   Citizen statement due (I page)
Th 4/13   no readings

N.   **Democratic rights**

4/18   Rousseau, Mill, Bay, Kateb, Young (intro, 32-36)

O.   **Democratic theory and practice VI: Contemporary rights issues**

Th 4/20   Immigration: guest speaker
            readings to be assigned
T 4/25   Issue of class's choice readings to be assigned
Th 4/27   Conclusion

May 3, 5 pm
            Final essay due

PS 38 THE DEMOCRACY SEMINAR: The Politics of Community Action
Spring 1995, T 6-9 pm, 3 1 0 Dartmouth Ave. 544-8104
Professor Meta Mendel-Reyes, mrnendel 1, x8O98, Trotter 8.
Office hours: Tuesday 1:30-3:30 (sign-up or drop-in), Wednesday 3-5 (by appt. only); student lunch: Thursday 11:45-1245.

The "Democracy Seminar," one of the core courses of the Political Science Department's Democracy Project, is a community-based exploration of democratic political practice. In the United States, such problems as poverty, racism, homelessness, inadequate education, lack of access to health care, unemployment, environmental pollution, etc., have become daily realities for many people. The pervasiveness of injustice and inequality call into question the meaning of American democracy. More and more people have given up on political participation, even as politics becomes more urgent. The recent elections make it even less likely that the national government will act on behalf of local, especially urban, communities. Yet, at the grassroots, in many American neighborhoods, people are organizing and trying to resolve the tremendous problems which confront them. How do communities empower themselves to take action? How can individual activists, from inside and outside the community, help to achieve democratic political and social change?

In trying to answer these basic questions of the course, we will encounter many others. Is it possible to achieve significant political change at the local level, when critical decisions are made at the national, and even international levels? How can communities have an impact on large, bureaucratic nation-states, and on multinational corporations? What role, if any, should outsiders play in community politics? How should an activist work with people who are different in terms of education, race, income, gender, etc.? Can people from one group understand, judge, or work politically with other groups? What is the relationship between community service and community action? What type of knowledge and education is appropriate to community politics? Does providing direct service to people undercut their political empowerment? Should community organizations be democratic in structure? Are there times when too much internal democracy makes it harder to achieve democratic political change? What is democratic leadership? How do activists sustain their work without burning out? How do community organizations sustain themselves?

In this course, each of you will explore the politics of community action in American democracy, through community-based learning. You will have many opportunities to integrate reflection and experience, primarily through public service internships, but also through dialogue with local activists, community-building within the class, reading and writing assignments, and group exercises which connect theory and practice. (Note: this version of the Democracy Seminar has been designed to complement PS 19. "Democratic Theory and Practice." also offered this semester)

Course Format and Assignments:

The main focus of the Democracy Seminar will be our public service internships; the course is designed to facilitate learning from our own experiences and from each other. Each of you will complete a n-minimum of 60 volunteer hours by the end of the semester (approximately five hours a week through the middle of April). The internship will give you the opportunity to explore in a sustained way a particular approach to community action. The internship experience is structured by the role and the responsibilities the host organization agrees to provide you, your own interests and learning objectives, and my course design. These three components will be formalized in a Learning Agreement, to be signed by the student, a representative of the host organization, and myself, as the professor of the course. It is important that the relationship between the intern and the host be as reciprocal as possible; the community organizations and activists who share with us this semester should be respected, not simply treated as "labs" or "data," for our purposes only.

Our weekly meetings will be conducted seminar-style, beginning with a shared meal. During our time together, we will share and reflect on our internship experiences, discuss democracy and the politics of community action, in light of our experiences, readings, and other class activities. In our discussions, we will integrate scholarly and other kinds of discourse and activities, with an emphasis on community "voices" which are not often heard in academic or public policy debates . Our sessions will also include individual presentations on internships, and dialogue with community activists. I have invited the first several community presenters; the rest will be people you invite from your host organizations.

The primary written work of the course will be a journal, intended to give you the opportunity to integrate reflection and experience on a frequent, regular basis. Plan to write at least three times a week, and to address the following topics at least once a week each: an issue or theme from the class readings, in light of your internship; the seminar discussions and activities, in light of your internship; a critical incident from or reflection prompted by your internship, which may not be directly connected to either the readings or the activities for that week. Feel free to add other topics, to include newspaper articles, photographs, flyers, or other material relevant to your topic, and to be creative. Remember that, although this journal is not expected to be a polished essay, it should not be purely stream of consciousness, either. Writing in your journal will be most valuable if you use it consistently to reflect, intellectually and emotionally, on specific issues and experiences. The journal must be typed or word-processed, double-spaced. You will hand in your journal every other week during the semester; the final entry will be a summary analysis of your internship experience. There will also be a community service writing assignments.

There will also be several activities scheduled to take place outside of class, including videos, and a class community work project. Additional information about assignments will be given in class. The assignments are indicated in the course outline below. It is likely like that the syllabus will change, in response to your interests as well as my perceptions of what the group needs to work on. Be sure to check email regularly. There will also be a folder for this class on the classes server, which includes a folder for you to talk with each other, and another internal folder containing this syllabus and other assignments, and all changes and updates, etc. (this is an experiment - I want to be able to communicate with you more efficiently, and conserve paper - You may also submit-tit written work to me electronically). The video classroom has been reserved for Wednesdays 4-11 (to make it easier for everyone to see the films, we will schedule two showings); a schedule will be posted in the class folder. So, you will also need to get in the habit of checking the classes server from time to time.

Because of the nature of this course, your participation is essential. You must attend all class meetings, having done the readings, and completed any other assignment for that session. I expect you to be equally responsible about your internship.

During our meetings, we will work together to create a class environment, in which we all try to express our views AND to listen to the views of others. This requires a degree of courage and trust; it is sometimes very hard to take a different stand on a controversial or sensitive issue, or to open ourselves to a very different viewpoint. But if we can't do it in the class, how will we ever be able to do so in our internships, or in public life?

Your final grade will combine your grades for the internship, based on the internship evaluation meeting, the internship presentations, and the community service writing assignment (33% of the grade, taken together), and for class. participation (33% of the grade), based on your participation in discussions and other class activities (33% of the grade), and the journal (33% of the grade).

Readings: The following required books are available for purchase in the bookstore; they are also on reserve in McCabe library. "Reader" refers to Writing for Change: A Community Reader. Readings marked with an asterisk will be distributed

> Melissa F. Greene, Praying for Sheetrock
> Peter Medoff and H. Sklar, Streets of Hope: The Fall and Rise of an Urban Neighborhood
> Ann Watters and M. Ford, Writin2 for Change: A Community Reader

Course Outline and Schedule of Assignments:

T 1/17   **Introduction: What is community action?**

> Dialogue with Zulene Mayfield, Chester Residents Concerned for Quality Living (neighborhood organizing against the incinerator)
> Leaming agreements distributed
> Praying for Sheetrock

T 1/24   **Community service and community action**

> Dialogue with Lisa Gaffney, Chester Community Improvement Project (housing)
> Handouts on service learning, housing*
> Internship presentation
> Leaming agreement due

Sat. 1/28 Community work project with CCIP

T 1/3 1   **Family and community**

Internship presentation
Reader, pp. 1-39
Roots assignment
Leaming agreement due
Journal due

T 2n   **Multicultural politics**

Dialogue with Fernando Chang-Muy (local activism)
Internship presentation
Reader, 40-8 1.

T 2/14   **The individual and community action**

Internship presentation
Reader, 86-135
Journal due

T 2/21   **Knowledge, education, theory, and practice**

Internship presentation
Reader, 139-199
Handouts on different ways of knowing*

T 2/28   **Health and community action**

Midsemester internship self-evaluations
Reader, 303-72
Journal due

Spring Break

T 3/14   **Outsiders and community action**

Internship presentation
Reader, Community service writing student projects at the end of each chapter
Handouts on community service writing*
Community service writing proposals due

T 3/21   **Power and empowerment**

Internship presentation
Reader, 206-50
Journal due

T 3/28   **Participatory democracy and leadership**

Internship presentation
Reader, 251-299

T 4/4   **The environment and community action**

Internship presentation
Reader, 379-446
Journal due

T 4/1 1   **The politics of community action: case study** Internship presentation

Streets of Hol2e, Chs. 1-5

T 4/18   **The politics of community action: case study, cont.** Final internship presentations and self-evaluations

Streets of Hol2e, Chs. 6-9

May 13 Complete journal and summary essay due

The Work of Citizenship and the Problem of Service-Learning

by Harry C. Boyte and James Farr

The debates about service-learning are not merely internecine squabbles among educators over methods and manners of out-of-class instruction. Or at least they don't have to be. For they reflect and are implicated in broader debates about community service and civic education more generally, as well as about citizenship, public policy, and even our understandings of American democracy and history. Take a couple of snapshots of these broader debates, now and then.

Throughout 1995, the national service initiative — AmeriCorps — became a sacrificial offering by the Republican leadership on the altar of a balanced budget. The question allegedly was whether government should be in the business of "promoting voluntarism": whether, in particular, AmeriCorps members should get paid for what citizens are supposed to do anyway on a voluntary basis. This rendering of what was at stake with a national initiative of this kind vividly illustrated how much had been lost from understandings of "service" — and of citizenship itself.

The debate about AmeriCorps and voluntary service can be contrasted with the public and political overtones that once existed in service initiatives such as the Civilian Conservation Corps (CCC) of the 1930s and early 1940s. The CCC enlisted more than three million young men, mainly poor and unemployed youth from rural areas and small towns, in public projects that ranged from contour farming to building dams, bridges, and national parks. Veterans from the CCC — men now in their late 70s or 80s, of all political persuasions — continue to meet all across the country, in commemoration of what for many was the transformative experience of their lives.[1]

There was never a question about whether CCC members should be paid. Indeed, monthly stipends of $30 a month were enough to support most members during the Depression. Service was understood to be work with civic overtones and implications: determined, hard civic effort to produce a public good, to meet critical public challenges.

These traditions and understandings continued. For instance, in the early 1950s the well-known educator Lewis Mumford warned about the rise of a bureaucratic, narrowly technical civilization and the loss of an ethos of citizenship based on public work. In The Conduct of Life — what he called the "culmination" of his career — Mumford argued that "our present civilization lacks the capacity for self-direction because it has committed itself to mass organizations and has built its structures from the top down, on the prin-

ciple of all dictatorships and absolutism, rather than from the bottom up."
Mumford believed technological civilization was "efficient in giving orders
and compelling obedience and providing one-way communication; but it is
. . . inept in everything that involves reciprocity, mutual aid, two-way communication, give and take" (1951: 276, 278).

To counter such trends, Mumford proposed a "public work corps" that
would put each young man and woman to work "doing a thousand things
that need to be done, from planting forests and roadside strips, supervision
of school children in nurseries and playgrounds to the active companionship
of the aged, the blind, the crippled, from auxiliary work in harvesting to fire
fighting." Broad education — including ways young people might experience
a larger public of different cultures, regions, points of view, and modes of life
unlike their own — was essential to his plan. Education for citizenship
through public work was, for Mumford, even more important than the particular tasks themselves.

Yet overall, Mumford's voice was the rare exception. The social, political,
and economic forces of the time dramatically eroded the explicit language
and the everyday experiences of public work, work that had larger public
purposes and overtones. With the loss of "public work," the concept of "service" changed its meanings as well.[2]

Today, participants in contemporary versions of the conservation corps,
part of the larger AmeriCorps service initiative, often see a clear distinction
between what they are doing and the way it is described; they lament the
absence of public urgency that once framed the CCC. "The Civilian
Conservation Corps of the 1930s was successful because it sought to address
a national emergency," argued Steve Guetterman, of Montana Conservation
Corps. Guetterman observes that "our problems today are more pronounced,
and embedded in social and environmental structures. Yet as a nation, we
have not declared 'war' on any of these problems" (interview, March 3, 1995).

AmeriCorps and other service initiatives, such as Campus Compact,
may well hold the potential to help revitalize the concept and practice of
public work, as well as to make service-learning explicitly contribute to the
education of citizens. But for such potential to be realized will mean understanding exactly what we want from service-learning, rethinking our history, and retrieving what we have largely failed to remember.

Service and Citizenship

American history can be told, in one of its most crucial dimensions, as a
story of the struggles of most of its denizens to become citizens: as a narra-
tive about conflict over the fundamental issue of membership, of exactly
who are to be included as citizens. This dramatic and tumultuous tale has as

its actors colonists, workingmen, (emancipated) slaves, women, and immigrants.[3] Today, this story of membership and inclusion continues, as can be seen in the often acrimonious debates over immigration or, especially on campuses, over multiculturalism and cultural pluralism.

Yet, American history can also be told in terms of another, rather less explored dimension of citizenship: namely, *what* is a citizen and what does a citizen do? Three main conceptions have arisen in our history, each tied to a distinctive conception of service. Citizens have been understood as:

1. rights-bearing members of a political system who choose their leaders, preferably men of distinctive virtue and talent, through elections;

2. caring members of a moral community who share certain values and feel common responsibilities toward one another; and

3. practical agents of a civic world who work together in public ways and spaces to engage the tasks and try to solve the problems that they collectively face.

Each of these conceptions may be thought of as an "ideal type" (in Max Weber's sense), picking out but refining, stylizing, and generalizing certain particular features of the real world of citizenship. In the actual debates of American history, these ideal types often run into and overlap with one another. But each is sufficiently distinctive, with clear and powerful voices behind it, as to organize our understanding of the past and our orientation to service and service-learning.

The first conception of citizenship, what is these days often called a liberal view of citizenship though it has roots also in a classical republican tradition, is based on the idea that a citizen is a bearer of rights. The liberal citizen's liberty is understood in largely negative terms: namely, as rights to protection from harassment, unjust imprisonment, or unwarranted interference from others. When it comes to acting and practicing their citizenship, citizens are mainly to vote, to petition for redress of grievance, and perhaps to organize with others into groups to convey their interests. But these citizen actions and practices are directed at or mediated by the government itself. Although its powers are to be kept as minimal as possible with respect to the rights of citizens, the government and the leaders who run government are at the center of action.

This was the view of citizens voiced by founders such as James Madison. In *Federalist* 10, as is well known, Madison distinguished between "democracy," where the entire citizenry participates, and a "republic," where authority is delegated to "a small number of citizens elected by the rest." Madison argued for representative government, based on his assertion that the deliberations of "a chosen body of citizens, whose wisdom may best discern the true interest of their country" would tend to "be more consonant to the public good than if pronounced by the people themselves" (Hamilton

1961: 81-82).

This approach was closely associated with republican ideas of public service as the mark of gentlemen who put aside their private interests to pursue the common good. Such men were to serve in government as members of a special class known for its virtue and talent. Service, in this sense, was sharply distinguished from work, especially manual labor. Over time, the republican elitism regarding service receded, only to be replaced within liberalism by a professional ideal. This ideal — the notion that politics and public affairs are what professionals do — dominates in our time. When analysts and activists refer to "politics," whatever their political persuasion or partisanship, they generally mean politics of this liberal, professionalized sort. Ordinary citizens still discharge their electoral activities, periodically voting to endorse or reject the policies that professional politicians create. Their role is institutionalized in this way.

The view of civic education that flows from such institutional citizenship is rather straightforward. It is what we know as "civics." If the center of action in governance and public affairs is government, then the key subject matter of education is what happens in government: How a bill becomes law; how professional lobbyists succeed; how parties mobilize constituency interests.

Service-learning is not generally a term of art for civics, though analogues of it may be found in those out-of-class activities that are preparatory for (later) public service of a professionalized kind. Student government, mock conventions, and leadership training activities are the conventionalized forms of such an education, as also are internships where students learn as they serve their legislative representatives or party officials.

These service-learning analogues of civics serve educative functions in our polity, of course; but they are open to the same criticisms that may be charged against the liberal, professional, institutional politics to which their view of citizenship and public service is attached. Today, for example, few would agree with Madison's sanguine view of the wisdom of elected officials or of the later liberal view of the expertise of professional politicians. People decry a separation between citizenry and officials. As a recent Kettering Foundation study discovered, Americans are angry that a seemingly unaccountable, self-referential group of politicians has effected a veritable takeover of the political process, turning the idea of "government of and by the people" into a sordid spectacle.[4]

The federal government stood at the bottom in polling about faith in major American institutions, with only 8 percent of respondents expressing "a great deal of confidence." According to a *New York Times* poll in August 1995, "frustration runs deep, perhaps deeper than any other time in modern American history." Seventy-nine (79) percent of the public, the highest in several decades, believed that the government is pretty much "run by a few big interests looking out for themselves." Fifty-eight (58) percent of those polled believed that people like themselves "had little to say about what the government did."[5]

Resentment of politics, politicians, and government is the tip of a larger iceberg of general discontent, anger about every institution, and fear for the future. Harvard political scientist Robert Putnam (1995) found that Americans' affiliations with civic institutions that have a face-to-face quality — from churches to PTAs to service groups such as Kiwanis — have declined over the last generation. In his much-discussed essay "Bowling Alone," Putnam pointed out that though more Americans were bowling — no mean statistic, since more Americans bowl each year than vote — far more were bowling by themselves. Bowling league participation has sharply declined. The industry was alarmed because alleys gain most profit from concession sales of products such as beer and pretzels, consumed mostly as a social activity. Putnam had other worries attendant to the isolation of bowling alone. In the 1960s, he observed, two-thirds of the public expressed trust of other citizens, while one-third was distrustful. By the 1990s, figures had reversed themselves: Two-thirds distrusted other people.[6]

The general citizenry itself is scarcely innocent in the problems with our democracy, however. Increasingly, Americans have come to think of themselves as clients and consumers. This is an even further step away from citizenship conceived as voting or the bearing of rights. While people complain, they look to government to provide answers or services. This means people see themselves as innocent, even victimized, as lacking any civic responsibility for what happens or for civic work that needs to be done. Such a view was epitomized on a talk show not long ago by one man who said none too coherently that "taxpayers shouldn't have to pay for the S&L mess. Government should pay for it!"[7]

Today, furthermore, the nation is in danger of splitting into a myriad of different rights groups that see themselves as consumers of professionalized government services: young Americans versus seniors on Social Security, blacks versus whites, suburbanites versus inner-city residents, environmentalists versus ranchers.

Fragmentation of groups and rights without responsibilities have led to the resurfacing of a second — essentially communitarian — view of citizenship, grounded in ideals of moral community and deliberation about the common good. In this perspective, voiced by people such as Robert Bellah, Amitai Etzioni, Michael Sandel, Michael Lerner, and many others, citizenship means participation in a shared way of life and a common system of moral values.[8] Thus, for instance, William Sullivan (1988), coauthor of the modern classics *Habits of the Heart* and *The Good Society*, proposes a vision of "commonwealth" involving a virtually unbounded "covenant morality." To Sullivan, the good society is one in which we "as citizens . . . make an unlimited promise to show care and concern to each other." Such a "way of life," in his view, "stands in opposition to the life of self interest." Its aim is "universal sympathy" that grows from a "mutual commitment to a common good."[9]

The reference to "convenant morality" recalls the important religious dimensions of American history, and thus of one tradition (or set of traditions) lying behind contemporary communitarianism. Communitarianism also recalls strands of the classical republican tradition as well, especially in terms of virtue and public service. However, communitarians have tried to displace the elitism of classical republicanism, finding in the people — or at least in members of the moral community — the repository of virtue and talent. Hostile to liberalism — especially to its preoccupation with rights and to (what Sandel 1984 calls) its view of an "unencumbered self" (1994:81-96) — communitarians have helped to reconceptualize citizens as moral selves, fully "situated" in a community. Such selves, to quote Sullivan again, make "an unlimited promise to show care and concern to each other," thereby invoking the importance of voluntarism within the communitarian conception of citizenship.

What do citizens do, then, on the communitarian account? They serve one another, but especially those who are most needy of sympathy, care, and concern. Citizens do voluntary deeds for the good of others in a community in which they themselves are situated (either geographically or morally).

A conception of service-learning follows almost seamlessly from this conception of citizenship. Indeed, the contemporary service-learning movement — if it can properly be called a movement — has, it would appear, a made-to-order ally in communitarianism. Students and young people learn about citizenship (by definition), as well as about themselves, when they serve others in the community. Thus, service-learning, its communitarian advocates claim, prepares an otherwise self-centered generation for citizenship. For instance, the Grant Commission's report *Youth and America's Future* stated that "if the service commitment begins early enough and continues into adulthood, participatory citizenship would become . . . traditions of local political participation that sustain a person, a community, and a nation" (see Grant Commission 1990: 441). Using this rationale, community service initiatives expanded rapidly in the late 1980s and the 1990s. Detroit schools now require 200 hours of community service for graduation. Atlanta adopted a 75-hour minimum requirement to increase "understanding of the obligations of a good citizen." Minnesota and Pennsylvania have developed statewide financing for service.[10]

Community service in this sense mainly refers to a variety of individual voluntary efforts, from work in food banks to homeless shelters, from helping in nursing homes or hospitals to tutoring projects and literacy campaigns. It is only a short step from here to philanthropy, with its injunction to "Do Good." In schools today, however, service-learning programs also stress personal growth. Educational objectives reflect this emphasis: "self-esteem," "a sense of personal worth," "belief in the ability to make a difference," and "consciousness about one's personal values."[11] It is only a short step from here to therapy, with its injunction to "Feel Better." Together, the philanthropic and therapeutic dimensions of service-learning lead us to "Do Good, Feel Better."

Service-learning understood in this way can make a number of educational contributions — connection with others, help to the needy, and personal growth. Communitarianism more generally has properly reintroduced notions of communal responsibility and civic values as central to the very idea(l) of citizenship. However, there are reasons to fear that communitarianism in theory and service-learning in practice tend to romanticize the idea of community and to sentimentalize the idea of the situated self. There can be many disturbing features about actual community life, especially for those whose "way of life" falls afoul of so-called community standards, much less a "covenant morality." There are also reasons to suspect that the conception of citizenship at stake here tends strongly to *purify* democratic politics and public life of power, interests, and practical purposes. It tends to assume or to aspire to a world, indeed "the good society" itself, terribly far removed from the complicated, complex, challenging, and everyday actions of citizens who work to get things done. In this way, it tends to overlook extraordinary lessons for civic renewal from American history. These lessons, in turn, help us revitalize a third conception of citizenship, one more attentive to practical problem solving, the public dimensions of work, and the very idea of public work itself.

Service as Public Work

As new scholarship has begun to emphasize, the distinctive feature of the American Revolution was neither a Lockean-liberal focus on rights nor a classical republican concern with civic virtue. Rather, America's revolution produced a political culture that was practical, down-to-earth, work-centered, and energetic. As Gordon Wood put it in his recent work *The Radicalism of the American Revolution*, "when [classical ideals of disinterested civic virtue] proved too idealistic and visionary, [Americans] found new democratic adhesives in the actual behavior of plain ordinary people" (1992: ix).[12]

Work on common projects of importance — in offices and schools, factories and farms, government agencies or inner-city communities, paid or unpaid — continued to be the way diverse people forged connections with one another and addressed the nation's problems and challenges. Through work, people developed trust in others different from themselves, gained visibility and authority, and reached larger intellectual horizons. They saw themselves as creators of their communities, stakeholders in the country, and guardians of the commonwealth.

Abraham Lincoln's idea of work-centered government, the instrument of common purpose, remained vibrant well into the 20th century. Belief in the dignity of labor fueled popular reform movements for change. For instance, in the first decades of this century the Country Life Movement, with land-grant colleges playing central roles, called for renewal of rural democracy and rural life, based on the long history of agriculture as "democratic public work," not simply commercial farming. Many jobs, local schools, community projects, and other experiences provided rich experiences in public work. In the Great Depression, images and themes of work, tied to democracy, filled popular culture — Will Rogers movies, Langston Hughes poetry, post office art. These experiences and the larger culture of public work formed the background for understanding service: as seen, for example, when millions of poor and unemployed youth put their talents to work in the Civilian Conservation Corps, building dams and bridges and planting forests.

Such experiences fired the imagination of mid-20th-century educators such as Lewis Mumford, whose call for a "public work corps" we quoted earlier, or John A. Hannah. In 1944, as president of Michigan State College, Hannah reflected on land-grant colleges such as his that were founded in strong work activities and dedicated to forging strong links between career training and citizen education:

> Our colleges should not be content with only the training of outstanding agriculturalists, or engineers, or home economists, or teachers, or scientists, or lawyers, or doctors, or veterinarians — it is not enough that our young people be outstanding technicians. The first and never-forgotten objective must be that every human product of our educational system must be given that training that will enable him to be an effective citizen, appreciating his opportunities, and fully willing to assume his responsibilities in a great democracy.

Words such as these and the work of generations of American citizens can and should still fire our imaginations today. They can help us rekindle a conception of citizenship as work with civic overtones, what we have called "public work." Public work is the expenditure of visible efforts by ordinary citizens whose collective labors produce things or create processes of lasting civic value. Public work is work by ordinary citizens who build and sustain our basic public goods and resources. It solves common problems and creates common things. It may be paid or voluntary, done in communities or as part of one's regular job. Public work takes place with an eye to general, other-regarding consequences. It is also work done "in" public — in places that are visible and open to inspection. And it is cooperative work of "a" public: a mix of people whose interests, backgrounds, and resources may be quite different.

What do citizens do, then, when they engage in public work? They work together in and through deliberation to specify and then try to solve problems and address the tasks that they face in a complex and complicated public world. Under such a conception, citizens are best thought of not as clients, customers, servers, or mere voters but as workers, collectively trying to solve problems and to create civic products. Emphasis falls upon the skills and productive capacities — not so much the virtues or values — of citizens who need to work together with their fellow and sister citizens, rather than do things for or to them. They share problems and labors; they need not share a profession, a party, or a moral community as such. The associations of this conception of citizenship are pragmatist and populist, fully attentive to the filiations between political action and productive economic life that, until recently, have been silenced in democratic theory or theories of citizenship.[13]

Substantial civic education through "service" in this third conception of citizenship view requires that young people be thought of as citizens-in-the-making who have serious public work to do. When thinking about "service-learning," public work means the creation and sustenance of projects for which young people are taken and take themselves to be accountable, serious creators and producers. It also means that young people themselves identify the problems that they wish to set themselves to solve through their collective labors in and around their own spaces — whether schools, churches, or youth group sites. Furthermore, for this form of self-consciously civic and work-oriented "service-learning" to contribute to generalized civic education, adults who work with young people in the field of youth development — including teachers, youth workers, counselors, clergy, and others — need to engage in public work with young people, both challenging and learning from them. Such experiences help youth develop a sense of themselves as effective, public-spirited citizens. In this way, they cultivate capacities for lifelong learning and for productive contributions through whatever jobs they do. Such a notion of service-learning is quite plainly a challenge to the analogues one finds in civics, where, we have noted, a professionalized and institutionalized notion of politics predominates. It is also quite plainly a challenge to the therapeutic and philanthropic orientation that pervades much of what passes for service-learning today.

A work-centered view of citizenship and service-learning must be sensitive to the problems it faces in the world we now live in. Today, unfortunately, opportunities for young people's public work are rare. Most youth development workers see young people themselves as "problems" to be managed, clients to be served, or as consumers of knowledge — in ways that unwittingly limit their talents and potential. Moreover, these youth development workers share in the conventional wisdom that teenagers and young adults are deeply disenchanted with politics and public issues. The Times-Mirror Center reports that for the first time since World War II, young people show less interest in public affairs than their elders. Only one in five follows major issues "very closely."[14]

In fact, youth today have a more complex set of attitudes about the world than polling suggests. More detailed probing finds a generation not so much apathetic as furious at adults' apparent inaction on mounting social problems. Young people are angry at what they perceive as adults' labeling of them as "problems." They are usually not enthused by 1960s-style protest. They worry about future work prospects and are uncertain about how to respond to the problems they see all around them. Senior trips to Washington, DC, or exhortations to be "good citizens" — the stuff of earlier generations' civic education — do not much address such problems.

The conception of citizenship as public work, tied to practical problem solving, not only has the historical legacy alluded to above. It animates the concatenated programs and practices that we have tried to develop at the University of Minnesota under the aegis of the Center for Democracy and Citizenship (and its predecessor, Project Public Life), including in the fields of service and service-learning. Indeed, the very idea of citizenship as public work was an emergent property of our efforts. The center originally grew out of a series of questions: How could the lessons from the "Citizenship Schools" of the civil rights movement as well as citizen action groups be translated to work settings? How could professional practices and identities be "liberated" into more productive public work? In order to answer these questions, we had to think of work as a kind of citizenship, as having civic or public dimensions and consequences. Having made this conceptual move, it was an altogether complementary one to think of citizenship itself as work, as public work. A virtuous circle was completed.

The center's strategy has been to develop democratic theory strongly enriched by practice. To this end, it engages with groups across many different work and institutional cultures to compare lessons from an array of experiments in civic renewal and the creation of cultures of public accountability. Settings have ranged from cooperative extension service to hospitals, middle schools, high schools, youth groups, a large nursing home, a Catholic women's college, a Korean youth center, a public health teen project, local government, and the Corporation for National Service. These settings were chosen because they provided ones that fit the center's efforts in the overlapping fields of youth development and community service, health, higher education, and citizen-government partnership. These have proved to be the seedbed for developing a theory and practice of public work, and thinking differently about service and service-learning.

The main vehicle for experimenting with a work-centered, problem-solving approach — or alternative — to service-learning has been Public Achievement, a youth and politics initiative spearheaded in 1990.[15] Sharing service-learning's intention to provide experiential learning and community involvement for students, Public Achievement has nonetheless been very self-conscious in trying to pass along to participants a conceptual framework about politics and civic engagement that we have found is largely missing from most service-learning activities. That framework valorizes not only public work and problem solving but also the unsentimentalized notions of power and interest. But it mainly strives to pass along the skills and civic capacities for teamwork, rule making, negotiating, deliberating, debating, public speaking, and "mapping" the environment in terms of powerful agents and diverse others with whom younger and older citizens must work.

While some Public Achievement teams have worked in various kinds of community service capacities, we have focused our greatest energies on working with young people. That is, college-age students have done their "service" with even younger students, in middle schools, high schools, theater programs, and other youth sites. The college-age students act as "coaches" (a term that the younger students themselves helped establish, as opposed to "teachers," "mentors," or "big brothers" or "sisters"). Coaches self-consciously work to pass along the conceptual framework, as well as the skills and civic capacities, that the younger students will need to negotiate the broader world of work and politics. The problems that the coaches take on are those that the younger students themselves have established as the important ones in and around their schools, neighborhoods, or youth sites. Sometimes these problems have standardly recognizable community service orientations — from violence prevention, neighborhood cleanup, or recycling to helping foodshelves, homeless shelters, or seniors homes. But sometimes the problems are quite plainly school related or youth-site related, from getting playground equipment or juice machines to changing uniform or playground policies. But whatever the problem specified, the younger students — along with help from their coaches — learn to engage a broader public world, to master its rules, to map its power, and to organize to change it. In short, they learn the skills — and the necessary concepts — to engage in public work.

Like any practical experiment, Public Achievement has faced challenges and difficulties. Many of these have been challenges that various community service programs or even internships have faced. Others have been brought on precisely because of the ambitious, self-conscious attempt to pass along a conceptual framework of politics that itself requires students to think about themselves and the world around them in civic terms. But challenges notwithstanding, the responses by younger students, college-age coaches, teachers, principals, parents, and community leaders have reinforced the importance of thinking of "service-learning" in these terms and thus of helping to revitalize a conception of citizenship as public work.

This form of youth citizenship and civic education "allows me to do something I want, not just something the teachers tell me to do," explains Tracy Veronen, an eighth-grader at St. Bernard's Middle School in St. Paul. Jeff Mauer, a teacher in the school, says the trick is to guide or coach instead of to lead or command. "Adults feel like they have to jump in and fix everything," explained Mauer. "I have developed a new appreciation and respect for my students as I watched them identify issues, devise strategies to deal with them, and evaluate their own progress." "I felt that we needed to have ways to take kids more seriously. That's why I was interested in Public Achievement," explains Dennis Donovan, principal of St. Bernard's. "We thought that learning citizenship skills would influence relations in schools, the curriculum, and the way we taught," says Donovan. "It has. Many kids are much better at expressing their interests and negotiating with teachers. Teachers have begun to base their teaching more directly on what kids are interested in" (interviews, August/September 1995).[16]

Young people's experiences in public work of this kind are not unique to Public Achievement. For instance, accounts from young people involved in Children's Express, a project that produces a youth perspectives news service to papers across the country, show the enhanced sense of civic efficacy and public involvement that these kinds of work experiences can generate (interview, August 24, 1995).[17] Other examples from the service-learning movement may well be found as well. These examples suggest the elements of a fundamentally different approach to youth development based on the revitalization of a notion of citizenship as public work. "Youth development to date has been defined within a human services framework that uses a language of personal growth," says Nan Skelton, a leader in the field. "It will require a major shift — a paradigm shift — to see youth as citizens who actually produce things of value. But this shift will also open up many new forms of work, new occupations, and new ways of understanding the social value of young people as coproducers and cocreators" (interview, September 6, 1995).

What is true of youth development in general is true of service-learning in particular. It is our strong belief that service-learning should be thought of as citizen education; and citizen education in turn should be thought of as an education in and for public work. Work is and should be at the center of citizenship, and this should be the problem for service-learning. Returning work to the center of discussion about democracy and citizen education opens up enormous new possibilities for democratic renewal. The service-learning movement should make the work of democratic renewal its own work.

Notes

1. For further discussion of the Civilian Conservation Corps in terms of public work, see Harry C. Boyte and Nancy N. Kari, *Building America: The Democratic Promise of Public Work* (Philadelphia: Temple University Press, 1996). Not everything in the CCC is above criticism, needless to say. See, for example, Eric B. Gorham, *National Service, Citizenship, and Political Education* (Albany: SUNY Press, 1992), chs. 4 and 7.

2. This is an important example of conceptual change amidst political innovation. In general, see James Farr, "Understanding Conceptual Change Politically," in *Political Innovation and Conceptual Change,* edited by Terence Ball, James Farr, and Russell L. Hanson (Cambridge: Cambridge University Press, 1989), ch. 2.

3. See, for example, James H. Kettner, *The Development of American Citizenship, 1608-1870* (Chapel Hill: University of North Carolina Press, 1978).

4. The democratic upsurge abroad has been accompanied by a sharp decline in partic-ipation in American politics, cited regularly as a model by our leaders and by aspiring reformers abroad. A growth industry of American consultants have visited — one might plausibly say plagued — new democracies. At the same moment, every index — from voter turnout to opinion polls — demonstrated increasing cynicism and anger about politics within the nation. See E.J. Dionne, *Why Americans Hate Politics* (New York: Simon and Schuster, 1991) for an insightful discussion of the moralized posturing that emerges from the political class's isolation; and Harwood Group, *Citizens and Politics: A View From Main Street America* (Dayton: Kettering, 1991) for the description of Americans' attitudes toward that class.

5. Figures from *BusinessWeek*, March 13, 1995; *New York Times*/CBS News poll, August 12, 1995. Fifty-nine (59) percent of the Times/CBS poll said there was not a single elected official they admired.

6. See, more generally, Putnam's *Making Democracy Work: Civic Traditions in Modern Italy* (Princeton: Princeton University Press, 1993).

7. Quoted in Harry C. Boyte, "Building Blocks for American Renewal," *Los Angeles Times,* December 25, 1991.

8. See, for instance, Robert Bellah et al., *Habits of the Heart* (Berkeley: University of California Press, 1986); Michael Lerner's editorials in *Tikkun* on "the politics of mean-ing," 1992-93; Michael Sandel, *Liberalism and the Limits of Justice* (Cambridge: Cambridge University Press, 1982); and Amitai Etzioni, *The Spirit of Community: Rights,*

Responsibilities, and the Communitarian Agenda (New York: Crown, 1993). For a balanced overview, see Will Kymlicka, *Contemporary Political Philosophy: An Introduction* (Oxford: Clarendon Press, 1990), ch. 6.

9. For the ties of service to communitarian philosophy, see the bulk of the essays in Kendall 1990.

10. Figures on service from Alonzo Crim, "The Obligation of Citizenship," in Kendall 1990, pp. 240-241.

11. For a representative listing of learner outcomes, see, for instance, Kendall 1990; also Sandra LaFave, "Letter to the Editor," *Harper's*, February 1991.

12. As Wood further observes, this "was momentously radical in the long sweep of world history up to that time," p. ix.

13. See Joshua Cohen and Joel Rogers, eds., *Associations and Democracy* (New York: Verson, 1995), and Benjamin R. Barber, *Jihad v. McWorld* (New York: Times Books, 1995).

14. For figures on youth disenchantment from politics, see, for instance, Michael Oreskes, "Profiles of Today's Youths: Many Just Don't Seem to Care," *New York Times*, June 28, 1990; "An Indifferent Age?," *Christian Science Monitor*, July 9, 1990; and "Children's Moral Compass Wavers," *Christian Science Monitor*, May 16, 1990.

15. For background and analysis, see the master's thesis by Melissa Bass, "Toward a New Theory and Practice of Civic Education: An Evaluation of Public Achievement," Minneapolis, Humphrey Institute, 1995. Also see the discussion in Farr's essay on "Political Theory" later in this volume.

16. Interviews at St. Bernard's Middle School were conducted in the course of an evaluation of Public Achievement.

17. Quotes from Children's Express staff are from *Report to Lilly Endowment* (Indianapolis: Children's Express Indianapolis News Bureau, 1995).

References

Grant Commission, "Pathways to Success: Citizenship Through Service," in Kendall 1990, pp. 439-455. [Excerpted and adapted from *Youth and America's Future*.]

Hamilton, Alexander, James Madison, and John Jay. (1961). *The Federalist*. New York: New American Library.

Kendall, Jane, and Associates. (1990). *Combining Service and Learning: A Resource Book for Community and Public Service*. Raleigh, NC: NSIEE.

Mumford, Lewis. (1951). *The Conduct of Life*. New York: Harcourt, Brace.

Putnam, Robert D. (January 1995). "Bowling Alone." *Journal of Democracy* 9:65-78.

Sandel, Michael. (1984). "The Procedural Republic and the Unencumbered Self." *Political Theory* 12:81-96.

Sullivan, William. (1988). *Reconstructing Public Philosophy*. Berkeley: University of California.

Wood, Gordon S. (1992). *The Radicalism of the American Revolution*. New York: Vintage.

Examining Pedagogy in the Service-Learning Classroom: Reflections on Integrating Service-Learning Into the Curriculum

by Karen D. Zivi

In recent years, service-learning programs have been praised for increasing the number of service-learning courses offered at a college or for involving more students in academically based community service activities. Indeed, many involved with service-learning have made it a primary goal to further "institutionalize," "integrate," or "infuse" service-learning into and across the curriculum, to make service-learning a standard practice on campus. During the 1995-96 academic year, I was involved in one such integration effort at Rutgers University. That year Political Science 101, Nature of Politics, became a service-learning course, or, more accurately, it offered a service-learning option for students enrolled in the course. For those who enrolled as service-learning students, service work became an additional requirement of the course, a requirement for which they received an extra academic credit. As the "service-learning" teaching assistant in charge of the specially designated "service-learning" discussion sections, it became my responsibility to move an additive model of service-learning to an integrative one. That is, I was to encourage and guide students to relate their service experiences to course themes, to make connections between the two educational experiences. It was during that year, as I struggled to integrate service into an already existing course, that I came to understand the work involved in such integration, work that requires an examination of and commitment to transformed classroom practices. While it is exciting to see new service-learning courses added to course listings and to involve new faculty, and while we have a long way to go to improve institutional commitment to service-learning, institutionalization of service-learning must be done thoughtfully. If we are committed to the promise and potential of service-learning to transform the educational experience of students, to challenge traditional models of learning, then we must identify classroom practices that promote or that hinder the learning goals of a service-learning course.

My concern, that in the move to infuse service into the curriculum we are too quick to lose sight of the learning goals of service-learning and the classroom practices that promote these goals, stems from my experiences with Nature of Politics. In that course, I struggled to identify classroom practices that would do justice to both course material and service experiences. I sought out an appropriate relationship between classroom practices and proposed goals of service-learning. I struggled to understand what was happening in our attempts to add and to integrate service into an already existing course. In this essay, then, I raise and explore the following questions: What happens to the learning goals of service-learning in the move to institutionalize service-learning into and across the curriculum? What becomes of the "learning" when service is seen as something that can be easily added to an already existing course, when service-learning becomes something that requires little or no pedagogical or curricular change? What happens when service is seen simply as a pedagogical tool through which to teach the same materials, themes, or ideas using traditional classroom practices? What is the implicit philosophical and pedagogical commitment of a service-learning program when it is praised in terms of hours of free labor provided to the community or in terms of the number of courses offered?

Service-LEARNING

In the answer to these questions and the evaluation of service-learning classroom practices lies a definition or conception of the potential of service-learning, the learning goals of such a classroom. Though there is much debate around the definition of service-learning or its necessary emphasis, there are some learning goals that seem fairly common, learning goals that are implicit in my understanding of "successful" integration. These include the potential of service-learning to encourage an active or experiential learning process that is reflective and community oriented. By this I mean that service-learning, first and foremost, is a form of experiential education that takes seriously that students learn by doing, that they learn from the work they do at their service site. This suggests that students are taking a more active role in their education by participating in rather than being passive recipients of knowledge already produced. Whether they learn to be more thoughtful participants in a community or they learn a particular skill, service-learning students are encouraged to recognize the service experience as an educational experience. However, service-learning also implies that the educational value of doing or experiencing can be enhanced by and through reflection. On college campuses, then, taking service seriously as an educational experience by encouraging reflection has often meant connecting it to a course or to academic materials. In other words, learning is furthered when students are encouraged to think about what they're doing at their service site in relation to academic work on topics such as child development, the law, or democracy. When service-learning ties academic pursuits to service experiences it becomes "community oriented." It approaches teaching and learning as occurring when the gap between the classroom and the world outside is bridged. Indeed, service-learning asks students and instructors to view the world outside the classroom as a place where academic theories are brought to life, challenged, and utilized. In a service-learning classroom, academic themes and service experiences are brought into conversation. Thus, service-learning encourages students to move beyond mastery of text to recognizing connections between classroom readings and service experiences. It encourages students to think critically not only about the texts they read but also about the way the world works and about what their education has to do with perpetuating, improving, or contributing to what they identify as problems in the world.

This kind of learning does not usually occur in a traditional classroom. In a traditional classroom, particularly in large lecture courses, students often assume a passive role. They become the passive recipients of knowledge transmitted by the instructor. In this scenario, instructors are placed in the role of knower, and student as receptacle of knowledge.[1] Service-learning demands transformed classroom practices. If students are to engage in active, reflective, community-oriented learning, the practices and roles of both students and instructors must be transformed. In a service-learning classroom, students take an active role in their learning. They learn not only by doing or participating but also by reflecting upon what it is they've done, often in conjunction with academic texts. As an experiential educational experience that brings classroom theories to life, that connects the "real world" with the world of the "ivy tower," service-learning places students in the role of the knower and instructors in the role of the facilitator. Indeed, for reflective learning to occur, students need instructors who offer guidance and encouragement, who challenge students to see ideas active in the world and to identify their service as a question for academic theories. Without an instructor who can model a particular way of questioning and connecting two often disparate realms of learning and students who are empowered to continue this practice, successful integration may be jeopardized. When traditional classroom practices are continued rather than transformed, the learning potential of service-learning may not be realized. It was just such a reliance on traditional classroom practices that jeopardized the potential for successful service-learning in Nature of Politics.

Nature of Politics – The Idea

My experience with integrating service into the 101 curriculum began, however, on quite a positive note. From my perspective, it seemed quite natural to make Nature of Politics a service-learning course at Rutgers University. After all, the Political Science Department was home to the original service-learning courses at the university and had given service-learning its specifically civic education emphasis at Rutgers. Nature of Politics, a course designed to introduce mostly first-year students to seminal works, concepts, and questions in the history of political thought, seemed like a perfect course in which to integrate service and learning, with which to establish a service ethic in students early on in their college careers, and through which to raise important questions about the nature of participation in a democratic society. It also seemed a fairly easy task. I was told that my job as the service-learning teaching assistant would not be significantly more difficult or time-consuming than that of a regular TA. In other large lecture classes, I was informed, the service placements worked out very well, helping students to understand the material better and offering instructors a tool with and through which to explain the course material. In fact, the service-learning students might even do better on exams because of the integration of service and learning, or so the argument went. This information was not difficult for me to accept at the time. I had just finished teaching a service-learning course on HIV and public policy, a course that, by my estimations and by many of the students', was a very successful and stimulating course. Service had enhanced the learning that occurred in the course, bringing academic theories to life and challenging students to see connections among disparate experiences and bodies of information. I was, therefore, very pleased to be teaching a service-learning course again.

As a teaching assistant for Nature of Politics, my teaching responsibilities were limited to working with students in discussion sections. In other words, service was not integrated into the lecture part of the course but, rather, contained in the weekly or biweekly discussion sections required of all 101 students. Initially, I expected to have approximately 90 of the 300 students enrolled in 101 engaged in community service each semester. In actuality, I had between 20 and 30 service-learning students; one or two service-learning sections. The students in these sections received an additional academic credit upon completion of 40 hours of community service done during the course of the semester and completion of required reflection exercises. Their reflection requirements included journal assignments and class discussions in which they were to make connections between their service experiences and course readings. It was my responsibility to help students do this, to facilitate this integration — a far greater challenge than I had anticipated.

Nature of Politics – The Tensions

As I suggested earlier, I approached the service-learning sections of 101 with a positive mind-set. I had just taught a course in which the service work enhanced and even furthered students' learning about a particular issue, as well as about membership in a community. Thus, I truly believed that service-learning could offer students a new and perhaps life-altering educational experience. On the other hand, I was concerned. I could hear the critics wondering whether a discussion of the service experiences would diminish the academic rigor or compromise the intellectual discourse of the course, as critics and skeptics seemed to believe. I wondered whether students' critical-thinking skills, skills supposedly learned and fostered in the "traditional" classroom, would be compromised by the "hortatory or even celebratory tone" associated with discussions of service (Barber and Battistoni 1993). Would grounding reflection in course readings and themes prevent such a compromise? And what kind of reflection exercises would be necessary to balance academic rigor with experiential learning? Should I ask questions about the role of the volunteer or the service organization in a democratic society? Or should my questions focus more directly on the themes chosen by the professor? If I were to take the latter route, would I lose the "civic education" element of service-learning? If I took this more "discipline specific" route, would it illuminate or would it cloud thoughtful reflection and integration?[2] Were reflection and integration the same thing? These were just some of the questions that were floating around in my head when I began the course, questions I had little time to ponder or answer once the semester was under way.

These questions and tensions presented obstacles early on in the semester. During the first week, I experienced a strong pull between academics and service, which Benjamin Barber and Rick Battistoni (1993) describe as a pull "between the democratic need to socialize students into patterns of responsible community and effective citizenship and the academic need to develop critical-thinking skills." They argue, in "A Season of Service," that by grounding reflection in carefully chosen reading material, instructors can alleviate this tension as well as promote critical-thinking skills. Academically based service-learning programs that have a specifically civic education emphasis might, according to the article, satisfy the needs of service-learning planners as well as silence the skeptics.

My experience suggests that the pull between service and academics is not so easily overcome, particularly when service is added to or, one hopes, integrated into an already existing course. Even though I was dealing with an academically based service-learning course, I found that the reading materials did not lend themselves to easy reflection and integration, especially in the early part of the semester. While the students were busy scheduling their service placements and making their first trips to the soup kitchens, after-school tutoring programs, women's centers, and nursing homes, lectures and readings focused on Antigone's conflict between laws made by her uncle and those made by the gods. While service-learning students were struggling to find or adapt to their placement sites, feeling excited, nervous, or confused, class discussions focused on whether or not Antigone should obey a higher moral law. Given what appeared to be a wide gap between concerns of the course and service experiences, I struggled with classroom plans. Should I encourage students to share and reflect on their experiences, roles, and responsibilities as volunteers, or should I guide them through an analysis of the importance of Antigone's dilemmas? Was my job to bring the two dilemmas together? Was that even possible? How could the service experiences and the course material be brought into conversation?

In the craziness that accompanies the start of any new semester, I was unable to find a satisfactory solution to my dilemma. With only weekly 50-minute meetings in which to review the literature, place it in the context of larger course themes, and discuss connections to service experiences, I opted for the familiar — emphasizing the readings and themes that would appear later in the semester on their exams. The pattern established in the first two weeks unfortunately became the pattern for the rest of the semester. That is, familiarity and competency with course readings and themes quickly took precedence over the more difficult, unfamiliar, and time-consuming practice of identifying and analyzing connections between coursework and service experiences, over even simple reflection on the experience itself. We had little time to think about what *Antigone,* the *Federalist Papers,* or *Lord of the Flies* had to do with the hassles, nervousness, and joys students were experiencing at their placement sites. Given our time constraints, we often left discussion sections feeling frustrated and confused. The students, because they could not see connections between their service and the readings, and me, because I felt as if I had not prepared them to be respectful participants or careful observers at their service sites. With little time to model and practice the kind of questioning and thinking required for integrating service and learning, it became clear early on that "traditional" academic needs were crowding out reflection and integration.

As the course progressed, I found myself involved in another debate about service-learning. It seemed that I struggled not only with the academics-versus-service dilemma but also with the discipline-specific versus civic-education models of service-learning. This is a tension identified by Edward Zlotkowski (1995; 1996). He suggests that we need to be critical not just of service reflection divorced from academic concerns but also of those service-learning courses that follow a particularly civic virtue model. In other words, Zlotkowski argues that service-learning as civic education is a model that privileges questions of responsible citizenship and civic virtue and is thus both discipline specific and ideological. In service-learning as civic education, he sees the educational value of service-learning being displaced by conversations about moral and civic values. According to

Zlotkowski, this ideology may be turning off or turning away faculty members who would otherwise be interested in service-learning. In order to encourage more instructors to engage in service-learning, Zlotkowski suggests emphasizing the practical, learning-enhancing quality of service-learning. "Advocates," he argues, "must begin . . . moving . . . from one-size-fits-all service-learning to service-learning as a pedagogy carefully modulated to specific disciplinary and interdisciplinary goals." Thus, Zlotkowski suggests deemphasizing the civic component of service-learning for a more practical, discipline-specific, experiential-education approach.

With Nature of Politics, I confronted a model of civic education that did not quite fit with the course I was teaching and a discipline-specific model that did not quite fit the service placements chosen. I began with a narrow civic education model of service-learning that identified integration and reflection with only a few questions. These included questions of civic responsibility, notions of community, the role of service organizations in a democratic society given these understandings of citizenship and community, and the role and responsibilities of volunteers in service organizations. These questions, I believed, were crucial reflection questions that would help prepare students to be thoughtful participants and observants at their service sites, as well as critical readers in class. Unfortunately, the reading materials and the professor's themes did not focus on these questions, and thus the questions seemed like yet another addition to an already overburdened discussion section.

Recognizing that this particular model of service-learning would not lead to integration in this particular course, I adapted a more course-specific approach. I changed my reflection questions to fit the themes of the course more directly. I asked journal questions that encouraged students to make connections between a course theme — authority, obedience, inequality — and their service experiences. These questions were to function as a means to promote reflection and integration of service and learning and as a basis for classroom discussion. Unfortunately, students were often unable to answer the questions posed. Students found that they had difficulty answering both very general and more specific framing questions. In the former, I'd ask them to pick any theme from the reading and relate it to a service experience. In the latter, I'd pick a key term or concept and ask students to frame their service experience in terms of this idea, to apply the concept to the events happening at the service site. Students, however, not only struggled to relate general themes such as community and freedom to their service experiences but also struggled with the more specific questions such as identifying the ideology at work at the service site and the function it served, evaluating whether or not it served a Machiavellian function. They were often unable to make any connections between their service and the readings.

These integration problems had at least two sources — the placement sites themselves and the privileging of academic concepts over service experiences. Placement sites hindered integration because they were varied and had not been chosen to fit the course themes specifically. Of the 25 students I had one semester, only 2 were at the same site, and very few were at sites that dealt explicitly with "political" issues. For example, though we were dealing with "political" questions in class, such as injustice and social change, students did not experience their service as political. That is, they could not see the work they were doing as arising from issues of injustice or inequality or contributing to things such as social change or redistribution of power. These issues were not coming to life at the soup kitchens, tutoring programs, or the nursing homes. The students were often unable to make what seemed to me like fairly obvious connections. This problem arose, in part, I think, because the conversation about these issues was not occurring on site; they were not discussing the social causes or the long-term remedies for problems such as poverty or homelessness. They could not see or were not being shown the institutional or structural factors that contributed to the need for their services.

However, this was not solely the result of poorly chosen placements. Students' unfamiliarity with the themes and terms of the course also placed obstacles in the way of integration and forced a change in classroom practices. As I discovered, simply making reflection discipline specific did not necessarily make it any easier or effective. The discipline-specific reflection assignments privileged, in fact, required, mastery of or at least competency with the terms prior to making connections. Recognizing that students needed work with reading comprehension, I changed not my journal assignments but rather my approach in class. I shifted the focus from integration to competency with texts. Integration, I thought, would come only after this competency. If the students could "get" concepts such as structural inequality, then they might have a better chance seeing it at work at their placement site. Unfortunately, what happened was that I ran out of time. I was rarely able to return to integration questions after spending time on conceptual issues and reading comprehension. I had to put aside the idea of radically altering the traditional model of teaching and learning, and instead ended up preparing students for exams, exams that required competency with themes and terms.

Rather than structuring class discussions around questions that took the outside world as an educational site, I found myself reviewing lecture notes and reading texts with them. Students seemed to need work on understanding unfamiliar and often complex ideas such as justice, higher law, inequality, revolution, civil disobedience, and freedom. Their ability to make connections to their service experiences seemed to depend upon their understanding of the terms they were being asked to consider. Thus, rather than modeling and practicing new ways of reading and reflecting, of being students and teachers, we spent time clarifying concepts such as the iron law of oligarchy, who the proletariat were according to Marx, and what Machiavelli meant by *fortuna* and *virtu*. These were the questions students would bring to the discussion section, concepts not obviously coming to life at their service sites.

Whether one chooses a discipline-specific or a civic-education model of service-learning, or some combination of the two, there may still come a time, as it did for me, when one is forced to focus on academics instead of service or integration. This choice, which I felt forced to make, stems, in part, from what I see as inadequate attention to the work involved in transforming an already existing course into a service-learning course. Those of us involved in the integration process assumed that we could easily substitute a service-learning discussion section for a regular discussion section. We did not recognize constraints built into the already existing course, nor did we recognize our reliance on traditional notions of pedagogy and learning. In both the fall and the spring semesters of 101, we did little to accommodate, facilitate, or encourage the different pedagogical approach necessary for successful integration of service and academics. We assumed that not much needed to or could be changed in order to integrate service into the course. No changes were made in the scheduling, little thought was given to placement selection, and both the exams and the syllabus remained unaltered. I tried to change some of the classroom practices by encouraging reflection through journal writing and class discussion, but, at the time, we recognized little need to change when and how much time students spent in the classroom, or to include readings that would be more likely to enhance the learning done at the service site, or even to worry too much about which service sites would be most appropriate to the course. We did not think to assess carefully our learning objectives or evaluation tools. The result was that the service-learning students were treated much like the other students. They were expected to be in class the same amount of time as the regular students, to read the same material as the others, to take the same exams, and to behave, in class, as the other students in 101. The only difference noted was that I would encourage them to use their service experiences to reflect on course themes.

It is this lack of awareness or recognition of necessary changes that, I would argue, exacerbates the gap or pull that can exist between service experiences and academic pursuits. It is the reliance on the traditional pedagogical practices and notions of learning that can and did cripple even an academically based, civic-minded service-learning course such as mine.

Successful integration, in this case, was hindered both by structural factors, such as scheduling constraints, inappropriate placement sites, and the use of traditional evaluation tools, and by theoretical factors, such as course themes and reading materials that did not coincide with or enhance the learning that was occurring at the service site itself. And while structural changes can be made fairly easily — extra classes can be scheduled or more appropriate service placements could be identified — it is more difficult to change classroom practices that rely on a traditional pedagogy. For example, the traditional pedagogical practice in both the lecture and discussion sections of 101 relied heavily on the model of instructor as disseminator of knowledge and student as passive recipient of information. Though theoretically, discussion sections are to foster discussion and debate about the meaning of the readings, they often become, in effect, mini-lectures. In other words, though the small group meetings are offered to provide students an opportunity to enhance and complicate their thinking about course themes and texts, to develop critical-thinking skills through closer readings of the texts and clarification of lectures, historically and primarily they have served a more rudimentary function. Discussion sections provide students an opportunity to raise questions from the reading materials and lecture notes and to clarify and expand on themes developed in lecture. And though teaching assistants might begin the process as facilitators of discussion and guides in the sharing of student ideas, more often than not they do a great deal of work explaining lecture notes and guiding students through close readings of texts. The more passive approach to learning modeled in lecture becomes replicated in discussion sections, even in service-learning sections.

During the second semester, I attempted to remedy some of these problems by adding extra specifically designated service-learning sections and by choosing more overtly political service placements, sites at which identification of social problems and work toward social change were explicit. Yet we ran into similar problems. Students still had trouble making connections between Machiavelli's ideas of political leadership and their service experiences. They had difficulty recognizing how ideology functioned at the organization. They were so unclear about the academic concepts that they did not even know what to look for at their placements. And even when the connections were more obvious and students felt empowered to integrate their experiences, such as in the discussions of the bureaucratic nature of the organizations, we often ran out of time. Fifty or 80 minutes was not enough time in which to discuss what Friedman, a classical liberal, would say about community service, what Machiavelli might say about the philosophy of the organizations, what the Federalists would say about the role of these institutions in our society, or to discuss the ways in which the service sites addressed structural inequalities in the Marxian sense. In the end, clarification of lecture notes, academic concepts, and readings became the primary goal of sections, such that we even replaced the last service-learning section meeting with a final exam review.

What became clear, then, was that overcoming structural limitations was only part of the problem. More important and more difficult, perhaps, would be overcoming what I consider theoretical limitations contained in the material itself, or, rather, perspectives on the material. As I mentioned earlier, no changes were made in the syllabi of the Nature of Politics course. Two different professors taught the course that year, and though each dealt with different themes, both had students reading similar material including the *Federalist Papers*, Machiavelli, Marx, Martin Luther King Jr. Both had students thinking about political concepts such as power, freedom, democracy, rights, capitalism. Yet neither course was designed to relate these concerns to service experiences. In other words, neither course prioritized questions of how these concepts contributed to our understanding of the need for or responsibility of community service organizations and volunteers. And though both often tied textual themes to current or historical events, neither professor designed lectures to address the relationship between course themes and students' service experiences. This is not to suggest that either professor would have been opposed to doing so or to having me give a lecture or two. It is, however, to highlight the extent to which we all assumed that a discussion section would provide enough space for a different kind of learning to occur and the extent to which we assumed that the culture of passive learning, of the transmittal of knowledge, could be reversed, overcome, or transformed in a discussion section meeting once a week or less.

What this experience also suggests is that the choice between civic education or discipline-specific service-learning is not always as clear-cut as Zlotkowski suggests. In 101, I was struggling with a model of civic service-learning that did not coincide nicely with the themes of the course, but yet I was dealing with civic issues. It is true that I did come to the course with a set of service-learning questions that were not addressed in the readings. The way I knew to make a service-learning course was to raise questions about and reflect on the nature of community service, community, citizenship. These, however, were not the questions driving the course. It was not that I wanted to encourage reflection on service unrelated to academic theories, as some critics of service-learning suggest, but rather that the academic theories I was given to work with did not address directly these questions. This is not, however, to suggest that the course was unrelated to questions of civic values. On the contrary, the course was built around other "civic" questions regarding democracy, justice, power relations, the rule of law, the rights of individuals. And though I did shift the reflection questions as Zlotkowski suggests, I did not leave behind civic education. Questions that ask students to reflect on what they are doing in the world, whom they feel connected to, what they understand to be their responsibility or right as a volunteer or a member of society — these are discussions about civic values. So, too, are questions that encourage students to make sense of what is happening at their service site, to recognize who has power, how it is distributed, and what is said about the function of the organization. The lesson here is twofold. First, I would suggest that it is not that a civic emphasis is misplaced, but rather a narrow definition of civic education may inhibit successful integration. Second, discipline-specific models are no guarantee themselves of successful integration.

Based on my experiences, I believe it is not necessarily critical-thinking skills that are at stake in the service-learning classroom, but rather the traditional and familiar classroom practices and roles played by both faculty and students. It is not that service is to be celebrated and academics pushed aside, but rather that traditional academic pedagogy is to be replaced by or transformed into a pedagogy of active and reflective learning. Furthermore, it is not that we should replace an emphasis on civic values with an emphasis on practical, experiential education, but rather that our understanding of what constitutes a discussion of civic values may need to be rethought and expanded.

Conclusions: Thoughts on Future Integration Efforts

Despite the tensions and obstacles I have identified, I still believe that already existing courses such as Nature of Politics can be transformed into service-learning courses. Integration of service into the curriculum, though at times difficult, is not only possible but often quite important. Indeed, even when students have difficulty connecting classroom learning and service work, they still learn valuable lessons from the service experiences themselves. For example, some of my students were introduced to and gained a better understanding of the difficulties particular populations, such as the elderly or poor children, encounter on a daily basis. Others learned that service organizations exist to address governmental limitations or to hold citizens and government accountable. Still other students learned how vital and tenuous outside funding is for service organizations. And despite frustrations with the integration aspect of the course, many students expressed a desire to continue their community service or to take another service-learning class. Given these responses and my belief that the learning that occurs at the service site is enhanced and enriched by academics, I have spent time thinking about how I would approach integration in the future. In this section, then, I share my ideas for integration, ideas that begin with transforming classroom practices.

Successful integration begins, as I have suggested, with an appreciation of the learning goals of a service-learning course. A successful service-learning course teaches students not only to master the course material or to recognize their service as a learning experience but, more important, to merge the two learning experiences, to use the academic knowledge to enrich the learning that occurs on site and to use the service experience to live, test, and challenge academic theories. Given this goal, some kind of connection must be made between the two experiences the students have. As this is not the usual goal of teaching, if we ask students to engage in integrative learning, we must be prepared to transform our classroom, to change the roles played by both the teacher and the student. Such transformation begins with "democratizing" the classroom.[3]

Democratizing the classroom changes the traditional hierarchical relations and responsibilities of members in the classroom. In a traditional classroom, the instructor is placed in a position of power as the knower, the one in control of what is learned and how it is learned. In a democratic service-learning classroom, the instructor plays the role of facilitator or guide. Knowledge is not already formed and to be transferred from instructor to students. Rather, knowledge is produced in the process of connecting service experiences and course themes. Students are no longer seen as empty vessels or receptacles of information, as passive recipients of knowledge. Instead, students are active learners bringing a certain expertise and information base, gained from their service, to the classroom, knowledge that the instructor has not given them, but that the instructor can help process. In this model of teaching and learning, the instructor becomes a facilitator and guide on the path toward learning.[4] In the democratic service-learning classroom, the instructor facilitates learning by asking questions that probe students' understanding of reading material and evaluation of service experiences, and by modeling a kind of thinking that connects academic ideas with service experiences. Rather than telling students how to read the *Communist Manifesto* or *The Prince*, an instructor guides students to identify key ideas in the readings, ideas that can be used to frame their interpretation of the service experience. The instructor also can encourage students to use key themes from the service experience as a lens through which to read the texts. These practices, unfamiliar to students and often instructors, would need to be modeled early in the semester and practiced continually throughout. These practices also encourage students to take a more active role in their learning, sharing the connections they see between their service experiences and course material.

Though the traditional classroom model may be a starkly drawn portrait of classroom practice and roles, it is often the kind of teaching that occurs in a 101 course. In other words, courses that rely heavily on lectures and that evaluate students' learning by measuring their familiarity with terms and ideas presented in reading materials often discourage reflection and integration. These practices leave little room or time for students to do the time-consuming and difficult work of integrating service and academics. Memorization of key concepts or comprehension of texts is only part of the goal of a service-learning classroom, though it is often the primary, if not the only goal of a traditional classroom.

For democratization to occur in the classroom, all parties must know what the learning goals are and how they will be assessed. In other words, students need to be informed about their responsibilities, the goals, and the practices of learning and teaching that will occur in the course, and they need to know at the beginning of the semester. These are the practices that must be modeled and practiced early on in order to institute a transformation of the classroom culture. Evaluation of students should be consistent with the learning goals as well, most likely necessitating changes in traditional evaluation tools and perhaps even syllabi. Taking Nature of Politics as an example, traditionally students and instructors measured learning through exams that assessed students' familiarity with concepts and readings. A more integrative service-learning approach might take this kind of learning and evaluation as secondary to a kind of learning that encourages students to notice and analyze connections between course themes and service experiences. Learning objectives and evaluation tools would therefore be designed with respect not only to understanding course materials but also to analyzing the service experience. With regard to syllabi, if reflective thinking is a learning goal, I might have looked more closely at which readings worked best in connection with the service or examined how much time would be needed to foster this learning. If the goal had been to model, encourage, and teach a new way of thinking about the world, of questioning and connecting theoretical ideas with real-world practices, the syllabi and schedule would probably have undergone some revision. For example, rather than reading a text a week, I might have spent two weeks on texts to be sure that mastery of material and connections to service were accomplished. Or I would have identified course themes that could be made explicit at service sites, themes that I would trace clearly and often through course readings. I would not, however, have reconceived the course along completely new thematic lines. Rather, I would have worked with already present themes, identifying the ones most likely to be present at service sites.

In the process of changing learning goals, evaluation tools, and course readings, the role of service may also be transformed. Rather than encouraging reflection and integration by privileging the academic materials, service is placed at the center of the learning process. It is understood as one among many "texts" to be read and analyzed.[5] As I suggested earlier, when students are encouraged to identify course themes that are present at their service sites they often have difficulty, in part, because they may not truly understand the academic concept. This process makes service secondary to mastery of texts and may discourage students from seeing themselves as active learners who have something to contribute to class discussions. If service is placed at the center, if integrative and reflective learning is a goal of the service-learning course, then perhaps mastery of texts will no longer be the primary learning objective. Perhaps reading comprehension would share priority with or become secondary to fostering students' ability to make connections between the themes of the readings and their service experiences. This latter ability may or may not rest on mastery of the text. My belief is that some students will be able to use the service experience to understand the texts and others will work from the service back into the text. In other words, mastery may or may not precede connection and reflection; mastery of course material may only come through reflection itself.

These course changes and the facilitation of reflective learning, however, rest on another important consideration — the selection of community service placements. As I mentioned earlier, not all placements are appropriate or relevant to course themes; not all placements coincide with or bring to life relevant course concepts. I learned the importance of this about two weeks into the first semester. I had students placed at nursing homes, soup kitchens, tutoring programs, women's organizations, and legal service sites. My nursing home volunteer had great difficulty connecting her work reading to an elderly woman with the discussion of factions in the *Federalist Papers*. However, those students placed in more overtly political organizations, such as the women's organizations or the legal service providers, were better able to recognize connections between political systems and their service. For example, these students could connect their experiences to a discussion of Marx's *Communist Manifesto* because they were witness to the ramifications of class and gender divisions in our society as they worked with organizations intent upon making social change. It is true that I could not make up a service experience in which they might confront structural oppression and inequality so that we could discuss Marx, or fix it so that they would attend a board meeting at which compromises were made for the sake of peace, or something even more Machiavellian. However, I could place them at sites where identifying social problems and working for social change were primary and explicit goals, goals that coincided with many of the course themes. During the second semester I did just that. I identified sites that would more readily illustrate key ideas such as the importance and limits of democratic rule, the role of citizens in making social change, the difference between elite rule and majority rule, and oppression and discrimination.[6] This change helped alleviate the frustration that many students felt about their service experiences not bringing to life concepts such as structural inequality or the accountability of government.

That second semester I not only addressed the structural constraints posed by inappropriate placement sites, but I also worked on the time constraint. In doing so, I recognized that integrative learning, as I suggested above, may take more time than traditional learning. Recognizing that we wanted to establish a conversation between service and academics in the classroom, a conversation that might start from the service, I established additional section meetings designed specifically for integration of academic materials and service experiences. In these meetings, we would start not from lecture notes or readings but rather from the service experiences themselves. Having already written a journal assignment connecting a particular theme, such as economic liberalism or bureaucracy, to a particular service experience, students would share the service experience identified. Together we would pull out themes relevant to coursework, turn to the texts to note similarities or differences, and raise questions about what a particular author might say or think about community service itself. In these meetings, we had more space and time for an analysis of service experiences, often leading students to new perspectives on issues such as the majority rule, bureaucracy, or civil disobedience. In these meetings, the service experience took priority or at least formed the basis of discussion. Rather than seeking to impose the theme of the readings onto the service experience, we put service at the center, working from the experience and together drawing connections to the course themes. In democratic fashion, we shared responsibility for this work.

I also learned, early on, that to encourage students to do this work, to promote active, reflective learning, these skills must be modeled and practiced often. A simple description of service activities will not encourage students to be critical about the experience or about academic theories. Nor will such an activity foster a concern with the role of community service in a democratic society; it is not civic education. Given this recognition, I redesigned journal questions during the second semester. And while I still found myself confronted with "theoretical" limitations — I wanted students to think about service organizations and service experiences as political, as practices of citizenship, as both foundational to and challenges of democracy, questions not always explicit, or even implicit, in themes of the lectures — I was able to produce better integration results. I was particularly pleased with the responses to the first journal question, which asked students to explain the mission or philosophy of their service organization, identify its clientele and its funding sources, and describe their role at the site. With this question students were forced to ask questions of their service sites and locate the organization within a context. From there we could begin the discussion of the relationship between the organization and the principles of democracy, theories about the rights and responsibilities of individuals, concerns about the proper role of institutions and ideologies, and so on. It was in this first journal assignment that students began to think critically and actively about the connections between service and academics.

This reflection work done in the journal assignments and practiced in classroom discussions must, however, be further reinforced by evaluation tools, as I alluded to above. As I found out in my experience, it is quite easy to forego the time-consuming work of modeling and practicing reflective thinking when exams cover different material and students are concerned about being prepared. As I mentioned earlier, the traditional evaluation tools for 101, the take-home midterm and final papers, did not ask service-learning students to integrate the service. Rather, they asked students to explore course themes through analysis of the readings. Students were not asked questions that provoked an analysis of the service experiences. We did discuss changing the exam questions so that students would be asked to analyze a course theme using the readings and their service experiences. However, I chose not to make these changes because I felt that we had not done enough work in class on integrating the two experiences to make these questions effective or fair. It seems to me, then, that encouraging analysis of service experiences through evaluation tools is a secondary step. Classroom practices must be transformed, learning goals should be clear, and reflective thinking and learning must be modeled and practiced before we evaluate students on their ability to do this work.

As I look back at both the difficulties and the potential that accompany this institutionalization or integration process, I realize, more than ever, that for a service-learning course to be successful, classroom practices must change, teaching and learning must be transformed. Despite the challenges I've encountered and identified in the process of integrating service into an already existing course, I remain committed to the service-learning model of education. While I am more aware now of the thought, risks, and challenges involved in this process, I will continue to seek out opportunities to teach service-learning courses and encourage others to do the same. However, I offer a note of caution. Integration of service-learning into already existing courses is not easy. It is time-consuming and requires radical changes in classroom practices. Service-learning requires students and instructors to engage in often unfamiliar and sometimes uncomfortable roles. And yet, I remain committed to the promise and potential of service-learning. The importance of service-learning, for me, is captured in the best of my own educational experiences, as well as in those somewhat rare but wonderful moments when a student sees an academic theory come to life. That student who recognized the advantages and disadvantages of the democratic process at his service site, seeing an inclusive process lead, at times, to the inability to decide or act, has lived the promise and problems of democracy in a way that he never could have if he had only read the *Federalist Papers*. This, to me, is an educational experience that is long-lasting, that involves the student in his or her own learning, and that places the instructor in the role of facilitator not disseminator of information and knowledge. It is with this in mind that I urge all instructors interested in service-learning to keep learning goals and classroom practices in mind and in view as they attempt to integrate service-learning into the curriculum.

Notes

1. For an interesting discussion of traditional classroom practices, see Paulo Freire's *Pedagogy of the Oppressed* (New York: Continuum, 1970). In particular, his notion of the "banking concept of education" reminded me of the work I often did in Nature of Politics.

2. See Zlotkowski 1995 and 1996.

3. This difficult task can become even more complicated when the integration of service into the curriculum is only partial, as it was in 101. We needed not only to think about how the service related to the coursework but also to examine whether or how the service-learning sections were to be different from the other sections. Were they to have different learning objectives? If so, would the teaching look different in the various sections? Would the students do different readings or focus on different themes? If teaching and learning were being transformed, what about our evaluation tools? How could we evaluate different learning objectives and different learning processes using the same evaluation tools? These are some of the questions I answer below thanks to the beauty of hindsight.

4. Expanding on principle 8 of Wingspread principles.

5. I thank Rick Battistoni for giving me a term, "text," to articulate the role of service in service-learning, and William Hudson for helping me understand where I wanted service to be placed in a service-learning course.

6. I selected sites such as New Jersey Citizen Action, a public-interest canvassing organization; Middlesex County Legal Services, an organization providing free legal counsel to poor people; and environmental organizations and women's organizations. I asked that students no longer be placed in nursing homes or in the after-school tutoring program, not because I think these are not "political" in nature but because their mission is not explicitly oriented toward making social change.

References

Barber, Benjamin, and Rick Battistoni. (June 1993). "A Season of Service: Introducing Service Learning Into the Liberal Arts Curriculum." PS: *Political Science & Politics* 26:235-240, 262.

Zlotkowski, Edward. (Winter 1995). "Does Service-Learning Have a Future?" Working Paper #18, New England Resource Center for Higher Education. Boston: NERCHE.

——————— . (January/February 1996). "Linking Service-Learning and the Academy: A New Voice at the Table?" *Change* 28(1): 21-27.

Community Service-Learning as Practice in the Democratic Political Arts

by Gregory B. Markus

Public opinion polls consistently show that a majority of Americans are deeply dissatisfied with politics and government today. The dissatisfaction extends beyond a distrust of current officeholders. Increasingly, Americans say they think something is wrong with the *system,* that America is heading in a fundamentally wrong direction as a nation. The irony, of course, is that this crisis of confidence has occurred just as democracy has apparently triumphed all over the globe.

The origins of Americans' dissatisfaction with politics are undoubtedly manifold, and no one-variable explanation will suffice. A rough consensus has developed among scholars and journalists, however, that an important cause of contemporary political disaffection is a widespread perception that citizens are no longer effective political agents, that politics in the United States is something done to people — or at best for people — rather than by people (Dionne 1991; Greider 1992; Lipset and Schneider 1987; Mathews 1994). As Lewis Lapham put it recently, "Ask almost anybody in the street about the nature of American government, and he or she will describe it as something that belongs to somebody else, as a them not an us" (1990: 53).

Disaffection with politics and government is particularly prevalent among younger Americans. In years past, most opinion surveys found mistrust of government to increase with age: The more one learned about government, the less one trusted it. Recent surveys suggest this has changed. A 1990 poll conducted by the Times-Mirror Center for the Press and Politics discovered that "Today's young Americans, aged 18 to 30, know less and care less about news and public affairs than any other generation of Americans in the past 50 years" (Cohn 1992). In the 1994 American National Election Studies survey, respondents born in 1975 or later were the most likely to express the belief that "the government is run for the benefit of a few big interests" (83%) rather than "for the benefit of all."

It is within that context that I offer a course at the University of Michigan entitled Contemporary Issues in American Politics [the syllabus from Fall 1995 follows on pp. 80-82]. The course is open to undergraduates without regard to their area of specialization, and for a fair number of enrollees it may be the only course in political science they will ever take. The class meets twice weekly as a group in 50-minute lecture sessions. Students also meet twice weekly (50 minutes per session) in small discussion sections led by political science doctoral graduate students.

As its title indicates, the course surveys a variety of prominent U.S. public-policy themes, including the federal budget, welfare reform, racism and race-related policies, the politics of economic growth, environmental policy, media coverage of politics, and so on. A key objective of the course is to provide students with some basic information about these issues and an overview of contending perspectives on them. Equally important to me is making the case to the 100 to 150 students who take the course each year that politics need not be a distant, confusing, and often distasteful activity performed only by politicians, professional lobbyists, and other connected insiders. I want the course to convey that politics is about *public* matters and that politics includes government but is not synonymous with it. Ordinary people — including the students themselves — have a place in politics, provided they claim it; they can be effective political actors, provided they develop their capacities for effective political action.

Why Service-Learning?

Making this case is not easy, even to students who are sufficiently interested in politics as to enroll in a course about it. Many of them are ambivalent about politics at best — hardly surprising given that they have spent their entire lives in an era in which the place of the citizen in politics has become increasingly cramped and unsatisfying.

When I redesigned my course a few years ago to reflect its evolving mission, I doubted that an unvarying diet of hortatory readings and lectures would have much lasting impact upon students' orientations toward politics and their personal store of knowledge about political issues and processes. If the course was to achieve its objectives, students would have to have an opportunity to engage those issues and practices firsthand. They would have to *do* politics, not just read, talk, or listen to lectures about it. I decided, therefore, to incorporate service-learning into my course for two reasons, one that pertains to the pedagogical goals of any academic course and another that is of special relevance to teaching and learning *about politics*.

The first reason was that service-learning held promise of increasing the breadth and depth of what students learned. From a pedagogical perspective, service-learning is one form of experiential learning, in contrast to the "information-assimilation model" that typifies classroom instruction (Dewey 1938; Coleman 1977). The information-assimilation model emphasizes a top-down approach to learning: Principles and facts are presented symbolically (through books, lectures, or videotapes, for example), and specific applications of principles are learned primarily through deductive reasoning or "thought experiments." The method's advantages are its efficiency in terms of conveying large amounts of information and its emphasis on the logical, coherent cognitive organization of that information. Its weakness is that students' actual acquisition and long-term retention of information are problematical — that is, students may not truly learn very much. Experiential learning is more of a bottom-up method, in which general lessons and principles are drawn inductively from direct personal experiences and observations. This approach is less efficient than readings and lectures in transmitting information, and general principles can be slow to emerge. On the other hand, experiential learning counters the abstractness of much classroom instruction and motivates lasting learning by providing concrete examples of facts and theories, thereby "providing connections between academic content and the problems of real life" (Conrad and Hedin 1991: 745). *Thus, when community service is combined with classroom instruction, the pedagogical advantages of each compensate for the shortcomings of the other.*

The more specific reason I decided to incorporate service-learning into my course stemmed from the fact that it was a course about politics, and in particular about public policy and citizenship. In his influential report to the Carnegie Foundation in 1985, Frank Newman wrote: "If there is a crisis in education in the United States today, it is less that test scores have declined than it is that we have failed to provide the education for citizenship that is still the most important responsibility of the nation's schools and colleges" (31). Among the various approaches that have been advocated for addressing this failure, perhaps none has received as much attention as the proposal that high school and college students should engage in community service as part of their formal education (see, for example, Barber 1992; Evers 1990; Moskos 1988).

Unfortunately, although well-intentioned service-learning programs often refer to enhancing students' understanding of their "civic obligations" and the "responsibilities of citizenship," it is not uncommon for such programs to be apolitical or even antipolitical in practice. For example, Serow (1991) found in his study of four public universities that the norms surrounding community service encourage students "to become directly engaged with the problems of vulnerable individuals rather than viewing them in terms of broader, abstract social or political phenomena" (553). Similarly, Boyte (1991a: 766) has found that students in community service programs "usually disavow concern with larger policy questions, seeing service as an *alternative* to politics." In a related article, Boyte argued:

> *Most service programs include little learning or discussion about the policy dimensions of the "issues" (such as poverty, homelessness, drug use, illiteracy) that students wrestle with through person-to-person effort. Volunteers — usually middle-class and generally white — rarely have occasion to reflect on the complex dynamics of power, race, and class that*

are created when young people go out to "serve" in low-income areas. (1991b: 627)

It is doubtful that such programs do much to advance students' understanding of, experience in, and commitment to participation in the political work of citizens. There is no good reason why community service programs must inevitably be apolitical or antipolitical in practice, however. Boyte's pilot program at the University of Minnesota, called Public Achievement, is one successful example of teaching young adults about politics through practical experience. The Citizenship and Service Education (CASE) Program at Rutgers University is another (Barber 1992).

Because mine is a course in politics, my graduate assistants and I try self-consciously to prepare and encourage students to reflect upon and draw lessons from the *political* aspects of what they observe and experience in their service activities rather than get caught up entirely in the "person-to-person" aspects of their work. For example, when college students work at a homeless shelter, they provide valuable service for the shelter and its clients, and the students typically feel a great sense of personal satisfaction from helping others. But students may not consider the broader social and political dimensions of the issue of homelessness unless they are provided regularly with the time and space within a classroom setting to discuss those dimensions: Why do substantial numbers of Americans go without adequate food and shelter within the world's richest nation? Is this matter a proper responsibility of government, or is it better left to charities, religious institutions, and private individuals? Why? How are such questions decided in the United States? Where do citizens fit in? Where do you fit in?

An Experiment in Service-Learning

The first time I used service-learning as part of Contemporary Political Issues (Winter 1992) was within the framework of an experiment on the impact of community service experience upon student learning (see Markus, Howard, and King 1993). Prior to class registration (and unknown to students registering for the course), I randomly designated two of eight discussion sections as "service-learning" sections, in which students would be assigned to engage in 20 hours of service over the course of the 13-week semester with their choice of one of a number of designated community agencies. The remaining six "control group" sections used a traditional format, in which section meetings were devoted largely to discussions of course readings and lectures. Students in the control sections were required to write term papers based upon library research intended to take an amount of time and effort equivalent to that expended by students in the service sections. Regardless of assignment to treatment or control section, all students attended the same lectures, were assigned the same course readings, and took the same midterm and final examinations, graded according to a common set of standards.

At the first lecture meeting of the course, students were informed in general terms that we would be experimenting with different types of teaching methods in the course and about the differing requirements associated with the two kinds of discussion sections. They were also informed that in order to prevent possible biases in the study, transfers between community service and traditional sections were not permitted. Care was taken to explain that the service component was not an "extracurricular" activity foisted upon the students in the service-learning section but was instead an integral, if alternative, part of the course curriculum for those students. As a result, and perhaps surprisingly, students raised few if any objections to the course design.

A total of 52 students were enrolled in discussion sections using the traditional format, and 37 students were in the service sections. There were no significant differences between treatment and control groups in terms of demographic factors (sex, race, and year in school), nor did the two groups differ in terms of student responses to a questionnaire about personal attitudes and values that was distributed early in the semester.

During the first two weeks of the term, the university's Office of Community Service Learning assisted in placing the designated students with local agencies and organizations that were selected from a larger list of ones with which the office had worked previously. The service opportunities included working at a homeless shelter, a women's crisis center, an ecology center, or tutoring at-risk primary or high school students. The particular agencies were selected because the focus of their activities meshed with the subject matter of the course and because the agencies reported that they could put students to work in meaningful and educationally worthwhile jobs immediately and without extensive training required on the part of the students. The graduate teaching assistant who led the service-learning discussion groups visited each agency at least once during the semester and contacted the agencies periodically to ensure that students were fulfilling their time commitments and that the tasks to which students were assigned were consistent with the goals of the course. A small grant from Michigan Campus Compact provided a salary increment for the service-learning sections' graduate assistant and covered miscellaneous costs, such as transportation and materials.

Over the course of the semester, a few students worked individually on their service assignments; the vast majority worked in teams of three to eight students each. Section meetings for the experimental group were devoted to discussions about the service in which students were engaged and how their experiences related to course readings and lectures. Students were encouraged to link abstract ideas and theories (for example, the dilemma of collective action) to their particular experiences ("the agency I work with is chronically underfunded"). Near the end of the semester, students in the service sections also wrote short papers and presented brief oral reports based on their experiences. The oral presentations were made during a three-hour evening session attended by all students in the service-learning sections, their graduate assistants, and the course instructor. Soft drinks and snacks were provided.

Effects of service-learning versus traditional instruction were assessed in a variety of ways (via pre- and postcourse questionnaires, course grades, and data on class attendance). Students in the service-learning sections differed markedly from their counterparts in the traditional sections on many measures of course impact. For example, the former displayed statistically and substantively significant pre- to postcourse increases in their ratings of the personal importance they attached to "working toward equal opportunity for all U.S. citizens" and "finding a career that provides the opportunity to be helpful to others or useful to society," while the latter did not.

As compared with their counterparts in the traditional sections, students in the service-learning sections were also significantly more likely to report that their participation in the course had increased or strengthened their "belief that one can make a difference in the world" and their "tolerance and appreciation for others" (Markus, Howard, and King 1993).

Students' academic learning was also significantly enhanced by their participation in course-relevant community service: As compared with students taught by traditional methods, students in service-learning sections were more emphatic in their judgments that they were performing up to their potential in the course, were more likely to affirm that they had "learned to apply principles from this course to new situations" and had "developed a set of overall values in this field," to mention some illustrative findings. Students in the service-learning sections also had higher attendance rates for both lecture and section meetings and attained significantly higher course grades on average.

Students' anonymous written comments in their course evaluations speak to the value of service-learning:

> The community service project was the most valuable part of the course. It made the issues discussed in class so much more real to me. It made me realize that there are social problems — but that they are not unsolvable.

> The community service gave me firsthand knowledge of the issues discussed in class. I also think my experience will make me a better citizen.

The community service project was a very good idea. I'm even working there again this week (at the shelter association). It provided me with a better understanding of the homeless problem.

I really enjoyed the community service aspect of this course, even though I didn't expect to like it. I actually saw the concepts we had discussed in lecture come to life. I think it should be continued.

Expanding the Service-Learning Component Course-Wide

In light of the positive results achieved in the pilot experiment, the service-learning component of Political Science 300 was expanded the following semester (Fall 1992). As in the previous term, the service commitment was for 20 hours over the course of the semester. This time, however, all 150 enrolled students were assigned to work with an off-campus agency or organization in the public sector. Another important change in the course was that the range of service-learning options was broadened to include assignments of an explicit political nature, including work with local party organizations, voter registration drives, and issue advocacy groups (for example, abortion rights) during the fall election campaigns. Approximately half the class selected one of these new options, while the other half chose from among the service agencies that had been utilized the previous semester. Students generally preferred to work in small teams of approximately three to eight individuals per team, a practice that worked well both logistically and educationally (Barber 1992: 253-261).

My decision to expand the service-learning component to include work in political party, candidate, and policy-related action reflects a view that public service encompasses far more than, and should not be equated with, advantaged individuals "helping the needy." It further reflects the thesis that the motivating objective of the service-learning activity is not to provide service as an end in itself but rather to expand the learning environment into settings beyond the classroom and to do so in a way that enables students to learn the arts of politics in settings that engage their own political interests rather than mine or the university's.

The university's Office of Community Service Learning once again assisted in placing students with local agencies other than political organizations. A graduate assistant contacted the latter organizations directly and arranged for student placements. The graduate teaching assistants also maintained communication with the community groups over the course of the semester to monitor the nature of the work students were performing and to ensure that students were fulfilling their commitments. Our experience was that, with only one or two exceptions, community agencies and political organizations were eager to make use of student volunteers.

As in the previous semester, section meetings were devoted regularly to discussions linking students' experiences outside the classroom to the subject matter of course readings and lectures. The graduate teaching assistants and I met weekly to share information about what students were accomplishing in the community, how well the service experiences were meshing with other aspects of the course, and any other ideas we had or problems we were facing. One side benefit of integrating service-learning into the course was that the graduate assistants found the discussion sections more interesting to lead, and they gained experience with new approaches to teaching.

As for the students, their assessments of the course via the postcourse evaluation questionnaire, their written and oral comments about their experiences in the community, and, especially, their performance in the classroom and on examinations all indicated that, even on this fairly large scale, classroom instruction and service-learning can be combined synergistically to enhance academic learning. For example, in their responses to the evaluation questionnaire, 45 percent of the students "strongly agreed" with the statement "Overall, this is an excellent course," and another 45 percent "agreed." Fully 51 percent strongly agreed with the statement "I learned a great deal from this course," and another 40 percent agreed.

What I'll Do Differently Next Time

In my initial effort to integrate service-learning into Political Science 300, I consulted with organizations experienced in the practice, such as Michigan Campus Compact and the university's Office of Community Service Learning; but I completed most of the work of designing the course on my own. In subsequent years, I brought the course's graduate teaching assistants more directly into the planning as well as the execution of the service-learning curriculum, but the undergraduate students in the courses still had relatively little influence over the course's content or plan.

Going forward, my intention is to engage undergraduates more directly in shaping their course and in selecting — and quite possibly creating from scratch — their civic service activities. In particular, I am interested in exploring with them the idea that the university is not separate from "the community" but is rather part of it. Indeed, for many students the university may substantially constitute their "community." One implication of this is that if the goal is to develop students' capacities as public citizens, perhaps the service-learning component of the course should offer opportunities for creating and implementing civic-minded activities within the university as well as outside it: What are the shared interests of undergraduates? How can they be effective, public-minded actors who take some responsibility for addressing and advancing their shared interests?

In addition, Political Science 300 still relies heavily upon a lecture format. Yet education in the arts of democratic politics requires doing things differently than they are done in traditional classrooms. It is difficult to imagine that individuals can develop their capacities as public citizens via a pedagogy in which students passively acquire knowledge dispensed from the expert at the front of the room. Instead, the classroom must model the practices it intends to teach (Barber and Battistoni 1993; Battistoni 1994; Stanton 1990). Surely there are ways in which students can engage in useful public discussion and active learning in the large-group setting of the "lecture room" in ways that are compatible with the responsibilities of the professor as communicator of, and guide to, knowledge.

Conclusions

Community service has many laudable purposes and outcomes — fulfilling civic responsibilities to one's community, helping persons in need, gaining an insight into one's values and prejudices, developing career interests and job skills, and so on, all of which are important. The primary focus of my experiences with Political Science 300 has been a less well understood aspect of service: its *academic* value. Students in the course were (and are) encouraged to engage in civic life outside the classroom as an integral part of their academic learning — to use the "town as text" (Lappé and DuBois 1994).

The academic benefits of having students engage in community service are substantial when that service activity is integrated with traditional classroom instruction. The key word here is *integrated*. Time in class meetings should be set aside consistently for students to reflect upon and discuss what they are learning in their service activity and how it illustrates, affirms, extends, or contradicts points made in readings and lectures. These recommendations are consistent with those of others who have studied service-learning (Barber 1992; Hedin 1989; Stanton 1990).

Integrating service-learning into a traditional classroom-oriented course requires a nontrivial investment of time and resources, especially the first time around. If one's institution has an office of service-learning, office of volunteer services, or similar entity that is experienced in placing students with service agencies in the community, using it can reduce the start-up costs considerably. It is also important to reach agreements with local service agencies in advance of the beginning of the course regarding the kinds of duties students will be expected to perform, how students will receive any necessary training, how many volunteers and how many hours of service should be anticipated, and so on. Finally, the instructor (or a course assistant) should monitor the agencies and students over the course of the term to ascertain that both are fulfilling their mutual obligations.

Through thoughtfully designed service-learning activities, young adults gain new insights into political, social, and economic issues. More than that, they acquire experience in articulating their interests in public settings, working with others to solve problems affecting their common interests, and holding themselves and others accountable. That is, they acquire explicitly political knowledge and skills. Robert Putnam (1993: 183) concluded in his widely cited study *Making Democracy Work* that "a conception of one's roles and obligations as a citizen, coupled with a commitment to political equality, is the cultural cement of the civic community." If so, then my experiences with service-learning suggest that it can fortify that "cultural cement."

There is no particular reason why experiential learning in the political arts need be restricted to the arena of higher education. Service-learning methods and approaches can — and should — be transferred to efforts at building civic capacities of individuals and groups in the broader community, whether those communities be here in the United States or in newly democratic nations around the globe. Surely this is a worthwhile endeavor for political scientists, on intellectual as well as practical grounds.

References

Barber, Benjamin. (1992). *An Aristocracy of Everyone*. New York: Ballantine.

————, and R. Battistoni. (1993). "A Season of Service: Introducing Service-Learning Into the Liberal Arts Curriculum." PS: *Political Science & Politics* 26:235-240, 262.

Battistoni, Richard M. (1994). "Education for Democracy: Service-Learning and Pedagogical Reform in Higher Education." Paper presented at the annual meeting of the American Political Science Association, September 1994, New York, NY.

Boyte, Harry C. (1991a). "Community Service and Civic Education." *Phi Delta Kappan* 72:765-767.

————. (May 13, 1991b.) "Turning Youth on to Politics," *The Nation*, pp. 626-628.

Cohn, Jonathan S. (1992). "A Lost Political Generation." *The American Prospect* 9(Spring): 33.

Coleman, James S. (1977). "Differences Between Experiential and Classroom Learning." In *Experiential Learning: Rationale, Characteristics, and Assessment*, edited by Morris T. Keaton. San Francisco: Jossey-Bass.

Conrad, Dan, and Diane Hedin. (1991). "School-Based Community Service: What We Know From Research and Theory." *Phi Delta Kappan* 72:743-749.

Dewey, John. (1938). *Experience and Education.* New York: Collier Books.

Dionne, E.J. (1991). *Why Americans Hate Politics.* New York: Simon & Schuster.

Evers, Williamsom M. (1990). *National Service: Pro and Con.* Stanford: Hoover Institution Press.

Greider, William. (1992). *Who Will Tell the People?* New York: Simon & Schuster.

Hedin, Diane. (1989). "The Power of Community Service." *Proceedings of the Academy of Political Science* 37:201-213.

Lapham, Lewis H. (November 1990). "Democracy in America?" *Harper's,* pp. 47-56.

Lappé, Francis Moore, and Paul Martin DuBois. (1994). *The Quickening of America.* San Francisco: Jossey-Bass.

Lipset, Seymour Martin, and William Schneider. (1987). *The Confidence Gap.* Revised ed. Baltimore: Johns Hopkins University Press.

Markus, Gregory B., Jeffrey P.F. Howard, and David C. King. (1993). "Integrating Community Service With Classroom Instruction Enhances Learning: Results From an Experiment." *Educational Evaluation and Policy Analysis* 15:410-419.

Mathews, David. (1994). *Politics for People.* Urbana, IL: University of Illinois Press.

Moskos, Charles C. (1988). *A Call to Civic Service.* New York: Free Press.

Newman, Frank. (1985). *Higher Education and the American Resurgence.* Princeton: Carnegie Foundation for the Advancement of Teaching.

Putnam, Robert D. (1993). *Making Democracy Work.* Princeton: Princeton University Press.

Serow, Robert C. (1991). "Students and Voluntarism: Looking Into the Motives of Community Service Participants." *American Educational Research Journal* 28:543-556.

Stanton, Timothy K. (1990). *Integrating Public Service With Academic Study: The Faculty Role.* Providence, RI: Campus Compact.

Political Science 300
Contemporary Issues in American Politics
Fall 1995

Prof. Gregory B. Markus
3030ISR 763-3284gmarkus@umich.edu

IMPORTANT! PLEASE READ THIS NOW!

This is a serious course for serious students who are genuinely interested in learning more about critical political issues and choices confronting the United States.

The course is aimed at undergraduates generally and not at political science concentrators alone (although the latter are certainly welcome). Curiosity, skepticism, energy, and a willingness to challenge yourself are the essential prerequisites. You will read, listen, discuss, write, and do a lot in this course, consistent with its four credit-hour value. (Translation: If you are looking for an easy, undemanding course in which everything is laid out for you step-by-step, look elsewhere.) In return, our goal is to make this the most educationally rewarding course you will take as an undergraduate.

Political Science 300 examines a variety of issues that are the focus of contemporary political debate in the United States, such as taxes and the budget deficit, the place of the U.S. within a global economy, welfare reform, the politics of race, and environmental dilemmas. This course stresses the utility of scholarly knowledge as a means to understand current events. Class discussions often move freely from assigned readings to the latest news.

Grading is on a no-curve 100-point system. The mid-term and final examinations are each worth one-third of your grade. The remaining third of your grade is based by what you do in your discussion section. As part of your section responsibilities, you will write a term paper of 8 to 10 pages in length. You may choose to write a paper based on your research on a topic covered in this course. Or, if you so choose, we can help place you in a course-appropriate community service project in which you will work 20 hours over the semester, and you can base your paper on that work.

Required Materials (all available in paperback):
Coursepack from Michigan Document Service, 603 Church St.
Edsall, Thomas B. and Mary D. Edsall (1991) *Chain Reaction: The Impact of Race, Rights, and Taxes on American Politics*. New York: Norton.
Krugman, Paul (1994) *The Age of Diminishing Expectations*. Cambridge: MIT Press.
Lappe', Frances Moore and Paul Martin DuBois (1994) *The Quickening ofamerica*. San Francisco: Jossey-Bass.
National Issues Forum (1993) *The $4 Trillion Debt*. Dubuque: Kendall/Hunt.
National Issues Forum (1 989) *The Environment at Risk*. Dubuque: Kendall/Hunt.

Course Outline

I. This Just In. Film at 11

Apple, R. W. (1995) "Poll shows disenchantment with politicians and
    politics," *New York Times*, August 12, p. A-1.
Wines, Michael (1995) "Bradley's exit is not just the Democrats'problem,"
    New York Times, August 20, section 4, p. 1.

II. First Principles

The Federalist Papers, Numbers IO & 5 1.
Will, George (1983) *Statecraft as Soulcraft*. New York: Simon & Schuster,
    ch. 2, 4.
Lapham, Lewis H. (1990) "Democracy in America?" *Harper's*, November, pp. 47-
    56.
Orren, Gary (1988) "Beyond self-interest." In Reich, Robert B. (ed.) *The
    Power of Public Ideas*. Cambridge: Harvard University Press.
Kelman, Steven (1988) "Why public ideas matter." In Reich. Robert B. (ed.)
    The Power of Public Ideas. Cambridge: Harvard University Press.
Lappe'& DuBois, ch. 1-4.

III. From Client to Citizen

Lappe'& DuBois, ch. 7-13.
McKnight, John (1995) "Professionalized service and disabling help," *The
    Careless Community*. New York: Basic Books.

IV. The Federal Budget: "Watch what we do, not what we say."

Peterson, Peter G. (I 993) "Facing up." *The Atlantic Monthly,* October.
O'Rourke, P. J. (1991) "Would you kill your mother to pave 1-95?" In
    Parliament of Whores. New York: Vintage Books.
Kinsley, Michael (1993) "When is it a tax?" *The New Republic,* December 27.
Krugman, ch. 7.
National Issues Forum, *The $4 Trillion Debt*.

V. The Politics of the Global Economy

Krugman, ch. 4, 10, 11, 14-17.

VI. Income, Poverty, and Politics

Krugman, Introduction, ch. 1-3.
Uchitelle, Louis (1995) "Wage stagnation is seen as a major issue in the
    1995 election campaign," *New York Times*, August 13, p. I 1.
Epstein, Gene (1995) "Still trickling," *Barron's*, July 17, p. 36.
Frum, David (1 995) "Welcome, Nouveaux Riches," *New York Times*, August 14,
    p. A- 1 1.
Murray, Charles (1984) *Losing Ground*. NY: Basic Books, ch. 4, 10, 12,
    15,17.
Jencks, Christopher (1992) *Rethinking Social Policy*. Cambridge: Harvard U.
    Press, ch. 2.
Wilkerson, Isabel (1995) "An intimate look at welfare: Women who've been
    there," *New York Times*, February 17, p. A- 1.
Toner, Robin (1995) "Resolved: No more bleeding hearts," *New York Times*,
    July 16, sect. 4, p. 1.

Pennar, Karen (1995) "Are block grants the answer?" *Business Week,* April 3.
Editors (1995) "Blockheads," *The New Republic,* March 20, p. 7.
Lappe'& DuBois, ch. 5.

VII. Race, Class, and Politics

Edsall & Edsall, Ch. 1, 6-12.
Loury, Glenn C. (1 995) "Let's get on with Dr. King's idea," *New York
   Times,* July 26, p. A- 1 1.
Kaus, Mickey (1995) "Class is in," *The New Republic,* March 27, p. 6.
Patterson, Orlando (1995) "Affirmative action, on the merit system," *New
   York Times.* August 7. p. A-11.
West, Cornell (1993) *Race Matters.* Boston: Beacon Press, ch. 1, 4.

VIII. The Politics of Health Care

Paton, Calum (1995) "Health policy: The analytics and politics of attempted
   reform." In Gillian Peele et al., *Developments in American Politics.*
   Chatham, NJ: Chatham House.
McKnight, John (1995) "The medicalization of politics." *The Careless
   Community.* New York: Basic Books.
McKnight, John (1995) "Politicizing health care," *The Careless Community.*
   New York: Basic Books.

IX. Politics, Values, and Ecology

Brown, Lester R. (1991) "The new world order." In L. R. Brown et al., *The
   State of the World* 1991. New York: Norton.
Easterbrook, Gregg (1992) "Green Cassandras," *The New Republic,* July 6, pp.
   23-25.
Schneider, Keith (1993) "New view calls environmental policy misguided,"
   New York Times, March 2 1, p. A- 1.
Schneider, Keith (1993) "How a rebellion over environmental rules grew from
   a patch of weeds," *New York Times,* March 24, p. C-19.
McElroy, Michael B. (1993) "Ozone debate," *Wall Street Journal,* June 17.
Boyle, Robert H. (1993) "All the news that's fit to twist," *Amicus Journal,*
   Fall, p. 9.
National Issues Forum, *The Environment at Risk.*

X. Media and Politics

Patterson, Thomas E. (1993) *Out of Order.* New York: Knopf, Prologue, ch.
   2.
Grossman, Lawrence K. (1995) *The Electronic Republic.* New York: Viking,
   ch. 8.
Lappe'& DuBois, ch. 6.

Service-Learning in the Study of American Public Policy

by William E. Hudson

During the spring semester of 1995, I introduced a service-learning component into my course American Public Policy — one of the oldest in my teaching repertoire. This is a report on this initial experience with service-learning in the course.

Over the years, American Public Policy has undergone a variety of permutations, and service-learning is not the first pedagogical innovation I have tried in it. Despite the course's changes and evolution in the 20 years I have taught it, my basic goals and objectives have been constant. The central goal is to develop students' capacities as "citizen policy analysts" — their ability to form critical analytic judgments about public policy arguments and proposals. The course emphasizes description and historical analysis over introducing sophisticated (and often arcane) analytic models and methods. In my view, making judgments about existing public policies and proposals for change requires, most of all, an understanding of the historical experience in addressing the public problems at which policies are aimed. This understanding includes knowing how the nature of the American political economy and the particular development of the American positive state shape and constrain all public policy. The first few weeks of my course always focus on political economy and the growth of the state as a prelude to in-depth study of a handful of specific policy areas. Analysis of specific policies aims at illustrating each of their links to broader problems in the evolution of the political economy and state development.

My goal for the community service component was to put students in contact with the consequences of public policy. I wanted them to encounter, and perhaps even get to know, people directly affected by the policies we would be studying. In my initial discussions with the college's service-learning coordinator, we explored what service sites and types of service would allow for encounters with welfare recipients and other people who might be affected by the Republican leadership's Contract With America, with recent immigrants, with urban school children, and with crime victims or those accused of crimes. Encounters with these people, I hoped, would provide a different perspective on public policy by "putting a face" on public policies and their consequences. It was unlikely that service sites corresponding to all policy areas discussed in class would be found, but our objective was to identify sites that would bring students in contact with at least some of the policy areas to be discussed in class.

In the end, four service site options were presented to students. Students could work in a Providence homeless shelter, Amos House, serving either a lunch or breakfast once a week. The second option was tutoring sixth- through eighth-grade students at an urban middle school, Esek Hopkins, located near the campus. The third alternative was working with Southeast Asian immigrant children in an after-school program sponsored by the Southeast Asian Development Corporation, a self-help civic group organized by recent immigrants. Finally, several students would work on a project for the community affairs vicariate of Providence's Roman Catholic diocese to interview welfare recipients and prepare anonymous case profiles that could be used in parish education on the welfare reform issue. Students would be given these options on the first day of class and asked to commit at least two hours per week to one of them.

Integrating service-learning into college courses requires attention to two important aspects of course development: (1) how to compensate for the additional student time and effort service requires and (2) how service will be factored into the evaluation of student performance. I believe thinking about the service requirement as analogous to other sorts of requirements, such as assigned papers or readings, helps in addressing both of these issues. Requiring two or more hours of community service a week needs to be taken into account in light of the overall course requirements, just as one must do in assigning an additional paper or book to read. In the public policy course, I could not simply add the service requirement on top of the quantity and type of assignments made previously. In this case, I decided to alter the course paper requirement to take into account the time taken up with service. Instead of a traditional research paper, I required students to write an analytic essay, without additional research beyond assigned course readings, on what they learned about public policy from their service experience. Students were required, also, to keep a weekly journal of their service experience that could serve as "data" for this paper.

The appropriate way to evaluate service and integrate it into the course grade seems to be a major concern for many service-learning practitioners.[1] My own view, one that reflects many discussions of this issue with my Providence College colleagues, is that we should concentrate on evaluating the "learning" side of service-learning and not the "service." The performance goal of service-learning is not how well a student *serves*, whether defined as how caring, how efficient, or how enthusiastically, but how well a student *learns* from the service experience. This approach is analogous to how I evaluate a student reading assignment — not by how well a student reads (speed-readers get no extra points) but by the learning that results from a particular book or article. Students are graded not on the service, per se, but on their reflections on that service and their ability to relate it to the subject matter of the course. In the public policy course, student journals and papers were the means by which I could judge what students had learned about public policy from their service. The service activity itself was evaluated only through monitoring whether students kept their service commitment and adhered to the basic rules of their service site (much as one might monitor class attendance or require submission of a paper by a certain date). No attempt was made to judge whether students were effective food servers, tutors, mentors, or interviewers — the basic assumption was that the service commitment included trying to do one's best. I was careful to make clear in both the course syllabus and my first-day introduction of the service component that students' reflections on their service experience and how these were related to public policy issues would provide the basis for the course grade.

The classroom portion of the course followed a conventional lecture/discussion format, with discussion predominating over the lecture portion. After the first couple of weeks, when I introduced basic concepts and the political economy context of American public policy, class sessions generally involved discussion around key questions or issues that I framed during the first 5 or 10 minutes of class. The final course grades were based on a midterm and final exams plus class participation — in addition to the service journal and analytic paper. Also, students from each of the four service sites made group presentations to the rest of the class at the end of the semester.

One advantage I had in organizing the service component of my course was the help of the staff of Providence College's Feinstein Institute for Public Service. Established in 1993 through a grant from a Rhode Island philanthropist, the Feinstein Institute promotes the integration of community service-learning into the college's academic curriculum. Along with the administration of a new academic degree program in public and community service studies, the Feinstein Institute staff offer support to faculty, like me, who want to integrate community service activities into their classes. A service-learning coordinator works with faculty in selecting appropriate service sites and in making contacts with staff of community organizations in setting up the service experiences. Already, the institute has established numerous community contacts that greatly facilitate identifying appropriate community service placements. An important aspect of this process is matching service sites with the particular goals of different courses.

In planning the service sites for my course, I met several times with the service-learning coordinator to discuss my course goals and review alternative sites. In addition, as a part of the new academic degree program, majors in public and community service studies are available to faculty as teaching assistants to help in organizing and coordinating the service components of courses. Throughout the course of the semester, institute staff keep track of service-learning classes and provide assistance for any problems that develop. At semester's end, the institute evaluates the service components of all service-learning classes.

The Service Experience

Most of the students who enrolled in my public policy class did not know before the first day of class that community service would be required, and many were not happy about the requirement when they learned of it. Based on comments during the first class, I estimated that about one-third of the students were hostile to the idea of service, one-third indifferent — although somewhat intrigued — and the remaining third excited about the idea. Those opposed to the service requirement were concerned primarily about the time commitment and fitting another two-hour obligation into their school and work schedules. Some accused me of being unfair in not advertizing the service requirement before course registration. My response was to point out that those opposed to service were free to drop the course, and that course requirements, like papers or specific reading assignments, are rarely advertized at course registration time. Beyond these comments, however, I tried during this first class to explain my rationale for including the service component and how it fit into course goals. By the end of the hour, I seem to have succeeded in converting most of those initially hostile to the service component, as all but three students remained in the course.

Besides the rationale for the service, each of the four service options was presented to the students on the first day of class. They were asked to rank order their preferences, and final service assignments were made by the end of the week. In most cases, the distribution of preferences allowed giving students their first choice. During the second week of classes, students attended a general service orientation at the Feinstein Institute and had an on-site orientation conducted by course teaching assistants and service site staff. Service schedules were worked out for each student, and all began their service by week three.

The service experience proved to be one of the most popular aspects of the course — despite the early misgivings of some students. Within a couple of weeks of beginning their service, I heard enthusiastic comments from students about their service. Early student worries that they would not have time for community service eased once the two-hour commitment became part of their weekly routine. One health services management major, for example, who wanted me to waive the service because of the time demands of her health management internship, soon became so enthusiastic about tutoring children at Esek Hopkins that she began volunteering extra hours.

By the middle of the semester, her service experience had led her to reorient her health services internship around devising a middle school antismoking curriculum. Another student, who had insisted on a Saturday service placement because of his busy work schedule, was soon showing up at Amos House both at his regular Saturday time and for one other breakfast during the week. By the end of the semester, many students said, in their course evaluations and journals, that the service experience was one of the most valuable aspects of the course.

The service experience in my course seemed consistent with the anecdotal accounts in the service-learning literature: Students find service meaningful, worthwhile, and appreciate its integration into the course. Most described service as a learning experience in itself — a means of contact with people and experiences they had not previously encountered. In their journal entries, students frequently mentioned how the service experience increased their awareness of social concerns and the life experience of those they met in their service. The service experience also seemed an opportunity for many for personal growth and the development of their own self-confidence. Many of the tutors at Esek Hopkins, for example, were surprised to learn, despite initial insecurity about their own math skills, that they knew enough to help the middle school students; several remarked that they "remembered" more basic math than they had expected. The students who interviewed AFDC recipients gained confidence in their ability to conduct interviews and, what several found most important, their ability to deal emotionally with the sometimes traumatic stories they heard. And, as has been my experience in previous service-learning classes, students found their service personally satisfying. Comments about "making a real difference" appeared in nearly every service journal.

My Perceptions of Service-Learning's Impact on the Course

Service-learning made American Public Policy different from any of the previous times I had taught it and made it better. Service-learning made a difference in what students learned, and students did connect their service experience well to the concepts and public policy issues we discussed. The student service experiences were a useful tool for raising questions, opening avenues of analysis, and offering illustrations of points I wanted to make in class. Most important, the service experience empowered students by making them "experts" on a portion of the material discussed in class. Because students were in contact with the people or concerns the policies we were discussing addressed, they found they possessed firsthand knowledge with which to react to the policy debate. Policy issues that had been remote and abstract in previous classes engaged these students on a much more personal level. I believe that the service experience was the key to making this happen.

Repeatedly during the course of the semester, I sensed students raising questions and issues with a sort of confidence and decisiveness that I have not experienced in previous public policy classes. This sense of empower-ment came through especially in two ways: first, in the quality of daily class discussion — student engagement and involvement in discussion was the best I have experienced — and, second, in the quality of the term papers stu-dents submitted.

As with previous semesters, the course focused on issues of equal edu-cational opportunity in our discussion of education policy. Jonathan Kozol's Savage Inequalities, with its dramatic and eloquent accounts of schooling in resource-poor districts, provided an excellent vehicle for raising these issues. Prior to reading the book, students raised the issue of social class difference in their discussion of their service experience. Coming from upper middle class backgrounds, they had noticed early on the contrast between their own experiences in suburban, predominantly white, public or private schools and what they observed in an ethnically diverse urban public school. They per-ceived a different and more impoverished educational atmosphere than they remembered from their own schools. Many comments were made about the lack of discipline and order in the school and absence of serious work going on in classrooms. They said the sixth- and seventh-grade stu-dents they were tutoring were working on math concepts they remembered covering in third and fourth grade in their own schools. Even before we got to Kozol, they were describing their experience in terms of class inequality.

After reading the book, the students brought up their service experience as confirming much of what Kozol described. At the same time, they drew on their experience to raise critical questions about his analysis. Most sig-nificantly, they found little to support Kozol's emphasis on differences in school resources as the source of educational inequality. While they were convinced that the quality of education at Esek Hopkins was inferior, they saw little evidence of a lack of resources. The school was in good physical condition (it had recently been completely renovated), and students seemed to have ample books and other materials with which to work. Rather than lack of school resources, my students brought up the social gulf between the middle class white teachers at the school and their pupils. Several of my stu-dents reported witnessing teachers directing abusive language at children, and their encounters with teachers left them with the impression that the teachers were largely apathetic and dismissive of the potential of those they were teaching.

While my students' perception of ample resources and abusive teachers at the school may not have been completely accurate, it led our class discussion on education policy in productive directions. Students used their experience as a springboard to seek other explanations, besides resource inequalities, to account for their service observations. They brought up issues such as teacher recruitment and training, school district organization and administration, school politics, and the segregation of the poor in central cities. Because students had a chance to learn about the chaotic home lives of some of the children they tutored and how that seemed to affect their learning, they began to think and discuss education policy in relation to broader social issues, such as growing income inequality, and the relationship to other policies, such as economic and welfare policies. Compared with my previous experience, this class explored educational issues more thoroughly and with greater sophistication. Having students in the class with direct experience with a public school made all the difference.

Students were able to bring their service experience to bear, in a similar way, when we discussed immigration policy. I organized discussion of immigration around a National Issues Forum booklet that offered three alternative policy "choices" on the issue.[2] After reading the booklet, the class deliberated about the alternatives and sought a consensus on a policy option. Student service with recent immigrants had significant impact when we discussed the option that focused on immigration as a threat to cultural unity. Rather than accept readily the claim that recent immigrants clung to their ethnic identity and refused to embrace American values, the students who had become acquainted with Southeast Asian children in the after-school program offered numerous anecdotes about the "American-ness" of the children — in their dress, games, musical tastes, and English language ability. At the same time, several students reported talking with the children about the children's home life, cultural traditions, and religion. They found the children seemed to be integrating well into the American cultural mainstream, while participating, at the same time, in their families' traditional cultures.

Service-learning had a major impact on how the class discussed welfare policy. To a greater extent than other policy issues, students in previous classes had addressed welfare policy in ideological terms, and students always divided on this issue along ideological lines. Given the attention to the new emphasis on welfare reform in the Republican's Contract With America, students were intensely interested in welfare and initially, as in the past, approached it in largely ideological terms, with the class conservatives praising Republican proposals and the liberals deriding them.

Interestingly, the welfare interview service option attracted some of the most ideological liberals and conservatives in the class. For both, as they made clear in class discussion, coming in contact with some actual welfare recipients caused them to modify the stance their ideologies dictated. While their general predispositions remained the same, the students became very critical of the terms in which the public debate was held and found they had to rethink the assumptions underlying their own predispositions. For conservatives, talking with AFDC recipients destroyed their assumption that recipients were lazy and happy about living on the dole. In their journals, several remarked on their surprise at how bright and resourceful the women they talked to were. In their final papers, several of the conservative students, while not rejecting the punitive approach of the Personal Responsibility Act altogether, argued for softening it with provisions for support for job training, child care, and mentoring programs. The more liberal students in this group became more critical of the welfare system as a result of their welfare interviews. These students were impressed with the demeaning, stigmatizing, and controlling character of welfare as revealed in their discussions with AFDC recipients.

One of the most interesting discussions of welfare policy during the semester occurred as a result of observations of students serving at the soup kitchen, Amos House. After several weeks of service, the students expressed surprise that they observed primarily men coming for meals. Talking about why this might be the case led to a discussion of the structure of the income support system in the United States and the near absence of basic income support for single men and women without children. Like many states, Rhode Island has recently effectively eliminated general public assistance (GPA), leaving no source of income for those without children. In following up our discussion, students talked with Amos House staff about how GPA cutbacks had increased the number of people coming for meals. In addition, they began to learn that some of those who came for meals had jobs, some of them full-time, but came to Amos House as a supplement to their low wages. As a result of these discussions, as in the case of our discussion of education policy, students were able to place the analysis of welfare policy in a larger context of growing income inequality, declining wages, and increasing poverty in America.

Finally, along with empowering students as "experts" in class discussion, service-learning helped them to write better papers and exams by empowering them to claim ownership of their own words. In my experience, undergraduates do not, typically, look on their course writing as something that belongs to them. Papers and exams are exercises undertaken at the behest of professors. The result is an artificiality of tone and absence of sincere commitment to the ideas expressed. Usually, papers in my public policy course reflected this context. The papers this past semester were different. In style and tone, they seemed to express the students' genuine commitment to what was written and desire to communicate about the service experience. Perhaps because they could claim ownership of their service experience, the students could assert ownership of what they wrote in their papers. Unlike the typical term paper, in which students merely synthesize the ideas of others, these papers drew on experiences unique to the writers and this improved immensely, in comparison with previous papers in this course, the quality of the work I read. While the paper and exam assignments required students to draw on course readings and their own additional library research, the link to the service experience seemed to give students ground upon which to think of what they wrote as their own.

Conclusion

Having had the experience of using a service-learning component in American Public Policy, I cannot conceive of teaching the course again without it. Service-learning made the course different and, I believe, better than the previous times I have taught it. Students did bring insights from their service experience into our classroom discussion of public policy. These insights allowed more enthusiastic, engaged, and informed discussion than I have experienced in other classes.

The most important contribution of service-learning to student learning in my course was through the way it seemed to empower students. Such empowerment may occur especially at institutions, like mine, with student bodies recruited from 18-to-22-year-olds. In my experience, one learning obstacle such students face is their youth; that is, their relative lack of life experience against which they can analyze and judge the material they encounter in the classroom. I notice this when I teach older students who do have such life experience and draw on it constantly in evaluating course material. Last semester, I discovered that community service gave my young students a quick and concentrated dose of life experience, their own and that of those they served. They used this experience in thinking about public policy. The result was a class of more mature and more empowered learners who gave this teacher one of the most satisfying teaching experiences of his career.

Epilogue

Spring semester of 1996, I taught American Public Policy again with a service-learning component. [The syllabus follows on pp. 93-97.] While some service sites were different and all students this time knew coming in that service would be part of the course (word of last year's experience traveled quickly through the political science major grapevine), the experience was quite similar to the previous year. However, having seen the value of the service component of the course for empowering student learners, I plan to alter the course significantly next year to make the service component even more central. My current plan is to reduce the number of specific policy areas studied in the class to only those related to student service experiences. This will allow an even tighter integration between classroom discussion and service. In addition, with fewer policy areas to cover, I hope to be able to spend more time, in class, on service reflection and developing specific relationships between these experiences and national public policy debates. In fact, because I hope to intensify the service-policy connection, I am considering reducing to three the number of service sites and policy areas. After a few weeks introducing general concepts, historical material, and theoretical material on the growth of the positive state, we will focus intensely on the three policy areas directly related to students' service experience. I hope this will give students greater freedom to explore in class those aspects of policy issues that emerge from their service site experience. In this way, the service component will be central to course learning and less of a supplementary field experience connected to only some class issues.

Notes

1. See, for example, Urban Whitaker, "Assessing Learning," in *Combining Service and Learning* (Volume II), edited by Jane C. Kendall and Associates (Raleigh, NC: National Society for Internships and Experiential Education, 1990), pp. 206-208.

2. National Issues Forum Institute, "Admission Decisions: Should Immigration Be Restricted?" (Dubuque, IA: Kendall/Hunt, 1994). These booklets are intended for use by community groups to promote citizen deliberation on public issues.

PSC 406 - AMERICAN PUBLIC POLICY

Instructor: William E. Hudson   Location: FC 307
               Howley 309   Series C
               865-2621   M, W, Thu: 9:30
               bhudson@providence.edu

Office Hrs.:   T and Thurs. 1:30-3:30 & by appointment

Description

This course has three goals: to improve your understanding of the nature
and content of existing American public policies, to improve your ability
to analyze competing explanations for why policies are enacted, and to
improve your ability to evaluate critically policy arguments and proposals
for reform. If this course is successful, by the end of the semester you
should be better equipped to address the following questions: What are
American public policies?, why do these policies exist?, and what policies
should exist? We will pursue these goals through study of several
contemporary policy issues.
        Because this course is about current policy concerns, much of our
attention throughout the semester will focus on day to day discussion in
the media of policy issues. For this reason, daily monitoring of these
discussions is a crucial part of our work, hence the necessity of the New
York Times assignment (see below). Our other readings and class
discussions will aim to broaden and deepen current policy debates through
study of the context and history in which they occur. Readings and
assignments are intended to provide a sophisticated understanding of
contemporary public policy debates.
        Student class participation will be crucial throughout the
semester. For this reason, students will be expected to complete reading
assignments prior to coming to class. The course outline below provides a
daily schedule of reading assignments. I will expect students to have
completed a given day's assignment before coming to class. In addition to
these reading assignments, I expect students to supplement their daily
reading of the New York Times through attention to other news sources like
periodicals and TV network news.

Service component

Every student in this class will be required to participate in a community
service activity. We expect students to complete a *minimum* of thirty hours
of community service over the course of the semester (about two hours per
week). Most service options will require a commitment of 2 - 4 hours per
week. During the first week of class, students will be provided
information on several service options. Students will select one of these
options for their service site.   During the first two or three weeks of
class, orientations will be organized for each site and individual service
schedules developed. Every effort will be made by both the course staff
and service site staff to fit schedules into your other activities.
        Either I or a Feinstein Institute Service Corps member will serve
as team leader for your service site. As team leader for your service
activity, we will be responsible for helping you with issues arising from
your service activity, including scheduling service hours; acting as a
liaison between your service site, this course, and the Feinstein
Institute; trouble shooting any problems that may occur; and leading

service reflection/discussion sessions with the students at your site.
        The purpose of this service activity is to bring you into contact
with how public policies affect people in American society. Each service
activity has been chosen with this purpose in mind. You are encouraged to
relate the experiences you will have at your service site to all aspects of
the course. Comments about service experiences are welcome in every class.
        Your service experience should be considered as one of the course
assignments of this course like the assigned readings, exams, and paper
assignments. You will be graded on your service through monitoring of a
service journal I will ask you to keep and submit weekly. (See journal
assignment) In assessing your service grade, I will hold you accountable,
at a minimum, for keeping your service commitment and, in addition, I will
assess the degree to which you relate your service experience to course
themes in your service journal.

Course readings

David Stoesz   *Small Change*
Gingrich, et al.   *Contract With America*
James Gimpel   *Fulfilling the Contract*
Joel Handler   *The Poverty of Welfare Reform*
Jonathan Kozol   *Savage Inequalities*
New York Times or other nationally oriented newspaper
Various hand-outs (these are marked with * in outline below)

Recommended:
weekly monitoring of some policy relevant periodicals (See: A List of
Public Policy Periodicals)

Written assignments and grade distribution

Two take home exams   20 %
Final   30
Final paper (10-12 pages)   20
Service, service journal,
  service group presentations, and
  class participation   30

Outline

I.   Introduction .... Jan. 17

II.   What is public policy? What does govt. do? .... Jan. 18-25
            Rushefsky "Process, Structure, Ideology" *
            (Jan.18- Select service preferences)
            (Jan. 22- e-mail training)

III. A Brief History of American Public Policy .... Jan. 29 - Feb. 8
            A. 1776 - 1932 .... Jan. 29
                 Linden pp.35-53 *
            B. New Deal and WW II .... Jan. 31 - Feb. 1
                 Linden pp. 54-63 *
                 Caro "The Sad Irons" & "I'll Get It for You" *
            C. Post-WW II to 1980 .... Feb. 5-7
                 Linden pp. 63 - 71 *
            D. Reaganism .... Feb. 8
                 Linden pp. 71-88 *

Community Service Placement Options
PSC 406   Hudson
Spring 1996

1. *Smith Hill Economic Development Project*

Agency contact: Richard Brien 885-3254/Bari Harlam 792-4356
PC contact: Bill Hudson 865-2621

This year the Smith Hill Center initiated an Economic Development project
to promote economic development in the neighborhood. Economic development
consultants, with the assistance of neighborhood residents and the
Feinstein Institute, have been collecting data on neighborhood assets and
the existing business base. This service project will involve providing
staff assistance to the economic consultants as they proceed with their
work. Students will perform a variety of tasks ranging from data entry to
formulating strategies for collecting additional data. Preliminary plans
suggest a need for students to research how public policies and
neighborhood social capital affect neighborhood economic development.
        Travel: initial meetings will be held at the Smith Hill Center,
                         110 Ruggles St. (two blocks from campus).

2. *McAuley Village*

Agency contact: Sister Holly Cloutier 467-3630
PC contact: Meg Stoltzfus 865-1256

McAuley Village is a residential facility that provides quality housing,
social services, and a supportive environment to assist welfare recipients
in ending their dependence on public assistance. Students electing this
project will provide child care assistance during early evening hours
(approximately 4-5:30 PM) once or twice a week for Village residents.
Each student will work (and play) with children in their apartments while
their mothers complete household chores or study. (All McAuley Village
residents are enrolled in educational programs.) Activities with the
children would range from helping them with their homework to playing board
games.
        Travel: by car or bus to 325 Niagara St. (South Providence)

3. *Esek Hopkins Middle School*

Agency contact: Ralph Campagnone 456-9203
PC contact: Nick Longo 271-1425

Esek Hopkins is a middle school (6-8 grade) located on Charles St. in
Providence's North End. The children at the school come from mostly low
income students representing many different ethnic groups. There is an
especially large Southeast Asian population at the school. Student
volunteers will tutor children in a variety of subjects in an after school
program.
        Travel: long walk (1 ½ miles) or five minute car ride

4. *Project HOPE/Proyecto Esperanza*

Agency contact: Stella Carrera 728-0515
PC contact: Christine Castagna 831-3217

Project HOPE/Proyecto Esperanza is an advocacy agency and social service
center funded by Catholic Charities, a Diocesan subsidy, and other grants
to address the needs of the elderly, low-income, and working poor in the
Blackstone Valley. This service project involves tutoring recent
immigrants as they prepare to apply to become US citizens.
     Travel: by car or bus to 400 Dexter St., Central Falls

Political Theory

by James Farr

The great American pragmatist John Dewey is presently undergoing a well-deserved recovery by philosophers, historians, and humanists.[1] His ideas, I believe, could prove even more valuable for political scientists, especially for those interested (as we all should be) in our discipline's historical mission to educate citizens.[2] Bringing political science and citizen education directly together, Dewey thought that the polity was a large classroom, and the classroom a small polity. He sought to overcome traditional dichotomies, such as those alleged between theory and practice. He also longed to go beyond a mass society to help create a Great Community composed of citizens who worked and served together to solve the problems of public life that they collectively faced.[3]

Dewey provides all the right elements, in my view, for thinking not only about political science and citizen education but also about political theory and community service in particular. Political theory is a subfield of political science that shares in the historical mission of the discipline as a whole, doing so with particular attention to the analytical, normative, and historical dimensions of citizenship. Community service (broadly understood) seems a particularly good vehicle these days to make the practical dimensions of citizen education all the more palpable by taking students out of classroom settings and placing them in community ones where they can directly engage and try to solve or at least alleviate the public problems that we face as citizens.

Courses in political theory can and should take advantage of community service opportunities — *especially* if these opportunities are thematized in expressly political and civic terms. Once thematized, community service opportunities can function as "civic laboratories" for the political theories being discussed in the course. This is self-evidently so for courses on democratic theory, as well as for those on competing contemporary ideologies — from liberalism and conservatism to communitarianism, feminism, or environmentalism. It is also so for courses that analyze key issues or concepts such as justice, rights, freedom, or multiculturalism. It is even so — if political theorists would only flex their imaginations — for courses in the history of political thought. What better way (if I can turn a point into a question) to teach students to think about the political issues that, say, Cicero addressed in terms of duty and virtue than to place them in a civic laboratory of community service where issues of (Ciceronian) duty and virtue emerge, even or especially if our understandings of these terms have changed, as arguably they have in the case of duty, or have been largely abandoned, as arguably they have in the case of virtue? What is true of learning about Cicero on duty and virtue is similarly true of learning about Augustine on charity, Hobbes on power, or Tocqueville on "self-interest properly understood." The learning here is decidedly two-way. Students learn more about their political theories from engaging in community service by "testing" them out in their "civic laboratory"; and they learn to think about the community and their service in terms of democracy, power, duty, multiculturalism, or self-interest (properly understood!).

The service-learning course in political theory that I teach and whose syllabus appends this chapter [pp. 106-108] reflects these general remarks. Indeed, it was designed to highlight the commitment of political theory to citizen education, and to adapt community service (broadly understood) to complement this commitment. The course — Political Theory and Citizen Education — investigates key episodes in the development of (mainly Western) political theory that are expressly directed to questions of the education of citizens. Over the course of a term, students are introduced to the key texts on education by some (so-called) canonical thinkers in the deeper history of political thought, including Plato, Machiavelli, Locke, and Rousseau. But they also make a more contemporary analysis and critique of political theory and citizen education in the works of John Dewey, Paulo Freire, Myles Horton, and others (mainly in shorter, article form). In the process, we focus critically and comparatively on the different general conceptions of politics, citizenship, and education at stake, as well as the more particular conceptions of, say, justice in Plato, virtú in Machiavelli, will in Rousseau, and the public in Dewey. The education of college students (discussed in the Matthews reader) is contrasted with the education of adults in radicalized situations (as found in Horton and Freire's book). Locke's "thoughts" on the education of a young 17th-century gentleman are counterposed to Dewey's "curriculum" for developing democrats; and both are contrasted with Plato's "blueprint" for educating guardians in philosophical truths and everyday citizens (with souls of baser metals) in noble fictions. Variants of the course with slightly altered reading lists have been offered under related titles such as Practicing Democratic Education and simply Political Education. But all of the courses attempt to communicate that much of political theory since Plato has been *about* citizen education, as well as being dedicated to the practice *of* educating citizens.

I could well imagine this course taking advantage of the many different kinds of community service opportunities available today. Most colleges and universities — thanks to Campus Compact, the YWCA, the YMCA, or local service organizations — have a number of such opportunities structured and available to students and instructors. Here at the University of

Minnesota, we have a particularly well developed set of options, thanks to our Office of Special Learning Opportunities (OSLO), as well as the activities of several faculty members, some of them having been crucial in the forming of the Campus Outreach Opportunities League (COOL) and other community service organizations. Also, off-campus but affiliated organizations — especially the YWCA — have been very oriented to service-learning. Most of the experiences that students have in community service opportunities such as these could be made to fit the cognitive goals of my course — or a course like it — at least if these opportunities were properly thematized as being a civic laboratory in citizen education. If this were done — and in more than a cursory, hand-waving fashion — then working at a homeless shelter, helping to build houses, staffing a public health clinic, cleaning up community grounds, or tutoring the young in math or new immigrants in English could all be made to fit under the penumbra of "political theory and citizen education." Surely matters of justice (as in Plato) or community (as in Dewey) would be raised; and if tutoring were the form that the community service took, the comparisons with Locke's tutor in *Some Thoughts Concerning Education* or with Rousseau's in *Emile* could be made to be quite precise and telling.

The above paragraph is quite consciously counterfactual; it attests to what *could* be imagined, by me or anyone else. Not only could I, counterfactually, imagine using most community service opportunities to fit the terms of my course, but I hope that *other* political theorists might take advantage of such opportunities for their own courses. I intend this as a strong form of encouragement. As a matter of fact, however, I have not relied upon the structured community service opportunities that are available. Instead I have been involved in a project to create an educational *practicum* that may be understood as an adaptation of service-learning (and that is briefly described in my article with Harry Boyte in this volume beginning on p. 35). Public Achievement, as the practicum is called, is expressly designed to realize the goals of citizen education — both for my undergraduate students and for even younger students with whom my undergraduates work at various middle schools and high schools. Since other political theorists and political scientists might think to craft a service-learning course along these lines, let me describe the practicum in a little more detail.

My students have as their service site, as it were, a particular school.[4] A partnership between the school and the university (or at least my class) has to have been reached in advance (just as at community service sites). The students, then, go as a group to the school once a week (and sometimes more often), and I always go with them. At the school, the undergraduates individually go to work with a particular group of younger students at the school. Each group is composed of from 6 to 16 younger students. Each group, moreover, is dedicated to working on a particular problem or issue in or around the school or the community in which the school is located. The younger students themselves have identified the relevant problems and issues, usually at a "convention" in which the student body (as a whole, preferably) participates. Then, when the problems or issues with the greatest interest are identified, the younger students choose the group to which they individually wish to contribute. The problems or issues can range quite liberally, as one might expect of younger students; and if we hope for better-educated citizens, they must be able to act as citizens do in articulating and choosing the problems on which to work. One group might work on fighting neighborhood violence; another might try to organize field trips or sporting events that otherwise would not be organized; yet another might strive to change the uniform policy or to get a juice machine at the school; still another might develop a strategy for helping the homeless nearby.

An undergraduate student functions as a particular group's "coach" (a student-friendly term of the younger students' design). The undergraduate, in a word, is there to coach the students along as they try to solve the problem or address the issue that they have identified. The coach has two general goals, and these are connected to the themes of citizen education in the history of political theory that he or she is addressing in readings and class discussions. First, the coach is there to help pass along a basic language or theory of politics and citizenship by means of which the younger students might better articulate their understanding of the political realities that attend their problem or issue. This basic language conceives of *citizenship* as *public work* where citizens are engaged in *teamwork* and the collective activities of specifying and *solving problems* of their own reckoning, attentive to the *powers* and *interests* that they have or that others have regarding the problems in question. For the younger students, the terms (in italics) contribute to a basic education in citizenship. For the undergraduates, the terms are themselves problematized and discussed in the course of readings and class discussions. Their higher citizen education thus consists in further articulating and challenging these notions in light of their more advanced understanding of political theory and public life. Second, the undergraduate coaches are there to help stimulate the *civic skills* and *capacities* that the younger students instinctively have but need more consciously to develop in order to do public work. These skills and capacities consist mainly in teamwork, rule making, negotiating, deliberating, debating, public speaking, and "mapping" the environment in terms of powerful agents and diverse others with whom citizens must work.

Week to week, then, during an hour time period during the course of the school day, the undergraduate coaches work with their groups, trying to develop a basic language of politics and some fundamental civic skills. They also help the younger students with the practicalities that attend solving their problem, usually by challenging them to think about what must be done; that is, what *they* must do as young citizens (from seeing teachers, organizing parents, writing letters, doing surveys, circulating petitions, making phone calls, developing curricula, practicing speeches, debating arguments, soliciting public officials, planning events, collecting funds, to coordinating actions). The problem in question invariably dictates the range of possible practicalities that need attention if problems are to find their solutions.

After the weekly hour-long session, the undergraduates reassemble as a group for another hour of discussion, evaluation, and mutual problem solving. I am an active participant in this session, having circulated during the course of the previous hour, checking in on my undergraduate coaches. The principal or teacher(s) at the school who is involved in the practicum is always invited to attend, and usually does so. This helps our work considerably. Besides reporting on their respective group's progress (or lack of it), the undergraduates discuss questions of politics, political theory, and even younger student behavior. There is an important educational component in this, as well as an element of sheer camaraderie. These discussion sessions are one forum in which the theoretical themes of the course are made to engage the practicalities of the service experience. Exams and a notebook (a term preferable to "journal," which, like "diary," sounds too privatistic) provide the other ways in which the theory and practice of the course are made to address each other.

Political Theory and Citizen Education with its practicum has been exceedingly well received by the students who have enrolled in it (or related practica) over the last four years. Indeed, they state that it ranks among their best academic experiences. This matches the reports of other students in other courses that have a community service component. Whatever the merits of this particular course in political theory or others in various fields, I am inclined to believe that students are starving for courses that engage them experientially as well as intellectually, and practically as well as theoretically. I can also confess that the course has been the best and most challenging experience that I have had in teaching. I certainly have received the education of my life.

This is not to deny that there have not been problems, with my course or with Public Achievement or with service-learning experiences more generally. I do believe that the Public Achievement practicum — or courses designed like it, should they exist or yet be developed — avoids some of the common complaints that have been raised against other service-learning experiences: that they are too philanthropic in orientation and insufficiently realistic about the politics and problems that "service" faces; that they are too therapeutic, overly interested in self-esteem, personal growth, or topics sappier still; that they are not well-integrated with the ostensible course topic and class readings; that they are too disparate, each student going in a different direction without much overall organization and integration; that the instructor is absent from the service experience, except for his or her exhortations.

However, Public Achievement, too, has its problems, some it shares with other kinds of service-learning opportunities, some unique to its aspirations. All such service activities entail almost excessive amounts of student effort amidst cramped undergraduate schedules; and they end up being enrolled in by self-selecting students who are already inclined to engage in service opportunities. Also, even when other faculty members express interest in service-learning or in Public Achievement, they complain — in advance — of all the time commitments, without even seeing whether they could make it work into their schedules. But it is hard to disabuse them of such complaints: It *does* take a lot of time, especially if you attend each and every session with your students. As for Public Achievement itself, I have found that younger students, perhaps because of their level of cognitive development, are better at picking up civic skills and capacities than they are at becoming fluent in a language of politics and citizenship. Also, the involvement of principals, teachers, and parents makes all the difference between different Public Achievement school sites. If there is not such involvement, then the ability of younger students and their undergraduate coaches to make a civic difference in the school or surrounding community is considerably limited.

Yet the difficulties do not overwhelm service-learning experiences or the promise that such experiences hold out for political theory, political science, or the education of citizens. They are, as Dewey would call them, the "hard stretches" that prompt us to "duty." "But what carries a person over these hard stretches," he went on, "is not loyalty to duty in the abstract, but interest in his occupation. Duties are 'offices' — they are the specific acts needed for the fulfilling of a function — or, in homely language — doing one's job."[5] As teachers, students, and community service organizers, it is our job — our civic duty — to educate citizens for a fuller, more meaningful life in a democracy.

Notes

1. See, for example, Richard Rorty, *The Consequences of Pragmatism* (Minneapolis: University of Minnesota Press, 1982); R.W. Sleeper, *The Necessity of Pragmatism: John Dewey's Conception of Philosophy* (New Haven: Yale University Press, 1986); Robert B. Westbrook, *John Dewey and American Democracy* (Ithaca: Cornell University Press, 1991); and Steven C. Rockefeller, *John Dewey: Religious Faith and Democratic Humanism* (New

York: Columbia University Press, 1991).

2. On Dewey and civic education in political science, see, for starters, David Steiner, *Rethinking Democratic Education: The Politics of Reform* (Baltimore: John Hopkins Press, 1993), chs. 5-6; Timothy Kaufman-Osborn, *Politics/Sense/Experience: A Pragmatist Inquiry Into the Promise of Democracy* (Ithaca: Cornell University Press, 1991); and, rather briefly but in the context of discussing democracy and community service, Benjamin R. Barber, *An Aristocracy of Everyone: The Politics of Education and the Future of America* (New York: Ballantine, 1992), esp. ch. 7. On the historic mission of political science to educate citizens, see essays in James Farr and Raymond Seidelman, eds., *Discipline and History: Political Science in the United States* (Ann Arbor: University of Michigan Press, 1993); and Stephen T. Leonard, "The Pedagogical Purposes of a Political Science," in James Farr, John S. Dryzek, and Stephen T. Leonard, eds., *Political Science in History: Research Programs and Political Traditions* (Cambridge: Cambridge University Press, 1995), ch. 3.

3. See especially *Democracy and Education* (New York: MacMillan, 1916) and *The Public and Its Problems* (New York: Henry Holt, 1927).

4. Over the past four years, a number of schools have provided such sites for my students, including J.J. Hill Middle School, a Montessori public school; and Calvin Christian School, a denominational middle school. But one school in particular — St. Bernard's Middle School, a Catholic school in a working-class, ethnically diverse part of St. Paul, educating students of many different religious orientations — has been a premier site because of the involvement of the principal, his teachers, and the students' parents, as well. While I am trying to speak in general terms about the practicum, the experiences that my students and I have had at St. Bernard's (and with its principal, Dennis Donovan) have been formative in my thinking about service-learning. It also deserves noting that there are other instructors and coaches — faculty, advanced graduate students, parents, and community workers — involved with Public Achievement at other schools and youth sites.

5. *Democracy and Education* (New York: MacMillan, 1916), p. 353.

Pol 5610: Abbreviated Syllabus
James Farr, University of Minnesota

POLITICAL THEORY AND CITIZEN EDUCATION

Course Description:

This course -- Pol 5610 -- will investigate critically some major texts and arguments in the history of political thought that address the question of political education, broadly speaking. It will be concerned to trace changing conceptions of "politics" and "education", as well as to articulate the various relationships between the discursive activity of theorizing about politics and the practice of educating citizens. It is driven by the renewed contemporary interest in questions of civic education; but it will address that interest in terms of some very important texts and arguments in the tradition of political theory. The principal authors include Plato, Niccolo Machiavelli, John Locke, and Jean Jacques Rousseau from the premodern era; and John Dewey, Myles Horton, Paulo Freire, and a series of recent writers from the contemporary period. The texts and arguments of these important authors should be understood as being about political education, as well as actually attempting to politically educate their audiences.

The course also has a required attendant course -- Pol 3090: Practicum (as described in the attached sheet). It will also address questions of democracy and education practically, in the form of an educational practicum. Students will put their education and democratic citizenship into practice by **serving as "coaches"** in our Public Achievement Project for middle-school students (at St. Bernard's Middle School or J. J. Hill Middle School, both in St. Paul). The younger students at these schools will be investigating and debating their own questions about politics, public problems, and social issues, in and around their school. The fundamental premise of the course is that we learn theoretically about citizenship and education in large part by being engaged practically as citizens and educators. Or to put it differently: to learn what must be learned about democratic education just is to be engaged in the practice of educating democrats. Overall, in short, we are interested in the theory and practice of political education.

Note well that the 5610 course has 4 credits, and the 3090 practicum has an additional total 4 credits, 2 credits in each of Fall and Winter quarters. That is, the practicum will continue into Winter quarter (in order to complete our work). Further credit will be available for Spring, should students wish to continue.

Course Requirements:

Requirements for 5610 and 3090 reflect their diverse goals. It will entail lectures, but also frequent class discussions. Thus it will be essential that class attendance be preceded by close reading(s) of the text(s).

Besides close reading and class discussion, the requirements of the course will consist in [1] a take-home midterm examination and [2] a take-home final examination. Both exams will be essay format.

The additional requirements for Pol 3090 -- especially regarding coaching and keeping a notebook -- are on the attached sheet.

Required Books:

Plato	The Republic
Niccolo Machiavelli	The Prince and the Discourses
John Locke	Some Thoughts Concerning Education
Jean Jacques Rousseau	Emile
John Dewey	Democracy and Education
M. Horton and P. Freire	We Make the Road by Walking
D. Matthews, ed.	Higher Education and the Practice of Democratic Politics

Weekly Readings:

1. Introduction: Political Theory and Citizen Education

2. Guardians, Forms, and Myths: the Engineered Republic
    Read: Plato, Republic

3. Humanists, Realists, and Republicans: Educating the Prince
    Read: Machiavelli, The Prince
                Machiavelli, The Discourses, selections

4. Civil Society and Liberal Education: the Englightened Gent
    Read: Locke, Some Thoughts Concerning Education
                Locke, selections from Two Treatises

5. Nature, Culture, and Gender: Tutoring Man and Citizen
    Read: Rousseau, Emile

6. Progress, Development, and Truth: the Self-Educated Liberal
    Read: Mill, Autobiography
                Mill, Inaugural Address to St. Andrews

7. Pragmatism, Progress, and the Public: Educating Democrats
    Read: Dewey, Democracy and Education

8. Radical Action and Social Change: Educating Adults Politically
    Read: Horton and Freire, We Make the Road by Walking

9. Citizenship and Liberal Education: Educating Students
    Read: Matthews, ed., Higher Education; selected essys

PS 3090: Practicum

The 5610 topics course on Political Education has attached to it an additional 4-credit course -- or practicum -- that involves students working as Public Achievement "coaches" at St. Bernard's Middle School or at J. J. Hill Middle-School, both in St. Paul. The middle school students are involved in year-long projects in which small working groups have identified issues and problems in and around their school that they are trying to address and solve.

The experience is intended to provide students with an exciting opportunity to integrate theoretical reflection on political education with some practical work in helping formative young citizens to educate themselves about the public world.

The practicum will begin this quarter, and continue into Winter quarter. Students are expected to commit themselves to the two-quarter project, in order to begin and hopefully bring to some conclusion the practical civic projects of the younger students at the respective schools.

Besides the theoretical readings for PS 5610: Political Education, the practicum has one text designed to help you as a coach: Making the Rules. This text has been designed by the Public Achievement staff of Project Public Life which represents the ongoing civic outreach component of the Center for Democracy and Citizenship at the University.

Requirements:

There are prerequisites for involvement in the practicum, or in PS 5610 more generally. Certainly students need not be majors in Political Science or the School of Education, or even intend to become professional teachers. A willing experimental attitude is all that is needed.

The 3090 practicum will entail weekly hour-long coaching sessions at the respective schools, as well as weekly hour-long follow-up evaluation sessions with all other coaches. Thus, besides travel to and from the respective schools, the coaching experience will be a two-hour weekly involvement.

Students will also keep a notebook that records weekly reflections on the practicum experience and that attempts to integrate the theoretical readings with that experience.

There will also be a final (4-page) evaluation of the practicum due at the end of the course.

Finally, there is a mandatory training session on Public Achievement coaching to be held on the first Saturday of the quarter.

Research Methods

by Daniel J. Palazzolo

An undergraduate course on research methods and analysis is fertile ground for service-learning in political science. Research methods courses teach students a variety of data-collection and analysis methods, and many community service agencies and nonprofit organizations typically benefit from research on how their services are provided and how such services can be improved. This essay illustrates how undergraduate students can use survey design techniques to help community service organizations collect data on program effectiveness and program development.

My undergraduate course in political science, Introduction to Research Methods and Analysis [its syllabus follows on pp. 115-118], introduces students to the fundamental tenets of political behavioralism and the basic aspects of the research process. The course is structured by the stages of the social scientific research process. Students learn how to define a research problem, how to formulate hypotheses, how to conceptualize and measure variables, and how to collect and analyze data using a variety of methods. I have concentrated on survey design for collecting quantitative data and participant-observation and interviewing for collecting qualitative information.

The service-learning project has the potential to meet several minimal course expectations, including mastering the basic elements of survey design, improving computer skills, and developing oral, written, and group communication skills. At a more ambitious level, I want the students to learn to appreciate research as both an intellectual exercise and an applied skill that can produce real consequences. In the social sciences, we do research because we want to explain the way people behave and also because we want to contribute to a dialogue about how to better the world in which we live.

The course assignments are meant to correspond with the objectives and expectations. The best way for students to learn research methods and analysis is to experience the research process. Students are required to complete six or seven projects (one of which is a group project) that apply the research and analysis techniques they are expected to learn. The students also make at least one oral presentation and take a final examination that asks them to reflect on the value of social scientific research based on their experiences in the course.

How can service-learning assignments help to achieve the course objectives and expectations of a research methods and analysis course? I had taught the course several times since 1990, but I had never tied it to a service-learning project until Spring 1995. It seemed to me that the course objectives and expectations were already being met — even before I assigned service-learning projects. But the service-learning projects certainly offered the potential for enhancing the class' capacity to attain the course objectives and expectations in several ways.

For the service-learning project, which I will describe in more detail below, students working in groups designed surveys for community service organizations, collected and analyzed the data, and wrote a paper on the survey design process and the results. In essence, the students were able to apply what they learned about survey design and help an organization that would benefit from the skills they could provide. Thus, the service-learning project enabled the students to learn as much as previous students had about group work and survey design. But, unlike other students who had taken the course before the Spring 1995 semester, these students experienced how a practical application of research methods could have real consequences for people and the programs that served them.

I am convinced that a general introduction to survey design is the best way to instruct students about the various aspects of the research process. Survey design requires thinking deductively about how to define a research problem; formulate hypotheses; and conceptualize, operationalize, and measure variables. I assign a book that covers the basic issues in survey design, and we cover the material in class.[1] Then the students construct the questions and the order of the questionnaire; they consider how to select a sample and how to administer the survey; and they enter and analyze the data produced by the survey.

Prior to the Spring 1995 semester, the class typically designed a survey on political attitudes and administered it to the student body at the university. But there is no reason why the techniques of survey design could not be used for other purposes. Indeed, with more at stake in terms of providing valid and reliable results to the service organizations, students might take the job even more seriously.

Though I had attended a service-learning workshop at the University of Richmond in 1992 and had directed numerous internships over the years, I had never attempted to assign a community service project in any course. I had always been intrigued with the idea, but worried about how it would work in practice. With a "nothing ventured, nothing gained" attitude and with the belief that a community service project might enhance the prospects of meeting the course objectives, I was encouraged by our Learning in Community Settings (LINCS) office to experiment. LINCS is designed to assist faculty in the process of incorporating service-learning projects into courses. With the advice and assistance of LINCS, I was able to find numerous organizations that were interested in having students do research for them, several of which wanted some kind of survey.

I selected four organizations that requested assistance on designing and implementing relatively short surveys to be distributed to fairly small target populations. The four organizations were Big Brothers and Big Sisters, the Capital Area Agency on Aging, the Chesterfield/Colonial Heights Department of Social Services, and the Virginia Poverty Law Center. While all of the organizations sought to ascertain information about the programs they provided, they had a diverse set of needs, both in terms of the questions they wished to ask and the type of survey they wanted to design.

Each organization was assigned to a group consisting of five students, including a group leader. While I tried to achieve gender equity, the most important selection criterion for creating the groups was the students' academic and extracurricular schedules. Group work requires students to meet outside of class, and for this project the students had to be able to travel off campus to meet with the program director of their organization. So, it was very important for them to have compatible work schedules.

After we spent a few weeks on survey design, the student groups were asked to complete the following schedule:

I. Meet with the program director of the organization and ascertain information on the following topics: (1) objectives of the survey, (2) sampling frame, and (3) a list of items (variables) to be included in the survey.
II. Meet with the instructor to discuss the interview with the program director and divide the workload for drafting survey questions.
III. Draft survey questions and arrange the order of the questions.
IV. Meet with the instructor to review the questionnaire.
V. Practice interviews with one another and check for validity.
VI. Present questionnaire to the class for review and critique.
VII. Clear the final survey with the program director.
VIII. Implement the survey and keep a record of phone numbers, nonresponse problems, unusual experiences.
IX. Enter the data (if applicable).
X. Write a report on the survey experience and the results of the survey to be presented to the program director and the instructor.

With one exception, the groups were able to complete this schedule in about one month.[2] Most of the work was done outside of class, so in class we were able to cover other topics while the survey project was under way.

From a traditional standpoint, it is difficult to assess the value of service-learning projects because it is impossible to oversee every aspect of the project. Group projects are even more difficult to evaluate because it is often unclear which individuals are responsible for the outcomes of the project. Nevertheless, in this case, several instruments were available for evaluating the service-learning projects: my general impressions, student evaluations of the project, and the final papers the groups wrote on their experiences. Before we evaluate the projects along these three dimensions, two caveats need to be addressed, both of which I brought to the attention of the program directors of the four service organizations.

First, it was important for the program directors to realize the limitations of the students' expertise in the area of survey research. I informed all of the program directors that the students would construct a good survey under my supervision, and that they could expect useful information about their respective programs. The results would be helpful in forming impressions about the program, and in some cases the data might suggest program changes. But I warned the program directors both before and after the surveys were completed against generalizing too much from the survey results and relying on them to legitimize policy change.

Second, it is important to bear in mind that the service-learning project was one of six research projects the students were required to complete for the semester. The course amounts to three academic hours, and unlike an internship or an independent study that might involve community service, the service-learning project for the course did not give students extra academic credit. Consequently, the value of having the students do a community service project, and do it well, had to be reconciled with the realistic time constraints posed by meeting other course objectives during the semester. The fact that it was a group project helped to spread the workload.

Nevertheless, the project had to be completed in a reasonable amount of time, since the grade for the project constituted just 10 percent of the overall course grade. This meant that the surveys would be relatively short, and the administrative time in implementing each survey had to be reasonable. We could not, for example, be expected to collect data on 200 or 300 variables for a sample size of 1,500. Fortunately, we knew in advance that the survey projects probably would not pose unreasonable time demands on the students.

My impressions of the projects were based on my observations of how each group was doing, my conversations with the group leaders and the program directors of the organizations, and voluntary comments students made about each group's work. With the exception of one group, the projects seemed to go well from the standpoint of group cooperation and the implementation of the project schedule. The group leaders were satisfied with the other students' work, and the leaders in turn were complimented by their colleagues in the group. The program directors were also generally satisfied with the process.

With a few exceptions, the program directors were also generally receptive to the two caveats I mentioned above. One program director bemoaned the fact that the students could not devote more of their time to the project, but the other three were content with the arrangement. Two of the four program directors wanted to use the results more aggressively as a means of advocating for their programs. We tried to reach an informal agreement about how to use the information from the survey, but I am not sure how convinced they were by my concerns about the validity and reliability of the data.

A second assessment instrument that helped to evaluate the service-learning project was a LINCS survey of the students that addressed questions concerning how the project related to the course. For example, one question was "What is the most important thing that you learned from your service experience?" Eighteen of the 19 responses could be classified into the following three categories:

1. Learned more about survey design and the problems associated with it (12 students made comments in this category).

2. Became more aware of the city of Richmond (four students made comments in this category).

3. Improved group interaction or communication skills (two students made comments in this category).

Another question was "Did your experiences help you to gain a better insight into the material and concepts of this course?" Fifteen of 19 students made positive remarks about how the project helped them to apply survey research. The other four thought the project helped only "a little" or "to some extent."

One of the interesting findings from the student survey was that the comments varied with the different groups and the organizations they worked for. For example, three of the four lukewarm comments to the second evaluation question about whether the "experiences helped you to gain a better insight into the material" came from students in the same group — the group that had a difficult time working with the organization and program director. This group had a difficult time scheduling meetings with the program director, and because of two irresponsible students, the group's internal cooperation suffered. This group's survey was finished later than the other three, and they did not even have time to implement the survey.

But it is also worth noting that the students from only one of the groups suggested that the project met the expectation that the course should make students aware that research has consequences for real people. Not surprisingly, this group did a study of check-cashing policies of stores and banks in poor neighborhoods. Their sense of efficacy was derived from the fact that they believed their survey had uncovered unfairness on the part of check cashers.

In sum, the student evaluations suggested that the service-learning project generally helped students to learn more about the problems and possibilities of survey design. The ultimate aim of realizing that research has consequences produced less encouraging results.

Finally, the written reports were another source of evaluation for the project. The assignment called for the report to contain information about the sample and sampling procedures, sources of error, the interviewing process, the interviewers themselves; a statement of nonresponse problems; a section on reliability and validity (about the pretesting questions, or problems that occurred in the data-collection process); and findings taken from the data.

Three of the four papers covered all of these areas and made very good observations about problems associated with survey design and administration of the survey instrument. The papers clearly illustrated that the students had benefited from the experience. Two papers reported findings that the organizations might use to evaluate their programs.

Certainly, a course in research methods and analysis offers the potential for conducting service-learning projects. This essay has indicated how survey design might be used in service-learning projects with reasonably encouraging results. Nearly all the students seemed to enhance their understanding of the problems and prospects for survey design by conducting surveys for community service organizations. Fewer students actually came away from the project with a strong sense that their research would influence the organization's programs. Meanwhile, some of the organizations were more satisfied than others in terms of how much they gained from the survey.

Notes

1. Floyd Fowler, Jr., *Survey Research Methods*, 2nd ed. (Newbury Park, CA: Sage Publications, 1993).

2. This group had a difficult time making an appointment with the program director, so their schedule lagged behind the other three groups.

Professor Palazzolo
Political Science 371: Research methods and Analysis
Spring 1995

Course Objectives: An introduction to the research process, including:
hypothesis formulation, research design, and various methods political
scientists use to collect and analyze political data. We shall construct
an original survey for a local service organization and we shall analyze
survey data and statistics on members of Congress.

Readings: Ethridge, Marcus, The Political Research Experience (2nd ed)

                   Fowler, Floyd Jr., Survey Research Methods (2nd edition)

                   Congressional Database

                   LIBRARY RESERVE

Assignments, Expectations, and Grading: This course has a demanding
workload, including six projects, several quizzes, and a final examination.
The projects involve research and analytic tasks, and the results will be
reported in typewritten papers. I will distribute an assignment sheet
specifying the tasks for each project well in advance of the due date.
Students are expected to be prepared for class on a daily basis. There
will be several "semi-pop" quizzes-- I will tell you on the day before a
quiz **might** be given, and you should prepare accordingly.
     I do not grade on a curve, each student is evaluated on his or her own
effort and progress. A ten point scale with letter grades from "A" to "F,"
including pluses and minuses, will be applied for each assignment as well
as the final course grade. A grade in the A range (100-90) is "excellent,"
B (89-80) "good", C (79-70) "average," D (69-60) "below average," and F (59
or below) "failing."

Due Dates and Grade Distribution for Assignments:

January 27   Project One: News Analysis (10%)
February 22   Project Two: Report on Observation of General Assembly (10%)
March 6   Project Three: Group Project on Survey Design (10%)
March 24   Project Four: Univariate Analysis (10%)
April 7   Project Five: Bivariate Analysis (10%)
April 17-21   Oral Presentation (5%)
April 21   Project Six: Multivariate Analysis (10%)
April 29   Final Examination: 9-12 (15%)
                Semi-Pop Quizzes (10%)
                Class Preparation and Participation (10%)

Attendance: Although attendance is only **mandatory** on days when quizzes and
exams are given and when projects are due, studies find that students who
regularly attend class earn higher grades on average than those who do not.
Since my experience is consistent with this general finding, student
attendance is considered in the 10% preparation and participation component
of the final course grade. To prepare for class, pay attention to my

announcement in class and complete the assigned readings before Monday of each week, as indicated in the course schedule below.

Late Policy: Projects are due at the beginning of class on the dates clearly marked on the syllabus and assignment sheets. Any project that arrives after the time and date specified on the assignment sheet will suffer a **full grade deduction** per day. Any project submitted 72 hours, or more after the time specified on the assignment sheet will receive a failing grade. Having said that, keep in mind that I am quite flexible in cases of emergency. Please contact me if special circumstances prevent you from completing class work on time. Emergencies, however, do not include: weekend trips, social engagements, extracurricular activities, sleeping late, or the infamous "work overdose" syndrome.

Office Hours: I am available for consultation in my office located on the top floor of the PS/MS building on Wednesday and Friday from 1:30 PM to 3:00PM. I am also available by appointment which can be arranged either after class, or by telephoning me at (home) 282-7575 or (office) 289-8973. If I do not answer, please leave a message at either number and I will return your call as soon as possible. **My only restriction on calling at home is that you do so before 8:00 pm, by then my daughter Sarah should be sound asleep.**

COURSE SCHEDULE

Week of January 11 **Introduction**
Readings: Ethridge, Chapter 1: *A Science of Politics* (pp. 1-17)

Week of January 16 **Doing Before Knowing and Hypothesis Formulation**
Readings: Schlozman, Kay Lehman, Nancy Burns, and Sidney Verba, "Gender and the Pathways to Participation: The Role of Resources," *Journal of Politics* (1994), pp. 963-90 (LIBRARY RESERVE)

Week of January 23 **Conceptualization and Measurement**
Readings: Ethridge, Chapter 2: *Measurement and Operationalization I: Variables Pertaining to Aggregate Units* and **Excerpt 1** Thomas R. Dye, "Taxing, Spending, and Economic Growth in the States" (pp. 18-38)

Ethridge, Chapter 3: *Measurement and Operationalization II: Variables Pertaining to Individual Behavior* and **Excerpt 3** Lyn Ragsdale and Jerrold G. Rusk, "Who are Nonvoters: Profiles from 1990 Senate Elections" (pp.57-81)

Squire, Peverill, "Challenger Quality and Voting Behavior in the U.S. Senate Elections," *Legislative Studies Quarterly*, May 1992, pp. 247-64 (LIBRARY RESERVE)

***January 27 Project One (News Analysis) is Due**

Week of January 30 **Survey Design I**
Readings: Ethridge, Chapter 7: *Surveys* (pp.177-85)

Ethridge, Chapter 6: *Sampling* (pp. 156-64)

Fowler, <u>Survey Research Methods</u>, Chapters 1-4

Week of February 6 **Survey Design II**
<u>Readings:</u> Fowler, <u>Survey Research Methods</u>, Chapters 5-11

Week of February 13 **Survey Construction and Observation of Assembly**
<u>Readings:</u> Rosenthal, Alan, "Soaking, Poking, and Just Wallowing In It," <u>PS</u>
(1986), pp. 845-50 (LIBRARY RESERVE)

Week of February 20 **Research Design and Survey Group Presentations**
<u>Readings:</u> Ethridge, Chapter 5: *The Logic of Research Design: Experimental
and Quasi-Experimental* and **Excerpt 7** Roy E. Miller and Dorothy L.
Robyn, "A Field Experimental Study of Direct Mail in a
Congressional Primary Campaign: What Effects Last Until Election
Day?" (pp.117-37)

*****February 22 Project Two (Report on General Assembly) is Due**

Week of February 27 **Univariate Analysis and Indexing**
<u>Readings:</u> Ehtridge, Chapter 11: *Univariate Analysis: Statistics of a Single
Variable* and **Excerpt 16** Fred I. Greenstein, "The Benevolent
Leader Revisited: Children's Images of Political Leaders in Three
Democracies"(pp.301-322)

Ethridge, Chapter 4: *Indexing* and **Excerpt 5** Jack Walker, "The
Diffusion of Innovations among the American States," and **Excerpt
6** Robert L. Savage, "Policy Innovations as a Trait of the
American States" (pp. 93-116)

Week of March 6 **Meet in Computer Lab (Jepson G-21)**

*****March 6 Project Three (Group Project) is Due**

Week of March 13 **Spring Break**

Week of March 20 **Bivariate Analysis I: Crosstabs and Chi-Square**
<u>Readings:</u> Dometrius, Nelson C., Chapter 13: "Contingency Tables (CROSSTABS)
and the Chi-Square Test" (LIBRARY RESERVE)

"Voting Behavior" (LIBRARY RESERVE)

*****March 24 Project Four (Univariate Analysis) is Due**

Week of March 27 **Bivariate II: Strength and significance**
<u>Readings:</u> Dometrius, Chapter 14: "Contingency Tables (CROSSTABS) and
Measures of Association" (LIBRARY RESERVE)

Ethridge, Chapter 12: *Bivariate Analysis* and **Excerpt 17** Edward R.
Tufte, "The Relationship between Seats and Votes in Two-Party
Systems" (pp.323-35)

*****We Will Meet in the Computer Lab on March 27, 29, and 31 (Jepson G-21)**

Week of April 3 **Control Variables and Multivariate Analysis**
<u>Readings:</u> Dometrius, Chapter 15: "Control and Elaboration" (LIBRARY
RESERVE)

Ehtridge, Chapter 13: *Multivariate Analysis: Statistics of More than Two Variables* and **Excerpt 18** Thomas R. Dye, "Taxing, Spending, and Economic Growth in the American States" (pp. 336-49)

***April 7 Project Five (Bivariate Analysis) is Due

Week of April 10   **Rethinking the Scientific Approach**
Readings: Ehtridge, Chapter 14: *Scientific Principles in Political Study: Some Enduring Controversies* (pp.380-392)

Almond, Gabriel, "Separate Tables: Schools and Sects in Political Science," Public Affairs, pp.828-841 (LIBRARY RESERVE)

Fenno, Richard Jr., "Watching Dan Quayle: Problems in Participant Observation," Public Affairs, pp. 1-10 (LIBRARY RESERVE)

Week of April 17 **Oral Reports**

***April 21 Project Six (Multivariate Analysis) is Due

April 24 **Conclusion**

April 29 **Final Examination (9-12)**

Women and Citizenship:
Transforming Theory and Practice

by Cynthia R. Daniels

Teaching about women and politics offers special opportunities for addressing the connections between academic scholarship and community service. In this field, as others, service-learning encourages students to "see" theoretical issues in practice in the real world. It also provides students with an opportunity to complicate seemingly abstract theoretical discussions with real-life experience. The courses I teach in the fields of women and politics, public policy, and citizenship provide particularly good opportunities for the integration of service and academic learning.

Most courses in the field of women and politics were introduced into the discipline of political science during the 1970s. These courses tended to build upon the accepted categories of the discipline, focusing, for instance, on women's political participation in (or exclusion from) formal political institutions and processes. Students in such courses were encouraged to extend their knowledge through participation in student internship programs, such as those in Washington, DC.

During the 1980s, the field of women and politics underwent profound transformations, expanding notions of "politics" and "political participation" to include those activities most central to women's lives. Courses on women and politics, therefore, focused not only on the role of women in state or federal legislatures, on voting behavior, or on activism within political parties but also on the activism of women in a wide range of public organizations — in their workplaces, in their churches, through educational institutions, and in their communities. In this way, "politics" came to be defined as any arena where women sought to challenge and transform unequal gendered power relations. Courses on women and politics might thus include, for instance, sections on the sexual division of labor at home, the history of women's standing in the workforce, or debates over women's position in religious institutions.

At the same time, a transformation occurred in feminist theory. Scholars, such as Carole Pateman and Susan Okin, challenged the fundamental categories of the discipline. A rich theoretical literature examined the philosophical foundations of concepts such as liberty, equality, autonomy, and privacy from women's historical perspective. What was the significance of formal political equality, for instance, while women remained economically dependent upon men? How could the state be "neutral" if it failed to address the violence against women that undermined women's political efficacy in both their homes and neighborhoods? By the mid-1990s, these questions came not only to enrich courses on feminist theory and politics but also to transform the core of questions addressed by the discipline regarding racial, class, and gender inequalities.

My seminar on Women and Citizenship [its syllabus follows on pp. 123-126] builds upon the complex questions of theory and practice suggested by this literature. We begin with an examination of certain key theoretical concepts such as citizenship to examine the question of whether gender equality requires the transformation of politics for all citizens. To what extent, for instance, does gender equality require us to rethink the distinction between public and private life, between public and private power? What might be the risks, as well as benefits, of using state power to regulate private relations of power in the home and the workplace?

The service component of the course provides students with a wealth of experience with which to address such questions. Students provide service through rape crisis centers, homeless shelters, and battered women's homes. They serve the elderly, provide health care to children, and staff literacy programs in the inner city. They work in welfare offices, community service programs, and day-care centers. In class, this combination of theoretical study and community-based service has produced a rich and complicated discussion of gender issues.

Let me provide a few examples from class. One issue central to the seminar was the question of whether economic dependency undermined one's status as a full citizen. Citizenship has traditionally been defined by the concept of self-sovereignty, essentially tying together ideas of self-ownership and self-rule. In early American history, self-sovereignty was defined by property ownership. As non–property owners, laborers and all women were excluded from the franchise. While such formal restrictions have been rescinded, the contemporary experience of poor women (and men) suggests that the antithesis between citizenship and property ownership has not been transcended.

Students explored these questions in practice through a variety of placements. One student worked at a homeless shelter providing daily services to women and their children. She often accompanied these women on trips through the state bureaucracy, as they searched for support for AFDC, health care, and permanent housing. This student was particularly struck by how difficult it was for these women to simply get the services due them — to get to state offices without transportation, to produce birth certificates for each child to prove they were, in fact, mothers. For this student, the humiliation of the welfare bureaucracy undermined any sense of citizenship — in the sense of self-ownership or self-respect — for these women. She was led to question whether the deep suspicion built into the welfare system is a necessary part of state dependency.

Two other students in class chose to explore questions of homelessness and autonomy in a different setting. Placed in an alternative housing program for women with children, they were able to visualize a transformed concept of citizenship. Unlike the shelter visited by the first student, this housing program gave families permanent housing for up to one year in a state-funded apartment complex. The stigma attached to the shelter was absent here. In addition, women received intensive employment training and support for educational programs (including college). Child care was provided in the complex, and all women and children shared responsibility for running and maintaining the property. The complex operated as a support group for the women, with staff available to help women work their way through various state bureaucracies. An alternative sense of community — and citizenship — grew at this housing complex.

In class, we read the work of Jennifer Nedelsky on the concept of autonomy. In traditional American political theory, individual autonomy is often cast as antithetical to collectivity or community. The maintenance of individual autonomy requires, from this perspective, the limitation of collective authority. Yet in this housing complex, these students argued, the collectivity helped to produce the conditions for individual autonomy. Through this experience, these students were able to examine the conditions under which a collective effort could contribute to alternative forms of empowered individualism. Conversely, they could then explore the conditions under which collectivity is coercive and disempowering. This combination of theory and practice produced some fascinating research papers on both the theory and practice of homelessness, autonomy, and economic dependency.

While placing students in the field proves invaluable to students, it also presents unique problems. Confidentiality is always an issue. One needs to build long-term relations with placement programs in order to avoid having women in the community feel as if they are simply guinea pigs for curious college students. Placements have to be appropriate to the skills (and not just the needs) of students. For instance, one student placed in the alternative housing project was an editor at the Rutgers student newspaper. Residents of the housing complex wanted to produce a newsletter but didn't have the computer skills needed to write, edit, and print it. This student was able to give something important back to this community, while taking away her own valuable experience.

Placement at battered women's shelters and rape crisis centers presents special kinds of concerns. Volunteers at such centers must always go through special training programs provided by the centers two or three times per year. Often these don't correspond with the semester schedule. For this reason, I've had to make special arrangements for training sessions to be held in September and January or February to accommodate students' needs. In return, I try to guarantee that I'll have students to place every semester so that these extra sessions don't go to waste. Community organizations must put a good deal of energy into training and monitoring volunteers. It's important, therefore, to establish long-term relations with organizations, so that they can plan on some regular basis for your students. Such centers, now so often underfunded, very much appreciate the needed help if they can prepare for students in some rational way. Such issues are not as critical for large-scale organizations, which may have scores of volunteers moving in and out throughout the year.

The semester concludes with the presentation of student research papers, which provide students with an opportunity to integrate their service experiences with the academic texts. While the service portion of the course requires a good deal of work on the part of both the instructor and students, it has produced for me some of the most rewarding and enriching teaching experiences — and some of the most sophisticated and moving research papers I've ever read. Particularly in the field of women and politics, service-learning has the capacity to transform and enrich the classroom — and students' lives — in unexpected and fascinating ways.

Political Science 440/03:
Advanced Studies in American Politics
Women and Citizenship

Prof. Cynthia R. Daniels   Course meets: TTh 11:30-2:00
Hickman 601/932-1919   Hickman 213
Office Hours: Wed 2:00-3:30

No longer wards of husbands, fathers or the state, women have gained important access to the rights of American citizenship. Yet women's self-sovereignty remains compromised by a social order which continues to privilege men. Those who occupy positions of state power remain disproportionately male. Women's claim to reproductive choice remains tentative, women are the targets of public and private violence and women's social and economic concerns remain peripheral to the state's agenda.

This course explores the meaning of citizenship for women in the United States through readings in feminist theory and practice. Feminist scholars have argued that the terms of citizenship must change for women to achieve gender equality. We will examine the feminist critique of key theoretical concepts including privacy, autonomy, property, individualism and community. We will then explore the connections between feminist theory and practice in a number of major areas of public policy.

This course explores the meaning of citizenship for women in the United States through readings in feminist theory and practice. Feminist scholars have argued that the terms of citizenship must change for women to achieve gender equality. We will examine the feminist critique of key theoretical concepts including privacy, autonomy, property, individualism and community. We will then explore the connections between feminist theory and practice in a number of major areas of public policy.

Throughout the semester we will also address questions regarding the necessity and efficacy of using state power for feminist ends. What have been the most effective strategies for implementing more equitable gender policies through the state? Is it possible to use government power without extending the regulatory power of the state over women? Drawing on the insights of both readings and student internship experiences, we will together explore the conditions under which the juridical, executive, legislative and symbolic powers of the state can be harnessed in women's favor.

Requirements:

Students will be required to participate in an internship in conjunction with this course. Placements will relate to the major themes of the course. Students will be required to volunteer at least 5 hours per week and will receive one extra credit for this work (under Pol Sci 399).

Students will be required to produce (1-2 page) "reflection" papers aproximately every other week reporting on their internship experience and reflecting on the connections between that experience and course readings. Each week one or two students will be asked to lead class discussion on the readings. Students will also be required to write one (6-8 page) mid-term paper related to course readings. In a final term paper (10-12 pages) and one in-class presentation students will have the opportunity to integrate

the semester's theoretical readings with their internship experience. Late
papers are not accepted except in cases of a documented illness or personal
emergency.

Course grade will break down as follows:
     Reflection papers (5):   30%
     Class Participation/discussions: 10%
     Mid-term paper: 30%
     Final term paper/presentation: 30%

Required books: (available at Douglass College Bookstore)
     Judith Shklar, _American Citizenship_
     Linda Gordon, ed., _Women, the State and Welfare_
     C. Daniels, _At Women's Expense_

Articles (available from me in class for a xeroxing fee):
     Pateman, "The Patriarchal Welfare State"
     Jones, "Citizenship in a Woman-Friendly Polity"
     Nedelsky, "Reconceiving Autonomy..."
     Package of N.J. State welfare regulations
     Parness, "Crimes Against the Unborn..."
     Daniels, "The Pregnant Citizen..."
     McDonagh, "Pregnancy and Consent..."
     Petchesky, "The Body as Property"
     Allen, "Women and Privacy..."
     Brown, "Reproduction and the Right to Privacy..."
     Freedom of Choice Act
     Acklesberg, "Communities, Resistance and Women's Activism..."
     Allen, "Playing the State..."

SYLLABUS

Sept 8:   Gender and Citizenship--Toward a Woman-Friendly State
          Dietz, "Context Is All: Feminism and Theories of
          Citizenship" (handout)
          Ackelsberg, "Communities, Resistance and Women's Activism:
          Some Implications for a Democratic Polity"

Sept 15: Political, Economic and Bodily Sovereignty
          Pateman, "The Patriarchal Welfare State" (handout)
          Shklar, American Citizenship

Sept 22: Does Dependency Undermine Citizenship?
          In Gordon:
          Gordon, "The New Feminist Scholarship..."
          Sapiro, "The Gender Bias of American Social Policy"
          Mink, "The Lady and the Tramp..."
          Nelson, "The Origins of the Two-Channel Welfare State"

          [First reflection paper due]

Sept 29: Poverty and Citizenship in Contemporary Politics
          In Gordon:
          Fraser, "Struggle Over Needs..."
          Piven, "Ideology and the State..."
          Pearce, "Welfare Is Not For Women..."
          Amott, "Black Women and AFDC..."

Oct 6:   Rethinking Individualism, Autonomy and Social Need
          Nedelsky, "Reconceiving Autonomy..." (handout)
          Fraser, "Struggle Over Needs..." in Gordon

          [Mid-term paper assignment will be handed out, due 10/20]
          [Second reflection paper due]

Oct 13:   Poverty and Reproduction: N.J. Case Study
          Package of N.J. State welfare regulations (handout)

          Report Back from interns placed with welfare organizations.

          Mid-term papers due

Oct 20:   Do Reproductive Relations Undermine Women's Citizenship?
          Daniels, At Women's Expense, Introduction and chapters 1-3.
          Parness, "Crimes Against the Unborn..."(handout)

          [Third reflection paper due]

Oct 27:   Citizenship and Maternal/Fetal Politics
          Daniels, At Women's Expense, chapters 4-5.
          Daniels, "The Pregnant Citizen..." (handout)

Nov 3:   Rethinking Bodily Sovereignty
          McDonagh, "Pregnancy and Consent..."(handout)
          Petchesky, "The Body as Property" (handout)

          [Fourth reflection paper due]

Nov 10:   Rethinking Privacy and Choice
          Allen, "Women and Privacy..." (handout)
          Brown, "Reproduction and the Right to Privacy..."(handout)

Nov 17:   The State and the Freedom of Choice Act
          Freedom of Choice Act (handout)

          Report Back from interns placed in the field of reproductive
          politics.

          Thanksgiving Break

Dec 1:   Reassessing Citizenship and Political Participation
          Dietz, "Context Is All: Feminism and Theories of
          Citizenship" (handout)
          Ackelsberg, "Communities, Resistance and Women's Activism:
          Some Implications for a Democratic Polity"
          Allen, "Playing the State..." (handout)

          [Fifth reflection paper due]

          Two-page paper abstract and bibliography for term paper due.

Dec 8:   Reflections on Feminist Theory and Practice

          Student Presentations (of term papers in progress).

Politics, Community, and Service

by Richard Guarasci

For many of us, our campuses are made up of diverse student subcultures seemingly with little interest in exploring campus life outside of their own immediate social milieux. These subcultures serve as safe havens within the larger residential and academic structure of our colleges and universities. In many cases, absence of a campus dialogue among these groups puts at risk the social, racial, and ethnic diversity we prize as a potentially positive foundation for that genuine, open inquiry and intellectual ferment so fundamental to robust and responsible academic institutions.

As disappointing and problematic as is this segregation of social and intellectual life on campus, we find many institutions also estranged and remote from the larger communities that surround and encircle them.

For those of us concerned with the conjunction of liberal learning and what Dewey would call "democratic education," the bridging of both these on-campus and off-campus disjunctions is imperative. How do we provide students with educational opportunities that allow them to encounter perspectives and experiences with students and community residents outside of their immediate orbits? How do we help them develop not only genuine respect for social and ethnic difference but also the skills and resilience to learn how to engage them? What curricular programs and experiential opportunities will move our students to begin to recognize differences — even those immediate to their own multifaceted biographies — and build from them to develop what I will call a democratic sensibility?

How do we help our students to become committed to those around them on campus and in the community while they discover the layers and complexity of their own biographies? How can we move them to reexplore the meanings of democracy, community, and identity within a multicultural and, ultimately, intercultural setting? The central question becomes "In a multicultural democracy, what does citizenship come to mean and what educational preparation is required for its development and enhancement?"

The sociological and cultural experiences of undergraduates for the most part are parochial. Their arrival from "the real world" (as some would characterize life outside the college) carries with it all the provincialism, ethnocentrism, and cultural myths circumscribed within their civic and personal biographies. When many of these students attending college arrive as residents on campus, they are virtually strangers to one another. For the most part they are prisoners of their particular socioethnic pasts, and they are likely to encounter meaningful and sustained racial and ethnic diversity for the first time in their lives.

In this context, social differences are, at best, tolerated. Normally students only are capable of constructing a social world composed of a crude version of cultural relativism. This leads to a secure but somewhat isolated set of racial and ethnic enclaves on campus, most unlike the very worlds from which they have migrated. Consequent to this social arrangement, political and social marginalization is sustained within the campus community, and it should be of little surprise when this type of cultural milieu produces harmful and wounding racial and ethnic conflicts.

Situated within this social context, it becomes evident that real community building and democratic citizenship, first and foremost, are learned and not inherited. They are not to be found within the ethos of students' personal experiences or their limited exposure within public and community institutions. And even more critically, intercultural experience is almost absent in the face of a society relegitimizing the impenetrability of racial, ethnic, and other social differences. Thus, one primary need for the curriculum and the cocurriculum is to connect issues of democratic participation, social difference, and critical judgment with an emerging need for the vibrant sense of intercultural citizenship. We need to help students understand their connection and begin to develop the critical capacities for imagining the possibilities of an intercultural and multicentric democracy, where community and difference become synergistic and generative.

The Community as Metaphor

For many of us, the communities that surround our campuses are themselves multicultural and desegregated. My community, Geneva, New York, is located in the Finger Lakes region of the state, tucked between Rochester and Syracuse. The city serves as a genuine metaphor for many of the racial, ethnic, and class differences found throughout the nation. Geneva is first a rural city, itself enigmatic. It sustains at least several different epochs of American economic history. A sizable portion of its socioeconomic composition is agrarian. In addition to traditional farming, a good portion of the surrounding area is dotted with a number of vineyards and wineries, which employ an extensive migrant workforce, mostly Latino. The city proper benefited until the last decade from a vibrant industrial base of manufacturing firms. The service sector is mostly framed around wholesale and retail franchises that provide low-paying, unsecured employment with very few, if any, benefits. Finally, a growing underground street economy is emerging, founded on illegal drug activities and supported by a seemingly nomadic population.

Socially, Geneva is populated by a diversity of ethnic and racial groups.

Since the antebellum period, African Americans have settled in Geneva. Originally brought to the area by rich Virginians spending their summers on the shores of Seneca Lake and ultimately benefiting from the emergence of the Underground Railroad, African Americans have long maintained a significant presence in the area. With the advent of mass-production industries after the Civil War, European immigrants, mostly of Italian ancestry, came to Geneva in large numbers. They now constitute the largest portion of the population, and they dominate the political structure of the city. In addition, Asian, Latin, and other European groups are represented in significant numbers in the population.

As a class-segmented society, diverse racially, and characterized by rural agricultural, migrant, manufacturing, service, and underground workers, Geneva captures a sense of diversity remarkable for upstate New York, particularly for a small community. It is a city suffering miserably from deindustrialization, and it has not found a path to economic prosperity in the "global competition" economy. The content of our course — democracy and diversity — and the composition of the community — hypersegmented and in economic eclipse — provide a natural coordinating point for the larger project of citizenship education.

At Hobart and William Smith, a private residential liberal arts college of almost 1,800 students, a number of initiatives for enjoying interculturalism can be found in the curriculum, residence education, and cocurriculum. One recent approach has been to offer students a direct experience in exploring issues of interculturalism and citizenship through the development of a sequence of courses involving community work. The development of a sequence of courses across the curriculum involving public service and joined to an on-campus residential base holds out the potential for joining a core of liberal learning to the biographies of students, faculty, and community residents. This is one approach to developing what Paulo Freire might characterize as "a pedagogy of hope" in addressing the atrophy of citizenship in and around our campuses.

The American Commitments Program

Hobart and William Smith Colleges maintains a comprehensive curricular program of community-based learning under the title The American Commitments Program. Approximately 22 faculty drawn from all the divisions of the curriculum regularly offer standing disciplinary and bi-disciplinary courses with field-service components. Courses range from a religious studies class on the Holocaust and a bi-disciplinary chemistry/religious studies offering on AIDS to a mathematics/computer science course and an Africana-Latino studies course on urban life in the United States.

Students in these courses work in local agencies, schools, hospitals, and with community organizations in and around Geneva. These sites range from rape crisis centers and economic improvement groups to neighborhood organizations and educational settings. In addition to the menu of service-learning courses, the campus maintains an office of public service, with a full-time administrative coordinator, a community service–focused residence, and two major organizations of student volunteers. These organizations produce a regular newsletter on community involvement and service.

The program is overseen by a dean, the coordinator of public service, and a faculty oversight committee. Community partners as well as the student organizations play a significant role in guiding the program. I teach one of the service-learning courses, and I want to share some of this work with you as a means of discussing the efficacy of this approach. [The syllabus follows on pp. 134-140.]

The Pedagogy of the Course

Most of the course revolves around the concepts of democracy, community, and difference, and it requires participants to be fully engaged in a term-long community service project. Indeed, it asks students to be fully engaged in the biographies of people within the community and to be involved in writing autobiographically about the effect of that service on their own lives, their perspectives on democracy, and their understanding of democratic citizenship.

Students are involved in community service from two perspectives. First, Geneva and its surroundings is a community in need of serious assistance as it encounters the limits, contradictions, and dramatic changes attendant upon postmodern capitalism. Work in service involves students in the everyday lives of individuals many times cornered by a very limited menu of social and economic choices. Geneva residents' experiences and student experiences with them are authentic and real unto themselves. We work with community members to enhance positive change in their immediate circumstances. This is the work of empowerment and social transformation.

Second, service work is, in and of itself, a project in citizenship. It explores the nature and limits of democratic citizenship in our time. This aspect of the service-learning experience involves an essential and quite important commitment in its own right. What does citizenship mean now? What ought it mean? How does it relate to various perspectives on justice? Democracy? Community? Difference? Service-learning ideally allows us to rethink these basic and critical concepts.

From both service-learning perspectives — social change and democratic citizenship — students need to bring together the experiential with the intellectual. Both experiences and ideas are ways of knowing the world, and our goal is to create a pedagogy — a way to learn — that joins the course readings with our field experiences so that students can use each to understand and critically evaluate the other. With this in mind, one course goal is to end the narrow approach to education that separates learning from experience. That perspective limits learning simply to the acquisition and absorption of knowledge. We are also attempting to end the equally false dualism of knowledge severed from personal experience. Hence, the course can be seen as an attempt to reconcile different realms of learning by joining readings and experience, intellectual development and ethical growth, and our individual academic experience with the unfolding of our own larger biographies.

Course assignments are meant to provide mechanisms for communication and reflection, allowing students both to *personally* engage the content (readings and service) and to begin creating a community of learning *within* the course. The assignments both in and outside of class are meant to help students collaborate so that they can expand their personal understanding of their experience and begin to see their involvement as a collective and cooperative enterprise where they genuinely learn from one another.

Students are required to do the following written assignments:

1. A dialogical experiential journal that carefully chronicles student reactions to and dialogues with the authors of the assigned readings; a second set of entries on field notes from the community involvement work; and finally, in a third set that brings the first two parts into play with each other, an integration and critique made possible by journeying from ideas to experience, and vice versa.

2. An ethnographic portrait of a person in the community. Here students meet persons whose lives tell a story about one or more key aspects of community life: class; gender; ethnic, racial, and other forms of social difference; political empowerment or political powerlessness. They encounter circumstances of material shortcomings and economic jeopardy, as well as anxieties brought on by semipermanent economic vulnerability and stories of great courage in overcoming seemingly insurmountable obstacles.

3. Two analytic papers carefully critiquing, integrating, contrasting, and synthesizing a rich array of work in democracy, gender, ethnicity, race, sexual orientation and identity, and cultural history — all from varying ideological and historical perspectives.

4. A final written assignment constituting an intellectual and ethical citizen autobiography. We explicitly ask the students to reflect on their experiences with the authors, the course discussions, and their community

involvement so that they become "texts" unto themselves — texts to be engaged, assessed, and evaluated. "How has the class helped you reexamine your personal, ethical, and political values? What does service-learning mean for your understanding of democratic citizenship?" In short, we ask them to articulate for us (and themselves) who they are by virtue of what they believe, what they do, and what they have read. By joining action to knowledge and reflection, we ask our students to consciously become the subjects of democracy, political actors in and around a community in which they are intimately involved. At their best, they are developing the democratic imagination and personal commitments required of an active citizen.

Fieldwork

Students are engaged in a wide diversity of community projects, ranging from literacy tutoring and helping staff the local food pantry to active work with the rape crisis center, the local hospital, neighborhood watch associations, and residential drug treatment centers. On average, they work between three and five hours per week over a 10-week term. Our coordinator for public service helps with placements, field assessment, and overall logistical support.

Individual student experience differs among the various sites. Some students have had major encounters with their own value systems, while others have had rather routine involvement with the agencies. One young woman working with a women's organization confronted issues of sexual abuse that resonated with her own personal experience. Her dialogical journal demonstrated deep reflection about the readings, particularly those discussing issues of gender and difference, as well as those analyzing conditions of empowerment. While her field experience was deeply personal, it was not that qualitatively different from those of many other students. Almost everything is related to reflective discussions about issues of equity, justice, and care. For most students, it is their first opportunity to frame their community work in a larger context of rigorous intellectual work and group reflection.

This last point can't be stressed enough. The conjunction of readings on citizenship with a larger context of social difference, pluralism, and economic justice proves to be formidable. When galvanized by direct encounters with persons and neighborhoods circumscribed by very real political and economic constraints, students see for the first time what C. Wright Mills once described as the interplay of "biography and history" or "personal troubles and public issues." They encounter the conjunction of personal lives experienced within the menu of choices constructed by public institutions and political cultures.

Summary

Foremost in this pedagogical approach to teaching citizenship with an ideal of intercultural democracy is the task of reenchanting our students with a belief in public life. Citizenship, after all, assumes that some larger public not only exists but is desirable and important. We are witness to an era when belief in public life is at a low point, with attendant correlates in feelings of personal powerlessness and social dislocation. Community-based learning, particularly when done with a dialogical pedagogy, allows for the revitalization of public life by offering our students, minimally, the opportunity to cross the borders of social segregation and ethnic rivalry. It starts with enhancing personal empathy for "the other" and, if developed, begins a merging of autobiography and interculturalism, so that "the other" and "the self" find coordinate moments of human recognition and acceptance. Citizenship begins, here, with the embrace of human connection and social obligation. It merges the sense of political and civil rights with the larger web of human need and social community. Service-learning allows us to identify the starting point, and, as such, it is a point on the larger spectrum of citizenship education. Though hardly the whole of citizenship and democratic education, it nonetheless appears, at this historical juncture, as a necessary component for restoring a democratic vision framed by equity, fairness, and participation.

Political Science 364   Richard Guarasci
Community Politics & Service   Hobart Dean, Smith Hall
Fall 1995 Mondays 6-9 p.m.   Office hours, Thurs. 3-5 p.m.
        Delancey House

Preface

This is a course about democracy, community and difference. It is a course that requires students to be fully engaged in a term-long community service project. It is a course that asks students to be fully engaged in the biographies of people within the community and to be involved in writing autobiographically about the effect of that service on their own lives, their perspectives on democracy, and their understanding of democratic citizenship.

This is also a course that prizes independent thought. We focus on the critical evaluation of both the readings and the field experience and how each serves to engage the other. We ask you to reaffirm one central precept, namely, that learning requires a serious commitment to both the subject at hand, and the voices and experiences of those engaged in the course and the community.

We are involved in community service from two perspectives. First, Geneva and its surroundings is a community in need of serious assistance as it encounters the limits, contradictions, and dramatic changes surrounding the realities of post-modern capitalism. Our work in service involves us in the everyday lives of persons many times cornered by a very limited menu of social and economic choices. Their, and your experience with them, is authentic and real unto itself. We work with them to enhance positive change in their immediate circumstances. This is the work of empowerment and social transformation.

Secondly our service work is, itself, a project in citizenship. We are exploring the nature and limits of democratic citizenship in our time. This component of service learning is an essential and, quite important, commitment in its own right. What does citizenship mean now? What ought it mean? How does it relate to various perspectives on justice? democracy? community? difference? Our work in service learning allows us to rethink these very basic and quite critical concepts.

From both perspectives in service learning, social change and democratic citizenship, we need to bring together the experiential with the intellectual. Both experience and ideas are ways to know the world and our goal is to create a pedagogy -- a way to learn -- that joins the course readings with our field experience so that students can use each to understand and critically evaluate the other. Toward this end we are attempting to end the narrow approach to educating that separates learning from experience. That perspective limits learning simply to the acquisition and absorption of knowledge. We are attempting to end the equally false dualism of separating knowledge from personal experience. The goal of this course is to reconcile these different realms of learning by joining readings and experience, intellectual development and ethical growth, and our individual academic experience with the unfolding of our own larger autobiographies.

Writing, Reading and Doing

Communication, experience and reflection are the means to intellectual and ethical growth. We grow by encountering and rethinking that experience. Writing, reading and action are the means to this growth. In this course we need to be constantly engaged in all three in ways that bring us together so that we can share, compare and contrast our thoughts and feelings. To these ends the course assignments are meant to provide mechanisms for communication and reflection allowing us to both personally engage the content (readings and service) and to begin creating a community of learning within the course. The assignments both in and outside of class are meant to help us collaborate so that we can expand our personal understanding of our experience and to begin to see our involvement as a collective and cooperative enterprise where we genuinely learn from one another.

The Dialogical Experiential Journal (15% of final grade)

Each student must regularly use a journal for this class. But we have a special type of journal in mind. We are after personal idiosyncratic notation, but we are after much more than that. We want you to write insightful and reflective reviews (not reports) of what you find to be key aspects of the assigned readings. In addition, we want you to write about your field experience in some detail, but also in contrast and comparison to the readings. What do they have in common or in opposition, or both? Finally, we want you to read each others journals so that you can share your ideas and experiences.

We will call our type of journal a Dialogical Experiential Journal. The journal may be a notebook or a binder. It must be organized in a specific way so that the readings being reviewed are followed by an accounting of field experience. One method is to use left side pages for the literature review and right side pages for a field work report. The goal is to then create third sections where the two are brought to bear upon one another.

A second method simply is to segment the journal by literature, field work, and synthesis (literature - field work comparison) sections. The journal needs to clearly demarcate these sections.

<u>Responsibilities: Attendance, Seminar Participation, Field Work</u>

Our work is collaborative by nature. The success of our discussions depends on preparation in advance and, of course, attendance at each session. In addition, our work will be as productive as the extent of our participation both in class and in the amount and quality of our efforts in field service. This class - our collective work - requires a full commitment. In addition, all assignments <u>must be submitted on time</u> in order to allow for serious evaluation and response.

<u>Weekly Seminar Organization</u>

a)   From approximately 6-7:30 p.m. we will discuss the assigned readings for that week. At each session one student will act as the <u>primary reviewer</u> of one of the readings. The role of the primary reviewer will be to present 5-7 minute <u>reviews</u> of the readings: offering a very short summary of the salient points, identifying the central <u>argument</u> or <u>thesis</u> of the text, and describing and assessing the main evidence or logic supporting the author's central argument. The primary reviewer <u>must</u> present her or his understanding of the importance, significance, and implications of the text. The primary reviewer needs to offer an assessment of the text. This may include a comparison to other texts read in this course or other texts outside the course but relevant to the topic. <u>The main function of the primary reviewer is to start our dialogue about the text and the topic. The Primary Reviewer must have a written outline to hand out to the class and it should include at least five key questions for our seminar to consider regarding this text.</u>

The secondary reviewer will be allotted 3-5 minutes to respond to the point of view of the primary reviewer. The secondary reviewer may support the perspective of the primary reviewer, or quite opposite, strike out in a different direction on the topic. The primary and secondary reviewer should collaborate in advance of the seminar meeting to compare ideas and stratigize about their presentations.

b)   From approximately 8-9 p.m. at each session one of our sites will be discussed at some length. <u>Students presenting this site must present a written outline</u> for the seminar participants. They may invite community guests to class to assist in the discussion. On occasion the instructor may invite community residents to participate.

The site presentations should include a history of the site, a socio-political analysis of the site, relate some of what the site is about to the relevant assigned readings (either in agreement or stark contrast to an author's point of view or analysis). The site presenters need to help the seminar understand the site, its participants, the range of problems it addresses, the range of social, political, economic, and other choices avialable to its directors, and the students' assessment of circumstances as they exist at the site. In short, our goal for the seminar is to gain a genuine understanding of the site, its people, its promise, limits, contradictions, and future. Robert Coles book may be of great assistance in helping you present your site analysis of your service commitment.

Community Service Requirement

Each student is expected to provide, on average, 5 hours per week of public service from the second through tenth week of the course. David Mapstone, Coordinator of Public Service, will be available to assist each student in their community placement. Each on site leader will be asked by the student to complete a statement of understanding regarding the student's public service, and at the end of the term the site leader will be asked to assess the student's work. Students will be asked to select a site from a list provided by the Coordinator of Public Service. Our goal is to get all of us working at 5-7 sites and to assign students in teams of 3 to 5. This will allow us to make a concentrated impact on select communities and organizations. If a student wishes to work outside of this grouping of sites, the coordinator of public service and the instructor will try to honor alternative assignments.

Two analytic Papers
(20% each)

(Due Friday, 10/6/95 by 4 p.m. in Smith Hall and Friday 11/3/95 by 4 p.m. in Smith Hall. No extensions granted.

You are asked to submit two analytic papers (approximately 10-12 pages each). These papers are your analyses of the assigned readings.

As writing assignments they have specific writing goals that inform how you should approach your writing. Specifically, you need to (1) identify central arguments of the respective authors; (2) identify the evidence and logical basis of their arguments; (3) evaluate their arguments by assessing the validity and strength of their evidence and interpretation of this evidence; (4) begin to construct your own argument on these issues as you sift through the various perspectives, voices, and information presented in the readings and influenced by your service field work.

More specifically each of these papers should include the following elements:

1. identification of the central thesis/arguments of the respective authors;

2. Identification of the evidence and logical analyses that each author employs to support these arguments;

3. identification of the issues and questions _absent_ in these respective pieces omitted or avoided in these respective arguments;

4. identification of the arguments that are most convincing and weigh their strengths and weaknesses; and,

5. reformulate the problems and responses in your voice and from your perspective by touching on the following points:

    a. draft a portrait of the central problems,

    b. identify the causal or essential relationships, cultural factors, institutions, political interests that shape the problems,

    c. draw upon the evidence you find most convincing and powerful,

    d. begin to formulate your responses to the central problems you identified in your portrait of the problems.

The journals are to be submitted for faculty review and reaction on three dates: Last Name

A-G	H-Z
9/25	10/2
10/16	10/23
11/13	11/13

Ethnography (15%)   3-5 pages Due: 1st draft, October 16, Mon.
                                       2nd draft, November 13 Mon.

Another assignment will further enhance our integration of the community work with our reflection about the broad themes raised by our readings. Each student will write a 3-5 page ethographic portrait of one of the individuals they encounter in their field service work. Like Kozol, Terkel, and other authors we read this term, you too are an intelligent observer as well as participant in the community. You too will meet persons whose lives tell a story about one or more key aspects of community life: class, ethnic, racial, gender and other forms of social difference, political empowerment or political powerlessness, the circumstances of material shortcomings, economic jeopardy, the effect of anxieties brought on by semi-permanent economic vulnerability, or stories of great courage in overcoming seemingly insurmountable obstacles. And of course there are any number of equally significant issues around education, health care, social services, housing, cultural conflict, immigration, and family. The key point to grasp is that you too are an author who has important insights regarding the telling of this person's story. Some of our assigned authors offer us fine examples of ethnographic reportage.   It is quite appropriate to borrow from their styles as you need.

<u>The Citizenship Autobiography</u> (20%) 7-10 **pages** Due: <u>No later</u>
<u>than 11/20/95</u>

How has this class changed you, if any? What personal,
ethical, and political values have you reexamined? How has your
service learning impacted on your life? Most importantly what does
service learning mean for your understanding of democratic
citizenship? Some of the readings will inform your autobiography
as you reflect on your service to the community, its personal
meaning to you, and how you believe it helps you understand what
citizenship means at this time in American history. In this sense
you are writing an intellectual and ethical autobiography, i.e. who
you are as virtue of what you believe, what you do, and what you
have read.

<u>Field Service and Participation</u>   (Journal & Service = 25%
                                    of final grade & class participation)

Your field service is an integral component of this learning
experience. Your participation must be consistent and thorough.
It must be critically assessed in your journal writing and in a
field assessment by the instructor, and the relevant field
supervisor.

<u>Required Readings</u>

<u>Books</u>

Robert Coles	<u>The Call of Service</u>
Audre Lorde	<u>Sister Outsider</u>
Andrew Hacker	<u>Two Nations: Black & White, Separate, Hostile Unequal</u>
Arthur Schlesinger	<u>The Disuniting of America: Reflections on a Multicultural Society</u>
Cornell West	<u>Race Matters</u>
Barber & Battistoni, ed.	<u>Education for Democracy</u>
Jonathan Kozol	<u>Savage Inequalities</u>

<u>Reprints/Handouts</u>

Guarasci & Cornwell	"Democratic Education in An Age of Difference" <u>Perspectives</u> v. 23, Fall 92
Farland & Henry	<u>Politics For The 21st Century: What Should Be Done On Campus</u>, Kettering Foundation
Doug Bandow	<u>National Service: Utopias Revisited</u>, CATO Institute, Policy Analysis #90, March 1993
Finger Lakes Times	Special Supplement on Economic Development in Geneva

Civil Rights and Liberties

by Bill Swinford

I begin by admitting that I have a relatively easy task when it comes to incorporating service-learning opportunities into the curriculum. I can think of few subjects that more readily or easily lend themselves to such endeavors than civil rights and liberties.

I first used service-learning as a component of my course Civil Rights and Liberties in the spring semester of 1995 [its syllabus follows on pp. 146-147]. As such, I am still relatively new to the enterprise, and there are, of course, "still a few bugs in the system." Still, I was, in general, quite satisfied with the extent to which the service-learning component complemented the other course material and assisted my students and me in the achievement of the objectives for the course.

I have three primary objectives for Civil Rights and Liberties. First, students should develop an understanding of the theoretical and historical foundations, as well as the current status, of American constitutional law, specifically as it relates to the Bill of Rights and the 14th Amendment. Second, students should learn to identify the strengths and weaknesses of current constitutional doctrine in those areas. Third, and perhaps most important, students should appreciate the practical realities resultant from the inevitable conflict between the desire for an ordered society and the premium Americans place on individual rights.

As to the first objective, the course is designed to expose students to the current legal status of the various components of the Bill of Rights and the 14th Amendment. As former Supreme Court Chief Justice Charles Evans Hughes said, "the Constitution is what the Supreme Court says that it is" (as quoted in Levinson 1985). Therefore, the readings for the course come primarily from the legal opinions of the U.S. Supreme Court in individual cases related to civil rights and liberties.

In attempting to achieve the second objective, considerable class time is devoted to engagement in analytical debates on the propriety of the Court's pronouncements in these cases.[1] As one can imagine, these are often spirited discussions, as the students wrestle with the application of vague phrases (such as "Congress shall make no law . . . abridging the freedom of speech")[2] to specific contexts and controversies.

However, given the classroom environment in which these debates take place, the discussions often evolve from analyses of whether "the Court got it right" in a particular circumstance to highly theoretical, abstract discourse. There can be little doubt that this exercise is valuable to students in the course of their education, allowing them to hone their intellects to deal with different levels of abstraction on important theoretical concepts.

But the negative side to such debates is precisely that: their abstract (or detached) nature. An understanding of the role of the Bill of Rights and the 14th Amendment in American society comes from much more than memorizing and analyzing Supreme Court opinions. The centrality of rights and liberties to American society means that the Bill of Rights is the subject of not only dialogue among Supreme Court justices but also street-corner discussions, state legislative deliberations, criminal investigations and prosecutions, lobbying efforts, election campaigns, political protests, and (most important) the conduct of every individual's daily life.

In essence, the life of the Bill of Rights is cyclical. The Supreme Court determines the legal parameters of rights and liberties. But Court pronouncements about these issues (or any issue, for that matter) can only exist as a result of the disputes brought before it through litigation by private and public (i.e., government) parties. The judiciary's pronouncements as to the resolution of these controversies, in turn, affect that society. Finally, American courts lack both the purse and the sword. They are therefore completely dependent on societal actors, be they private or public, for the institution of the practical impact of judicial decisions. I constantly worry that classroom discussions about components of the Bill of Rights will become too detached from the actual society that the Constitution governs. Thus, the third objective of the course is to expose students to the practical realities of the application of and adherence to the Bill of Rights as our society seeks to balance respect for rights with the desire for order. An understanding of the Bill of Rights must also include a sense of the society from which rights-based litigation rises.

Service-learning has proven quite valuable to the achievement of this objective. My expectation of the service component of the course is that the students, in working with various community organizations during the semester, will gain a better understanding of the practical impact of the Bill of Rights's existence and reaffirm the fact that civil liberties are not simply the subject of legal debate at the High Court.

In terms of administration, the students have the option of committing 20 hours of work to service-learning during the course of the semester (versus writing a more traditional research paper). With the assistance of the Learning in Community Settings (LINCS) Program at the University of Richmond,[3] students were matched with private-interest organizations located in the Richmond metropolitan area. The organizations were chosen on the basis of whether there was some aspect of their mission that related, in some capacity, to the protection or advocacy of or research on some area of individual rights and liberties. Certainly, this is a rather broad definition.

But it affords students the opportunity to choose from among organizations representing diverse missions and ideological perspectives.

Perhaps, at this point, it would be appropriate to provide a few examples of student service-learning experiences from the course during Spring 1995. The opportunities to which students availed themselves seemed to fall into four general categories. First, students worked with organizations designed to represent the interests of and provide information to those who deal with rights and liberties as part of their professional responsibilities. For example, students volunteered with the Virginia Chapter of the Fraternal Order of Police.

Second, students worked with organizations that concentrated on advocating the rights of the criminally accused. For example, students volunteered with the Virginia Civil Liberties Union and Virginians for Justice.

Third, students worked with organizations that concentrated on lobbying for or against legislation pending before the Virginia General Assembly. For example, some students worked with organizations such as the Virginia chapter of the National Rifle Association. Last semester, these organizations were deeply involved in the debate over legislation pending in the Virginia Assembly that would have broadened the accessibility of permits for carrying concealed weapons. Obviously, views on the propriety of this legislation are often the result of interpretations of the Second Amendment.

Fourth, students worked with organizations that assisted those whose rights are perceived to be adversely affected by government policy. For example, a student conducted research for the Virginian Interfaith Center for Public Policy on the impact of a state law that denies in perpetuity the right to vote to individuals convicted of a felony. Another example is the research conducted by a student for the Office of Refugee Resettlement on the impact of California's Proposition 187.[4]

For the purpose of assessment, the students were required to keep a written journal. The journal served two purposes. First, it was to be a diary of the students' activities with their organizations. More important, though, the journal was designed as an opportunity for the students to reflect on their experiences. In order to provide some broad structure to the reflections, students were asked to respond to general issues throughout their journal: to describe the existence and day-to-day meaning of the right(s) with which the organizations are concerned (that is, how are those rights viewed and experienced by those who are affected by them?); the relationship between that reality and judicial decisions on those rights (that is, to what extent do decisions affect that reality?); whether societal implications should be considered when the judiciary makes decisions related to civil rights and liberties; and the extent of the influence of the students' practical experiences on their views on the theoretical issues we address in class.

In addition, I kept myself up-to-date as to which organization with which each student was working. Occasionally throughout the semester, I would ask particular students to supplement our class discussions with their personal experiences. For example, in various discussions of Supreme Court decisions related to the rights of the criminally accused, students working with the Virginia Civil Liberties Union, the Virginians for Justice, and the Virginia chapter of the Fraternal Order of Police were asked to comment on their group's perception of the propriety of various decisions and the impact such decisions would have on the system of criminal justice in Virginia.

I was, in general, satisfied with the success of the service-learning component in complementing the in-class material in the effort to attain the course objectives. In reading the journals and in various informal discussions with students, I found that most were pleased with the opportunity and felt the project was worthwhile. All students agreed that they came away from the experience with a better understanding of the impact of the Bill of Rights on individual lives and how debates about rights and liberties are not limited to the classroom.

There were, however, two major problems that I found with the project. First, as you might imagine, most students gravitated toward organizations with which they already shared ideological predispositions. For example, more-conservative students found their way to organizations such as the National Rifle Association and the Fraternal Order of Police, while more-liberal students were likely to sign up with the American Civil Liberties Union or the Virginians for Justice. It was thus often difficult for students to assess whether the experience had an impact on their views. I have considered requesting (or requiring) that students sign up for an organization whose members maintain views that are not aligned with theirs. Obviously, this approach raises concerns about the level of participation in service-learning among students, their comfort with the project, and the quality of their contributions to the work of the organization.

A more general problem lay in my inability to fully articulate my goals for the journal. Several students expressed frustration throughout the project as they tried to figure out "what the journal was supposed to be about." My repeated attempts to explain the purpose of the journal were, in many cases, only marginally successful. Part of the problem, I think, was that I did not dedicate sufficient time in class to discussing the very questions the students were asked to respond to in the journal. Working through some of those issues in class will probably clarify things a bit.

As I remarked at the beginning, I cannot imagine another course that lends itself more easily to service-learning than Civil Rights and Liberties. I plan to continue to use this approach in this class and others in the future.

Notes

1. I am always adamant in class that there is a difference between adhering to and agreeing with Supreme Court decisions. Tradition dictates that the Court's application of components of the Constitution to specific legal controversies is binding on all of us. However, as the syllabus states: "The Court, composed of nine fallible human beings, does not have a better, more truthful view of the meaning of the Constitution's language than either you or me. You can, and are expected to, decide for yourself whether or not you agree with the Court on the meaning of particular words or phrases."

2. U.S. Constitution, Amendment I.

3. This program is designed to assist faculty members interested in pursuing service-learning as part of their courses. The LINCS staff matches students in these courses with community organizations that seek volunteers and meet the specifications established by the faculty member.

4. Proposition 187 was a referendum approved by California voters in November of 1994. Proposition 187 allowed for the denial of state government services — such as free public education, welfare benefits, and emergency health care — to illegal immigrants.

Reference

Levinson, Sanford. (1985). "On Interpretation." *Southern California Law Review* 58: 724.

ABBREVIATED SYLLABUS

POLITICAL SCIENCE 333 -- CIVIL LIBERTIES AND CIVIL RIGHTS

Over the course of the next 15 weeks, we will journey through the two most important components of American life: the Bill of Rights and the Fourteenth Amendment. our collective experience here will thus be about the most basic issue of our existence: what rights we possess as American citizens and as human beings.

Because "the Constitution is what the Supreme Court says it is", our attention in class will focus primarily upon the decisions of the U.S. Supreme Court. But it is critically important for you to realize that, on one hand, what the Court decides becomes "the law of the land." On the other hand, while you must abide by the decisions of the Court, you do not have agree with them. The Court, composed of nine fallible human beings, does not have a better, more truthful view of the meaning of the Constitution's language than either you or me. You can, and are expected to, decide for yourself whether or not you agree with the Court on the meaning of particular words or phrases.

BOTTOM LINE: Constitutional interpretation is NOT like math. There are few, if any, rules that are considered to be absolute!

In order for this class to be a meaningful and lasting experience, we must prepare for class by carefully reading the Supreme Court cases before us and seriously reflecting on the issues involved. You therefore have a responsibility to your colleagues and me to come to class prepared and willing to discuss the topic(s) at hand. You should be prepared to discuss the issues involved in each case, the written opinions of the Justices, and your personal view of the appropriateness of the decision and logic of the Justices. It is an obligation that you are expected to take seriously.

READING:

      Constitutional Interpretation: Rights and the Individual
      (Fifth Edition) by Craig R. Ducat and Harold W. Chase.

GRADING
Your grade for the course will be based on three components (each worth 33% of the final grade):

    1)   oral/written discussion of the cases
    2)   participation in Supreme Court decisions and written opinions
    3)   research paper

ASSIGNMENTS

3) Research Paper -- The purpose of the paper is to provide you with the opportunity to research and discuss the practical implications of a court decision or series of decisions which deal with civil liberties. You have two options from which to choose:

OPTION 1: You can volunteer 20 hours (during the semester) at a community organization that deals, in some form or fashion, with civil liberty/civil rights issues. An organization here at the University of Richmond known as LINCS (Learning In Community Settings) will assist you in finding an organization with which to volunteer. Alternatively, you can search out a community organization on your own. If you have a particular organization with which you would like to work, you must clear it with me in advance.

Your grade will be based upon the competence of a written journal which you will maintain during the course of the semester. The journal should perform two functions. First, it is to be a diary of your activities with the organization. More importantly, though, the journal is designed as an opportunity for you to reflect on those experiences. As you reflect on your activities, consider: the existence and day-to-day meaning of the right(s) with which the organization is concerned, the relationship between that reality and judicial decisions on those rights (i.e. the implications of the decision for reality), the'extent to which such a relationship should be considered when the judiciary makes decisions related to civil rights and liberties, and the extent of the influence of your practical experiences on your views on the theoretical issues we address in class.

OPTION 2: You can interview ten individuals (over the phone or in person) who, because of employment or volunteer activities, deal directly with the implications of court decisions in a given issue-area. For example, you can interview eight members of the Richmond Police Department regarding their views of the appropriateness and impact of Miranda v. Arizona (which requires police officers to inform an arrestee of his/her rights). Another example would be for you to interview eight individuals associated with primary and secondary education (school teachers, administrators, etc.) regarding their views of Engel v. Vitale (which outlawed school prayer). You will then write a paper, no more than 15 double-spaced pages in length, in which you discuss the views of those whom you interviewed. You should focus your attention on 1) their views regarding the appropriateness of the decision and its impact and 2) your personal view of those same issues.

You must inform me by FEBRUARY 1 as to which of the above options you have chosen. The journal or research paper (whichever is appropriate) is due no later than MONDAY, MAY 1 AT 5:00 P.M. (NO EXCEPTIONS).

Service-Learning and Comparative Politics: A Latin American Saga

by Robert H. Trudeau

PSC 336, Introduction to Latin American Government and Politics, is an upper-division course in the Political Science Department at Providence College [its syllabus follows on pp. 160-166]. For students who are majors in the department, it satisfies a "field requirement" in comparative politics. Over the years, it has been a relatively popular course, running at or nearly at capacity most years, that is, at about 20 to 25 students, most of whom are juniors or seniors. Occasionally, a student enrolls who has had some significant, meaningful experience in Latin America, but generally students are drawn to the course by the usual variety of factors, including time of day, feelings about the instructor, curiosity about the region, and/or the need to fulfill a program requirement. Consequently, a major factor in planning for this course is the question of bridging cultural and experiential gaps between students, some of whom are relatively parochial and almost all of whom are quite uninformed, and a vibrant, complex, and fascinating region with which they have had little direct contact beyond cultural stereotypes and professional athletes.

Community service seems easily integrated into courses whose subject matter operates in the "real world" close at hand. However, it is somewhat counterintuitive to try to integrate service into a course that focuses on a world a hemisphere away. Nevertheless, in the fall semester of 1995, I undertook to incorporate service-learning into a course in Latin American government and politics. This paper describes my motivations and expectations, the structure and process, some of the exercises and the service sites, and the mixed results. The variation in the results leads me, in the conclusion, to suggest some lessons learned.

Choosing the Adventure of Service-Learning

How did service-learning come to be a part of this course? As the reader will have discerned from my introductory paragraph, I have long felt that an approach based entirely on textbooks, even when novels and other "soft" materials were used, would not be adequate. As a result, I have integrated videos into the course for several years, not to mention more polemic materials focusing on Central America or Cuba.[1] I use these materials partly to spark debate, but also to substitute for the lack of basic factual knowledge about Latin America that most of my students share. That is, it seems ped-agogically more valid to use these materials to spark interest in an area or a specific topic, with the hope that this will motivate students to pursue more information, analysis, and so forth.

In other venues, moreover, I have had some very exciting experiences with service-learning in teaching introductory courses, both in the Feinstein Institute for Public Service and in the Political Science Department.

In sum, I was inclined to try something new to motivate my students in the Latin American politics course, and service-learning had shown itself to be very appropriate in that regard. These two factors, both of which pointed toward the adoption of a service-learning component in this course, were counterbalanced by a substantive concern, however. In introductory cours-es, such as American Government and Politics and Introduction to Service in Democratic Communities, establishing direct connections between the aca-demic content of the course and the types of service activities I could expect from students was a fairly straightforward process. I believe that this kind of close correspondence is important in service-learning, the goal of which, after all, is to improve the quality of academic learning in my courses.

I would certainly enjoy, for example, taking a service-oriented trip to a site in Latin America. This would provide direct experience for my students, which would translate directly into more academic concerns when the for-mal course took place. But that model of combining service with a semester course was impossible to undertake prior to or during this course. Therefore, I stuck to the model I had successfully used in the two courses mentioned; that is, I wanted to integrate weekly community service activities with fre-quent reflection classes throughout the semester. But given this model, it was difficult to imagine how I could get students to perform any communi-ty service that could be connected to the topic of politics and government in Latin America: It's hard to imagine how community service in Providence, Rhode Island, could directly enhance knowledge about, or analysis of, party or electoral politics in, say, Argentina.

My solution was to accept that I could expect only indirect connections with the course's materials. This led to a second expectation, which would be that community service would therefore serve as a motivational tool — not unlike my prolific use of video and polemic materials. The questions then became these: Could I get students more interested in the region *via* community service? Could I get them to understand a little more about pol-itics, or at least to ask better questions, after some experience working with people from the region? Because my aspirations were now primarily moti-vational and cultural, I sought service placements that would involve direct, one-to-one contact with relatively newly arrived individuals from Latin America or the Caribbean, of any cultural or national origin. In other words, my goal for student community service would be indirect, not direct, relevance to the subject matter of a course on Latin American politics. The goal was motivational: I hypothesized that my students would be more interested in the course's subject matter if they could put a human face on the topics via this interaction.

I explicitly avoided, to provide contrasting examples, certain other possible activities. For example, I did *not* want my students engaging in any direct or inappropriate interviewing of individuals who had recently arrived in the United States. Although the course included an important unit focusing on human rights violations in Central America and on the role of U.S. policy in those violations,[2] I did not expect my students to interview any recently arrived immigrants about their experiences, views, or recommendations on this question. In fact, I explicitly warned them not to do so unless their "client" insisted on discussing these topics. To interview recent arrivals on these questions would have been totally inappropriate, in my view, for a variety of reasons: Not only were my students, on the whole, too naive in the topic to conduct a good interview, but the prospect of being questioned about these topics would be quite unwelcome to most recent immigrants from the region, especially if their personal experiences had been tragic or if their documentation status were questionable.

To turn to a second, perhaps less volatile illustration, I did not ask my students to conduct interviews about elections or political parties in the countries from which their service "client" might have emigrated. Again, although these questions were perhaps less inappropriate than those from the previous example, my goal in assigning community service was for students not to do research but to engage in some kind of service activity that would (at least indirectly) affect their academic performance in the course by (to repeat) letting them put a human face on the subject matter and by improving their cultural understanding of people from the region we were studying.

To conclude this section, I knew from experience that there would be administrative and infrastructural issues to resolve were I to adopt a service-learning approach to this course, as is the case in any course. The primary example being finding service sites that were more specialized than those used in other (introductory-level) courses, where the type of service mattered more than the ethnic origin of an agency's clientele. I felt quite comfortable with those "problems," however, largely because of previous experience in other courses and because of the excellent support provided by the staff of the Feinstein Institute. Conversely, I was far more concerned by the substantive question of the ways to connect service with the academic content of the course. My decision to proceed was based on the resolution of this academic question, as I've described above, not on the administrative or infrastructure questions.

Structure

Most students did not know, before taking the course, that there would be a service-learning requirement as part of the syllabus.[3] The general response was surprise, followed by curiosity, a lot of questions, and some, but no more than one or two, defections. During the first week of the course, students heard presentations by representatives of the three service sites chosen for the course. Students had some choice of both their site location and type of service. There were site orientation visits as early as the second week in the semester, and for most students community service began during the third week. Thereafter, service was performed every week, up to, but not including, the week of final exams at the end of the semester; this meant 10 or 11 weeks of service. The community service component in the course did not exceed four hours per week, for a total of about 40 hours, depending on the site. There were a series of reflection classes scheduled, during which we discussed service experiences in the light of other course material. I was assisted by an undergraduate teaching assistant, a student who had been directly involved in service-learning, both as a student in a service-learning course and as a teaching assistant in an earlier class. The teaching assistant helped with reflection classes and other administrative duties associated with the community service activities.

The community service component of the course was not an optional assignment, nor was there the possibility to earn a fourth credit for community service. Service was a requirement, much like a term paper or an exam. The service component was graded on a pass-fail basis, however, and therefore did not figure directly into the mathematical formula for the final grade for the course. Nevertheless, and this was stressed in the syllabus, students had to pass this component of the course in order to pass the course and earn academic credit, no matter how well they performed on other, more traditional class assignments. Particularly outstanding (or especially poor) community service was reflected in the participation portion of the grading formula, however.

Besides the direct assignment, the community service itself, I tried to integrate service with other assignments, so that students would seek (or be forced to seek) to connect their service with other course materials. My goal was to avoid having the community service seem to be merely an appended component, an extra, with relatively little to do with what really mattered. I did not completely trust the reflection process in this regard; that is, I thought that reflection classes would help students connect service with other, more traditional academic material, such as the texts, but I wanted to ensure that more of this synthesizing would happen. Hence, I required students to prepare an oral presentation as well as a written term paper synthesizing service with broader questions relevant to the academic content of the course.

The basic assignment was to integrate the community service experiences with the course's reading and video assignments. Each student had to develop a more specific theme beyond the simple idea of "connecting," and we spent class time throughout the semester discussing this, especially during the reflection classes. For example, I urged students to think in terms of developing themes around the central concepts in the syllabus, such as democracy and social justice. I further urged them to refine their approach by using themes taken from the *Americas* video series and from the course texts. The oral presentations were made by groups of students, according to the service sites, during the last weeks of the semester, but each individual student was required to hand in his or her own individual paper. This component of the course was worth about one-third of the student's grade in the course, an intentional decision on my part to add weight to the idea that service had to be integrated to be of value.

Results and Commentary

This experiment in service-learning was adopted as a way to improve academic learning in a specific course, not as a pedagogical research project. Consequently, my commentary on the results of the experiment is based on anecdotal evidence, not on systematic surveys of my students. Based on these observations, my feeling is that the results of this experiment in service-learning in a course on Latin American government and politics were decidedly mixed.

For some students, remarkable levels of insight and motivation seemed to be reached. This could be seen in the relationships that were developing with people at their service sites, in questions and responses during class discussions, in exams, etc. On many occasions, both in class and in conversations outside of class, I could just see the wheels turning in the heads of these students, as they incorporated a completely different level of understanding than they were used to achieving in most classes. These students seemed especially good at appreciating assigned videos throughout the semester. Some students invited people from their service site to attend a session of our class, which produced lively and interesting classes that I believe profited all sides. In short, for students for whom service worked well with their academic learning, things worked well indeed. Had this been the general experience, I would simply conclude at this point with an endorsement of the logic and the structures I described earlier in this report.

But the results were mixed, as noted earlier. For other students, the course, perhaps — but only perhaps — because of the community service, seemed to become onerous and more confusing as the semester proceeded. There are always "good" and "poor" students in the random mix of any class, so some of these less-successful students might simply have been turned off by other parts of the course, or by their lack of motivation, other problems affecting them, etc.[4] However, it became clear during the semester that for many of the students in this less-successful category, community service was not helping them learn about Latin America. Indeed, for some of them, community service was worse than irrelevant: It was becoming a problem affecting their survival, let alone success, in the course. For example, since the term paper writing assignment in this course was specifically pegged to the community service activities, as described above, students for whom service was not easily integrated with other course materials became increasingly concerned as the end of the semester approached. Unfortunately, for many of these students, this course was probably not a very positive experience.

Because the results were mixed, we need to reflect on the possible sources of the failures. I see several potential bases for analyzing the less-successful outcomes. The first is generic to the question of service-learning, and the second is more specific to the question of comparative politics courses, at least for Latin American courses.

The generic topic is the question of community service itself. In the Feinstein Institute at Providence College, the gateway introductory course is entitled Introduction to Service in Democratic Communities. In my experience teaching that course, and I know this to be true of colleagues, as well, ample time is given to extensive discussions of what it means to be part of a community, what it means to do service, how it is that one can learn (or otherwise profit developmentally) from community service, etc. Students not only perform community service, they have well-structured reflection sessions, and enjoy the assistance and support of teaching assistants. Moreover, it is a reflexive course: The service itself is a central topic of the course, with time spent analyzing how students learn, how service affects how students learn, etc. Students know this before taking the course, and usually choose it because they are interested in service and its impact on themselves, if not on their communities. So students leave the course well steeped in the concepts, problems, expectations, and so on of community service in the context of an academic class. That is, that course is an introduction to a complex and relatively new way of learning. For the Institute, the gateway course is the prerequisite for other courses in its program.

But in the Political Science Department, prerequisites for upper-division courses tend to reflect disciplinary concerns. For my Latin American course, for example, I might variously require that students have taken an introductory survey in American government or an introductory course in empirical research methods. Students, at least political science majors, come prepared in some ways, but not in the complexities associated with doing community service. But because my course is an upper-division course in a rigorous department concerned about politics and political science, I cannot devote any significant time to these complexities. One result is that there is a built-in tendency to have less-effective and valuable service. It would take extraordinary conscientiousness on the part of the instructor, extraordinary work by experienced teaching assistants, extra seminars outside of class, and probably even more direct participation by the faculty member to overcome this problem. I cannot see how this can be resolved unless one were to add, as a prerequisite, a course with a service-learning component, just as one adds prerequisites reflecting one's discipline or the course's specific methodologies. Based on my own teaching experience in the two situations, my hypothesis, therefore, is that students who have taken an introductory course involving service-learning, including reflexive discussion of same, would be far more successful in my upper-division course in Latin American politics than students without that experience. To solve this, we either must develop better reflection materials or reduce our expectations in terms of the impact of service-learning in this sort of course.

A second theme for discussing the mixed results in this course is more specific to the goals and content of the course itself. As implied earlier, in the section on structure, I felt that the choice of service sites and service activities was critically important. Our experience in the Feinstein Institute for Public Service introductory course, described above, was that practically any kind of simple, straightforward service activity at a supportive site was more than adequate for the course. In other courses, especially upper-division courses, we have accepted the idea that more complex service activities might be appropriate.

In a Latin American politics course, however, the question is much more complex. It is an upper-division course, with sophisticated students quite capable of complex analysis. But the general level of knowledge about the region and its politics is low, resulting in a course in which the instructor must often combine an introductory-level posture with an upper-division course's complexity of analysis. Add to this the indirect, motivational goals for community service that I described above, and the resulting situation is even more complicated: Sophisticated students capable of complex political analysis are asked to perform fairly simple, straightforward service that may be, for many of them, "beneath" the appropriate level for a senior course. Students who might have, in another course, done research on political parties or interest groups were now being told *not* to conduct interviews on these topics, for example.

The mixed results in this course reflect different answers to the dynamics just described. The course offered three choices to students. Officials in all three programs (which were located at two physical sites) were very cooperative; they were quite supportive of the students and of the concept of service-learning. The following paragraphs describe each of the three programs the students were involved with, as well as the results. From these three examples, I will try to extract some general conclusions in light of the questions raised above.

About one-third of the students helped in a citizenship training program at Project Hope/Proyecto Esperanza, a comprehensive community service agency located in Central Falls, a largely Hispanic city near Providence. There, they helped individuals apply for U.S. citizenship: They helped applicants fill out the citizenship application forms, and then, on a weekly basis, worked with them to prepare them for the citizenship interview they would have to undergo at the offices of the U.S. Immigration Service. Of the three student-service sites, this was the most successful in terms of academic learning. Students in this group became very interested in the individuals with whom they were working, and this translated into concerns shared in the class. This group's reflection meetings centered on immigration law and policy, for example; they invited people from Project Hope to speak in class; and their class presentation at the end of the semester spoke eloquently to the problems Spanish-speaking people might encounter in an English-speaking ambience.

Another third of the students were involved in either small-group teaching or in one-to-one tutoring in a relatively unstructured English-as-a-second-language (ESL) program, aimed at adults with little or no English language ability. The ESL activities were sponsored by the South Providence Neighborhood Ministries, a small community support agency in the South Providence neighborhood, generally a lower-income area. This group's experience was also somewhat successful, in slightly different ways. Like the Project Hope group, they became interested in specific individuals, but instead of focusing on immigration policy in the United States, they seemed to collect more anecdotes about the places of origin of the adults they worked with. It is difficult to say, however, how, or even whether, this translated into greater motivation in the class: Neither the group presentation at the end of the semester nor the individual research papers showed much attributable impact from this service activity.

The final third of the class also worked at the South Providence Neighborhood Ministries location, but were assigned to an after-school recreation program, which included tutoring, help with homework, participation in games and recreation, and other specific projects that would involve children. In this setting, three things combined to make the experience much less successful in terms of the academic goals of this particular course. First, it was very difficult, practically impossible, for students to develop one-to-one relationships over time. Second, due to the nature of the program, it was impossible to discriminate within a very diversified clientele, distributed among Southeast Asians, Latinos, Haitians and other Caribbean children, African Americans, and Anglo Caucasians. Third, most of the children were either native born to the United States or had immigrated at a very young age, and hence could do little to motivate my students in the ways I had hoped for, even if there had been the possibility of developing ongoing relationships with children from Latin America. The boisterous, unstructured quality of time spent in this particular program also added to some of the students' problems, but that was not an insurmountable problem, had the other factors been in place.

In terms of the goals of the course, the students in this last group understood what was asked of them in terms of integration and synthesis. But very early in the semester, they became, first, quite concerned about how this was to be done and, soon thereafter, quite adamant about not being able to connect service with the course. For the most part, they were correct; but unfortunately, for a variety of reasons, including the fact that other program opportunities were foreclosed, it was impossible to remedy this situation during the semester itself. As a result, a good deal of class time was spent on topics other than those originally intended in the syllabus, and some assignments had to be modified during the semester. Reflection classes became discussions of poverty in the United States or discussions of the effect of family structures on children perceived as being "at risk," etc. While these (like U.S. immigration policy) are important topics, they had not been part of the scope of this course. The experiences of these students, as well as my own in grappling with these problems, were not happy ones, nor were they productive.

Summary and Reflection

To summarize, I believe my instincts were correct when I sought only indirect, motivational impacts from community service in this course. I further feel correct in assuming this would come from one-to-one relationships with individuals who had recently arrived in the United States. The experience in this course confirms these feelings, and reinforces the primary lesson I can pass on to others, and that is that the choice of service sites and activities is probably more crucial in specialized, upper-division courses than it is in other, more general courses. But even in the most successful of the three student groups described above, the "connections" centered on a topic foreign to the major concerns of the course's syllabus, namely, the question of U.S. immigration policy. So even that site, which would be an excellent site for an upper-division course in public policy, for example, was less productive in terms of my course.

A second lesson suggests itself: that not only are reflection classes absolutely essential but careful preparation of materials for these classes is even more essential, especially to the extent that service is seen as indirectly connected to the course or as a motivational device. Students will feel free to discuss their experiences and their emotional reactions to their experiences — that is not the problem. The problem is to get them to academically analyze what they have observed in light of other course materials. What is needed, then, are framing questions, themes, or other types of conceptual assists that can get students thinking (as opposed to "remembering" or "feeling") about their experiences. The more indirect the impact of community service is expected to be, the harder it will be to prepare these materials.

In conclusion, this report has presented descriptions of my motivation and goals in deciding to incorporate service-learning in a somewhat counterintuitive situation; a description of the structure and process involved; and discussion of the results. Measured against the narrow definition of the academic goals of this course, the use of service-learning was not particularly successful. More careful attention to service sites, types of service activities, and reflection materials would help, but there may be generic problems that will always limit the direct connections between community service and a course whose content is focused on distant worlds.

There are, nonetheless, two consolations, besides the opportunity of trying to improve results within the limitations just described. First, many of the students in the course were clearly motivated to pay a lot of attention to recent immigrants living in the local community; many of them learned much that will be of value to them in the long run about connecting readings with the "real world," about interacting with individuals not exactly like them demographically, ethnically, economically. Second, the best learning in this course occurred when students used community service to focus on politics and conditions in the United States. Since my goal for a course in comparative politics is to use the study of other nations to help students understand U.S. politics with fresh eyes, this is an acceptable denouement in this course.

It is hoped this report will stimulate dialogue. Faculty interested in pursuing the pedagogy of service-learning, among whom I count myself, must work on the hard cases, the situations at the edge, where success is harder to achieve. I hope this paper contributes to this process.

Notes

1. Among the more successful video series I have used include two PBS series: *South American Journey* and *Americas*. I have used other, more polemic videos in connections with Central American issues, such as *When the Mountains Tremble* and *If the Mango Tree Could Talk*. I periodically use specific issues of newsletters from solidarity organizations, etc.

2. In addition to some of the video materials mentioned earlier, this unit relied on Douglas Porpora's book *How Holocausts Happen: The United States in Central America,* which uses research from social psychology to discuss citizen reaction to policy. The book provoked excellent discussions, which I discuss in this chapter.

3. There remains a debate about whether or not to announce beforehand that a course includes a community service component. In this case, I did not announce it, nor did I keep it a secret. Any student who asked me about the course was told that service would be required, but most students didn't ask. Professors do not routinely describe all requirements in a course prior to its opening-day syllabus, and this is an argument for not announcing community service beforehand. However, service is relatively unusual and has a greater practical impact on students. Consequently, I am now of the mind that if service-learning is part of a course, that should somehow be actively communicated by faculty when students are preregistering.

4. The samples in each category and service site are small; so with the appropriate note of caution in place, it is interesting to note, however, that there seemed to be none of these "poor" students among the group in the successful service sites.

Political Science 336
Introduction to Latin American
Government and Politics
Fall, 1995

Instructor: Robert H. Trudeau, Howley Hall 301; 865-2629;
rtrudeau@providence.edu
Political Science Department Office: Howley 315; 865-2434; fax: 865-1222
Class Meetings: Series J (Monday and Thursday, 2:30-3:45)
My Office Hours:
-    Monday, 4 PM to 5 PM
-    Tuesday, 11:45 AM to 5:00 PM, but after 2:30 only by appointment.

A. **Introduction and Texts**

 Welcome to the study of Latin American politics. This course meets the
Political Science Department's field requirement in comparative politics.
This is a lengthy syllabus: please skim it immediately, but read it more
carefully before our next class meeting.
 The texts (all paperbacks) for this course are ordered in the PC
Bookstore:

•   Michael J. Kryzanek, LATIN AMERICA: CHANGE AND CHALLENGE (New York:
     Harper Collins, 1995).
          This is a basic, generally descriptive, relatively short overview
     of Latin America and its politics and economics. There is relatively
     little general geographic material, for example, but more on current
     issues, as you'll see from the Table of Contents.

•   Douglas Porpora, HOW HOLOCAUSTS HAPPEN: THE UNITED STATES IN CENTRAL
     AMERICA (Philadelphia: Temple University Press, 1992 (paperback
     edition)).
          This is a short, provocative book focusing on political violence
     in Central America and the role of the United States (and therefore
     our own role) in supporting that violence.

•   Bernadette M. Orr, AMERICAS: STUDY GUIDE (New York: Oxford Univ.
     Press, 1993).
          The *Americas* video series, described below, is an integral part
     of the course, and it has its an analytic framework, etc. This text
     will help you learn more from the videos in the *Americas* series. You
     could consider sharing this Guide with another student.

     There will be additional readings as needed, usually Xeroxed or on
reserve in the Library.
     Besides the **readings,** there are several **video** assignments. These are
mostly programs from the *Americas* video series, and are accompanied by
Orr's *Study Guide*.   Each of these programs runs about 55 minutes -- we
will schedule showings in Howley Hall room 300, but you may wish to view
these at your leisure in the Audio Learning Center (still in Meagher?).
There is additional information below on this series and your assignments.
In addition to the reading and viewing material, this course includes a
service-learning component. This means that students in the course are
required to perform community service at a local site. A good deal of
class time is devoted to integrating this experience with the more
traditionally viewed academic materials of the course.   There is more on
this requirement below.

B. **A Course Synopsis**

This course will provide you with a broad overview of Latin America and its politics. We study several aspects of Latin American life, including politics but extending well beyond the narrow view of politics to incorporate society in general, economics, and international relations issues. The major goal of the course is to provide you with not only some information about an important region of the world, but also with a set of analytic tools which you, as an informed citizen, can use in the future first: to analyze developments in Latin America and in U.S. relations with Latin America; and second: to act upon your knowledge, i.e., to be a better citizen of the Americas.

In brief, the course looks like this: we begin with a section that provides an overview of many facets of Latin American life. Then, we try to establish a comparative framework for looking at Latin American government and politics, using some of the concepts in the paragraphs that follow below. Then, we shift to a focus on U.S. relations with Latin America, including an attempt to explain U.S. complicity (if any) in the horrible violence that has afflicted Central America for several decades. Throughout, we will seek to integrate our community service experiences with the readings and videos, through a series of reflection classes. We conclude with your semester presentations (about which more below).

It is important for you to be aware of a couple of key assumptions that I make in this course. First, I assume that understanding Latin American politics is impossible without a sound foundation of basic factual and background material, beginning with geographic data and other basic socio-economic data. Most people in the class will not have any extensive experience in, or information about, Latin America. But since you have selected this course from a wide range of options, I assume you are willing to work to improve your background knowledge of Latin America. Basic background information will not be a major item on our agenda during class meetings, so you will need to review some of this on your own. The *Americas* videos and *Study Guide* should help.

Second, I assume it is impossible to understand either the interactions between political participation and public policy in Latin America, or the demands for social change in Latin America and elite resistance to these demands, without an understanding of economic forces in the region. To understand Latin American politics means to study the economic context as well as the political institutions and processes themselves. Students need to work to understand the economic aspects of Latin American politics.

Following on those two basic assumptions, the course focuses more on public policy than it does on institutions or political history. Public policy means the choices political leaders make (or don't, or can't, make), as they strive (or don't strive) for (1) better lives for their citizens and/or for (2) political stability. In a sense, then, this is a course on public policy in Latin America, and the course includes an agenda of questions like: what are the conditions (social, political, economic) that engender demands for public policy; what institutions respond to these demands (what decisions are made, or not made); what are the outcomes (stability, fewer demands, better lives, democracy, social justice, violence)?

If "public policy" is one focus, another angle is to look at democracy and therefore at political participation, with another corresponding set of questions on the agenda: who makes demands and why; who has the resources to "win," and by what rules do they play. And again, what are the outcomes (stability, more participation, more (or less) democracy, human rights

...)? In a sense, public policy is "elite" response to citizen
participation, and modes of political participation are often a "public"
response to elite policy decisions: it's an ongoing tension in all
political systems, and a good framework for beginning our analysis. (You
will see that the *Americas* series has a similar framework, which we will
outline and begin using early in the semester.) Although many readings
won't specifically ever mention the kinds of questions in these paragraphs,
these are the themes in my mind as I prepare lectures and facilitate class
discussions, and those are the themes I will pursue in exams and that you
should pursue in papers and other work.

Finally, besides those analytic themes, it is extremely important that
we evaluate our answers to the questions listed in the previous paragraphs.
For this, I recommend using standards of judgement such as democracy and
social justice. We will discuss these standards early in the semester,
when we outline "procedural democracy" and "social democracy," Robert
Gamer's notion of a Stable Personal Environment, etc.

In this course, therefore, students should:
- build up a base of factual knowledge about the region;
- include economic perspectives as they study the region;
- focus on public policy and political participation; and
- evaluate empirical findings and analytic points against standards of
judgement.

C. **Exams, Papers, Grades and Other Requirements**

The rough formula for grades in this course is:
- 20% for the midterm exam (a take home essay assignment);
- 30% for the student presentation, including (and primarily based on) a
    written paper;
- 30% for the final exam;
- 20% for class participation.

In addition to information in this section of the Syllabus, read the
Academic Policies, at the end, for additional information about how I
calculate grades.   Some details on course assignments:

1.   The **midterm exam** is a take-home essay. In this assignment, I
will give each student a different journal article or book chapter to
analyze in the light of the course's materials so far. Your task is to
write an essay of between 5 and 10 pages. The midterm exam essay is due at
the beginning of class on Thursday, October 19.

2.   The **student presentation** consists of both a verbal report in
class and a written paper. The basic assignment is to integrate the
community service experiences you have done with the course's reading and
video assignments, including the specific material you read for the midterm
exam. Each student must develop a more specific theme beyond the above;
this aspect will be discussed in class throughout the semester, especially
during the Reflection classes listed in the Course Outline below, but for
now, you can think in terms of developing themes beginning with the broad
standards of judgment described above: democracy and social justice. Then,
you can further develop themes along the lines of the themes in the
Americas video series.   The presentations in class will be done by groups,
according to the service sites, during the last weeks of the semester, but
each individual student must hand in his or her individual paper.

This **semester paper** is a very important assignment and represents your
best chance to show what you've learned this semester. I envision papers

in the 10 to 15 page range. The final version of your paper is due on the day of our last scheduled class meeting, which is **Thursday, December 7**. Please mark the date on your calendar. If you wish to have me read a draft of your final paper, I am willing to do so: in order to make sure I have enough time to read it and make comments, AND that you will have enough time to make changes that might be recommended, the due date for draft submission is **Monday, November 20** (before Thanksgiving recess). I cannot comment on partial drafts; if you want me to comment on your paper, you must give me what is essentially a complete draft on this date. If you haven't noted these two paper deadlines on your calendar, do so now. Be sure to read the Academic Policies sections on deadlines and on plagiarism so that you don't run afoul of these provisions.

A Note on Style in doing papers: don't use footnotes or endnotes for simple citations; instead, cite references in the text of the paper itself, for example (Brockett: 213), and attach an alphabetized bibliography that includes sources that you cite in the paper as well as other sources that you read but didn't cite directly.[1] WordPerfect, the wordprocessing program in the College's computer labs, automatically places and numbers footnotes and endnotes -- it's worth learning how to use the computer to do this.[2]

3. The **final exam** is comprehensive and covers all of the material from the beginning of the semester. The final is your opportunity to use what you have learned: its goal is to see if you have the skills to use the course materials in the future. The final exam will probably be an open-book exam, since in the future you can and should use reference material to help you analyze events. The final in this course typically asks you to use course materials to analyze an editorial, an Op-Ed column, a news article, even a political cartoon, or some other items taken from the press around the time of the final exam. (One semester, the final for this course included the option of viewing a videotape and writing an essay on it, as a "take-home" option.)

The final exam for Series J is scheduled for **Saturday December 16, at 9 AM.**

4. **Community Service.** As mentioned in the introduction to this syllabus, there is a service-learning component in this course, hence a requirement that students perform community service as part of this course. Normally, this requirement will not exceed four hours per week, for a total of about forty hours, and may well be two or three hours, depending on the site. Early in the course, you will hear information about the four or five sites chosen for this course, and students will have an opportunity to exercise some choice in their site location and type of service. There will be site visits as early as possible in the semester, and community service should begin the second or third week at the latest. There are a series of reflection classes scheduled, during which we will discuss

---

[1]   If a section of your paper is based on several sources, though, you can use a footnote or endnote to say so and to list the sources, rather than putting a long list of sources in parentheses in the text itself.

[2]   If you do use footnotes or endnotes in the paper, they should be used either to explain a point that is not central to your argument at the moment, but which you think might be of interest to the reader, or to clarify other arguments you are making, as this footnote is doing.

service experiences in the light of other course material. The class will be assisted by a Teaching Assistant, who will help with reflection classes and other administrative duties associated with our community service activities.

The community service component of this course is a requirement, much like a term paper or an exam. The service component is graded on a pass-fail basis, however, and therefore does not figure directly into the mathematical formula for the final grade for the course. Nevertheless, you must pass this component of the course in order to pass the course. To repeat, if you do not successfully complete the service requirement for this course, you cannot pass the course and earn the academic credits. Particularly outstanding (or especially poor) community service will be reflected in the participation portion of the grading formula.

5. **Class Participation** is an important part of the course. Besides questions and answers about assigned readings and videos during classroom discussions, "current events" is an additional dimension. You should keep up with current events in Latin America: reading the *New York Times* should help, as will a general news magazine. You might also wish to read a specialized newsletter, some excellent examples of which are available in the Political Science Department's Data and Research Center in Howley Hall, or in Howley 300, the Department's study and conference room. I also recommend listening to *All Things Considered* (5 to 6:30 PM) on National Public Radio (WGBH Boston, 89.7 FM). For viewing, a good newscast is the *MacNeil-Lehrer News Hour*, on Public Television (Channel 2 WGBH Boston, or 36 WSBE Providence). Speak Spanish? if so, watch the news on Univisión.

Course Outline

This Course Outline lists the assignments for each week, with references to specific meetings when something new is being introduced mid-week. This Outline is the Instructor's best guess at the start of the semester, and it's subject to change, as circumstances dictate. Since most of the material is being used for the first time this semester, there may well be changes in the schedule. Changes will be announced in class, and students are responsible for keeping up with any changes. Stay tuned. Please note that assignments, including videos, should be completed **before** the class meeting in which they will be discussed. At the end of this Outline, there is a Table summarizing the assignments, for quick reference.

A Note about the *Americas* video series: some of the material in Orr is based on readings that you are not assigned, but the overviews, questions, and themes are excellent preparation for viewing. So you will want to peruse these Units, reading some of it carefully and skimming other parts that are less relevant. Note: **the video "program numbers" do not correspond to the Unit numbers in the Orr *Study Guide* -- be careful, so that you prepare the correct material**. The entries below try to include both numbers.

Week 1: September 4 Introduction

    Thurs. - Syllabus review and clarifications of Academic Policies; introduction to service-learning component. Service Site information should be available today. Students should make site selections today or Friday (by phone). Details in class.

Week 2: September 11 Overview of Latin America; Race, Gender Issues

   Mon.   - Kryzanek, Chapters 1 and 2; Orr, read or skim, as
              appropriate, from beginning through page 21
   Note: Monday; Service site assignments announced.

   Thurs. - Americas videos, #4 and #5; Orr, Units 6 and 7.
   Note: Hopefully, service site visits will happen this week. Service
              should begin as soon as possible. Site visits need to happen
              in groups, for orientation, so please try to be as flexible as
              possible for this assignment.

Week 3: September 18 Historical Background

   Mon.   - Kryzanek, chapters 3 and 8

   Thurs. - Americas video, #1; Orr, Unit 3
   Note: Community Service should start this week at the absolute
              latest.

Week 4: September 25 Standards of Judgement

   Mon.   - Kryzanek, chapters 4 and 5

   Thurs. - Americas video #2; Orr, Unit 4

Week 5: October 2 Public Policy

   Mon.   - Kryzanek, chapters 6 and 7
              Americas video #8; Orr, Unit 10

   Thurs. - Reflection class on service

Week 6: October 9   Introduction: The United States and Latin America

   NOTE: This week, Providence College is running the Monday schedule on
              Tuesday, so we have two class meetings, in spite of the
              Columbus Day Holiday.

   Tues.   - Kryzanek, chapters 9 and 10
              Americas Video #9; Orr, Unit 11

   Thurs. - Continued
   NOTE: Assignment readings for the midterm exam essay assignment to be
              distributed Thursday.

Week 7: October 16 Introduction to Guatemala

   Mon.   - Porpora, chapters 1, 2, and 3
              Video: "When the Mountains Tremble"

   Thurs. - Reflection class on service
   NOTE: Midterm exam essay must be handed in at the start of class
              today, Thursday, October 19

Week 8: October 23 The United States and Central America

   Mon.   - Porpora, chapters 4, 5, and 6
             Video: "Guatemala Death Squads"

   Thurs. - Continue the above, plus return midterm essays

Week 9: October 30 The United States and Violence

   Mon.   - Kryzanek, chapters 11 and 12
             Porpora, chapter 7
             Americas video #6: Orr, Unit 8

   Thurs. - Reflection class on service

Week 10: November 6 Migration, Emigration, Immigration

   Mon.   - Kryzanek, chapter 13
             Americas videos #3 and #10; Orr Units 5 and 12

   Thurs. - Continued

Week 11: November 13 Environment; Children; Democracy; Social Justice

   Mon.   - Kryzanek, chapter 14; Video: "Under the Mango Tree"

   Thurs. - Reflection class on service

Week 12: November 20 (one meeting) Some Conclusions

   Mon.   - Orr, Unit 13

Week 13: November 27 More Conclusions

   Mon.   - Kryzanek, chapter 15

   Thurs. - Student Presentations: Integrating Service into the study of
           Latin American Politics

Week 14: December 4

   Mon.   - Student Presentations: Integrating Service into the study of
           Latin American Politics

   Thurs. - Conclusions

The Police Corps:
Researching Teaching and Teaching Research

by Milton Heumann

In the fall of 1994, I taught Rutgers University's first course on the "Police Corps" [its syllabus follows on pp. 176-181]. The Walt Whitman Center at Rutgers, headed by Professor Benjamin Barber, had received a grant from the Fund for New Jersey[1] to explore through a course with an experiential component three policy areas, one of which was President Clinton's "Police Corps" proposal. Since I am our department's resident student of the criminal justice system, and since I have looked at police behavior many times in my more general political science courses, I was asked to develop and teach the course.

To be sure, I was most interested in the proposal, one that envisioned an ROTC-type plan for future police candidates. In return for agreeing to serve in a police department for four years, college students would receive stipends of as much as $10,000 for each of their years in college.[2] Harking back in recent literature to the well-known study of the President's Commission on Crime and Law Enforcement,[3] increasing education for the police, if not a panacea, was certainly almost a "given" prescription in the sense that it was so self-evidently smart.[4] From a substantive perspective, all this was quite interesting. Either we would be studying a "good thing," a desirable and widely endorsed reform, or, to me equally tantalizing, we might be calling into question, qualifying, or at least adding some caution to a conventional wisdom, maybe even partially debunking a pillar of the police reform literature. And after all, debunking a myth (even qualifying it) in our world is second only to writing a seminal study in terms of attractiveness.

But alongside this interest, even surpassing it, was the opportunity to teach this course in a way that time and resources generally do not allow. Specifically, as part of a course on the Police Corps, an internship component was expected. What was wonderful about this expectation was that students were not simply set adrift to "gain experience"; instead, internships were part and parcel of the larger course.

In this paper, I discuss in greater detail the structure and operation of the Police Corps class. The bottom line for me, and I think for my students, was that the course was one of the most exciting, most productive, and most interesting courses that I, and they, have taught or taken. I will try to put flesh on this claim in what follows; what remains uncertain is what were the necessary and/or sufficient conditions that made this course so special. This is a question that I still mull over, and one in which I invite readers to share their views. Lots that was special happened in the course; and without the rigor of a controlled experiment, it is difficult to sort among contributing variables. I will tell the whole story in this paper, for this will at least allow better informed guesses about necessary and sufficient variables to be made. In turn I will talk about resources, the subject matter, access, and the pool of students I accepted into the course. Finally, I will turn to the title of the paper and, by way of concluding, address the ways the class informed, and was informed by, research considerations; the point here will be that the oft-employed teaching/research dichotomy is too stark; at least in this class, teaching and research genuinely, and not in platitudinous or boilerplate ways, reinforced the other.

Resources

First, the course was as a seminar, with a desired enrollment of about 15 (actual enrollment was 13). Since we had a difficult task — to study the Police Corps and to develop prototypes for what future Police Corps programs might include — the seminar format was necessary. Second, I was able to select a graduate student to assist in literature review and in supervising some aspects of the course (for example, the internships).[5] Third, the grant included some money for student travel and guest speakers. From a teaching perspective, this situation was a dream come true. It is not often that we teach small classes with teaching assistance, and with resources to provide "just a little extra." The culture of the class, I believe, was also changed by these factors. I, and the students, felt that this was indeed a special seminar, and I think this belief dovetailed nicely with the expectations I placed on the students (more about this shortly). It is worth stressing, furthermore, that to get this "extra" was not a terribly expensive proposition. For probably $5,000, most of what I describe could be replicated; no small amount to be sure, but in light of the many ways grant money is expended, the amount is not huge either.

Subject Matter

The subject matter choice was not straightforward. As already indicated, two Police Corps–specific purposes colored the course. First, not surprisingly, we wanted to learn about the Police Corps: its origins, its components, its political history, the kind of reception(s) it might receive in various kinds of police departments (large versus small, rural versus urban, etc.), its link to community policing, the consequences of serving in the Corps for subsequent citizen participation in their communities, etc. Second, we saw our charge as developing materials and practices useful to future courses for Police Corps students. This is to say, from what we read, from what the students were familiar with in other areas, and from their experiences in this course, we reflected on what readings and internships would prove useful to future Police Corps students. So, while evaluating the Police Corps proposal, we were simultaneously designing a Police Corps curriculum for the future.

Less straightforward were the complementary requirements of the seminar. The most important of these was a linked, but separate, one-credit course required of all students in the seminar.[6] This was a straightforward internship requirement, and I insisted that students work one day a week for the duration of the semester on this internship. Some service-learning courses appropriately include internships for students "to do good things," to help an agency or its clients. This "service" approach is fine, and I can imagine many criminal justice internships in which "doing the right thing" would be desirable. But, the internships attached to this seminar were not of that sort (though, of course, "doing the wrong thing" was not expected either!). I wanted students to observe what their agencies were doing, or to provide professional help (data collection, research, analysis). I wanted the students to learn about the places in which they were working, and not to have as their primary responsibility providing intensive service assistance. In short, my goal was to provide internships for the students that enhanced their research skills and contributed to their professional development. I want to repeat that the "service" approach has many, many values; it just was not what this class was about.

In addition to criminal justice system internships (I will describe these in more detail below), all students were given the opportunity to ride (or walk) with patrol officers for a minimum of one shift in two different departments. Also, during several class sessions, police chiefs and police scholars were invited to participate in panel discussions (for example, three police directors discussing the Police Corps and community policing) or talk about their research on current policing policies.

Collectively, the Police Corps readings, the criminal justice internships, and the police rides and police speakers were designed to afford students the opportunity to evaluate the Police Corps and, as noted, to reflect about future Police Corps courses. *But,* I really attempted much more with the readings and with the internships. It was my goal — and I think this would apply to many criminal justice proposals quite different from the Police Corps — to "use" the Police Corps to justify a theoretical foray into policy reform and the criminal justice system. The assigned readings, and my class goals, were consistent with these purposes. At every turn, I tried to use the very interesting, and seemingly quite straightforward, Police Corps proposal to force the seminar to consider (1) the nature of policy reform in general and (2) the effects of reform on the criminal justice system more broadly. With respect to reform, we looked at a rich array of policy material (implementation, performance measures, political attractiveness, claims of success, etc.); with respect to the criminal justice system, we placed on our collective agendas the now well understood "hydraulic" model of criminal justice and attempted to understand how a Police Corps would affect, and would be affected by, the other parts of the system. Indeed, one reason I did not limit internships to "police-only" situations was my sense that students interested in the police could profit from understanding the system more generally. The world of criminal justice is filled with recriminations between members of the same "system" (police blaming courts, courts blaming police, both blaming jails and prisons, etc.).

These were the most important dimensions of the class. Yes, the Police Corps is itself significant; yes, affording students an opportunity to intern as part of a structured class setting is also very valuable. But most valuable was validating the significance of the more theoretical policy and criminal justice research by employing it to assess a specific policy proposal. And I should also note that the experiential dimensions of the course(s) allowed us as a group to collect a substantial amount of data about current criminal justice processes, and these data, in turn, moved us to a critical assessment of the theoretical literature. Thus, what began as a course about the "Police Corps" fruitfully broadened into a course about policy reform and criminal justice, a course in which we both used and challenged the extant literature. The Police Corps was a hook to make the theoretical literature more significant; our internships allowed us to advance theoretical arguments shaped by the readings *and* by our own data.

Access

Through a combination of service activities to various criminal justice agencies in the metropolitan area, teaching experiences with many judges (I was a coteacher of a law school seminar on criminal sentencing), and my own research, I had met many individuals working in different parts of the criminal justice system. Knowing practitioners firsthand allowed me to prepare a list of the "best and the brightest" in many areas of criminal justice; unless students could construct convincing cases otherwise, the presumption was that they would select from among the internships I offered.

The internships proved to be spectacularly successful and yielded an incredibly rich body of data that we incorporated in our seminar discussions, and which, in many cases, was also invaluable for the students' seminar papers. Four students opted to work for criminal court judges — one in

Philadelphia, two in Manhattan, one in the Bronx. Three students worked for the new Mid-Town Court in Manhattan. Three worked directly for police departments — one walked along with community patrol officers in the East Village, while the others were participant observers in the Rutgers and Trenton Department. Four students worked in prosecutors' offices (in Hudson and Middlesex counties), and one worked with juvenile offenders. Running the risk of sounding hackneyed, I watched — and it was a delight to behold — the world of criminal justice open to these students. The Police Corps proposal and the policy and criminal justice literature were seen through lenses informed by the reality of criminal justice. Of course, any single experience can be skewed; but to limit this risk, I incorporated into the seminar almost weekly reports on the internships (these formal reports were in addition to the many ways the internships informed our more general discussions) and tried to make the internships a kind of collective data-gathering experience. This allowed us to confront hypotheses from the policy and theoretical criminal justice literature with our own "data set," an exhilarating and productive exercise.

Student Commitment

I set very high expectations for this seminar, and for the associated internship. Many, though not all, of the students were honors students, and my goal with them, and with the others, was to engage them in a learning experience that was truly memorable. I expected excellence (and preparation) during our seminars, and excellence and commitment to their internships. The writing requirements for the internship were relatively straightforward — a diary of experiences, coupled with a separate essay on the relationship between the internship experience and the Police Corps proposal. The writing requirement of the seminar was the major expected product. There I urged a major research paper of almost publishable quality. I stressed that a literature review alone would generally be insufficient; in most cases, I expected students to collect their own data and undertake a journal-quality social science analysis.

Student papers were presented during our final class session.' This truly memorable class testified to the students' commitment to the course and to the seriousness with which they approached their research. Each student gave a presentation, and I expected that the class, which began at 3:00 pm, would end about 6:00 pm. Instead, the presentations were not completed until 1:00 am! Also, unique in my teaching experience was what happened after a presentation by one of the students at about midnight. The class ought to have been numb by this point, having listened to nine hours of research. Instead, this particular student's research and his presentation were so remarkable (he conducted interviews in several New York precincts about the relationship between college education and police corruption) that when he completed his talk, the class spontaneously burst into applause. This event remains one of the most special moments in my many years of teaching.

As noted earlier, sometimes the internships directly contributed to the research, at other times they did not. In the corruption paper, the student interned not with the police but with a criminal court judge, though the judge was helpful in smoothing the way for some of the interviews with the police. Another student interning for a judge did a completely different kind a paper — an economic analysis of the Police Corps; a third undertook a more ethnographic study of police/community relations.[8] What most of the papers had in common, though, was an enormous amount of student input, an effort to write professionally acceptable papers, and, for many, a first foray into social science research. And again, though many of the students began as "high achievers," others had more checkered college experiences. In this class, the combination of my exhortations and, I hope, the attractiveness of the seminar/internship link led almost all the students to excel, and to complete the seminar with pride in their work and sensitive to the complexity of social science scholarship.

Conclusion: Researching Teaching and Teaching Research

The Police Corps seminar worked. I am not sure if it worked because of its size, because of the teaching assistance I received, because of the resources available for student travel and guest visits, because of the internship, because of the visibility of the policy we were analyzing, because the policy literature and the criminal justice literature could be applied fruitfully to a "real-world problem," because students were forced to dedicate themselves to major writing projects, which when completed gave many much pride, or for some other reason(s).

I know that we made lots of progress toward both of our goals. We reflected about the materials that future Police Corps courses might use, and engaged lots of nonobvious hypotheses about the Police Corps. For example, we concluded that future courses ought to look carefully at the literature on the relationship between college education and performance. Why? In our preliminary readings, in our panel discussions, in the internships, and in some of the papers, arguments questioning the necessarily positive relationship between college education and police performance were raised.[9] Also, we concluded that future courses ought to more systematically address the citizenship aspect of participation in a Police Corps: what differences the veterans of this program will bring to their communities?[10] And time and again, we heard concern expressed about the four-year Police Corps "term." Above and beyond these direct Police Corps matters, students embraced the notion of general criminal justice internships as part of Police Corps training. The assumption I made in allowing these broader internships was supported by student experience: The empathy gained by looking at the police from multiple vantage points provided a rich and valuable perspective on the specific Police Corps idea.

In addition to learning much about what might be reexamined in future Police Corps courses (and we also spent some time on specific readings), the course also was successful in giving students research experience. I have already noted some of the methods used — participant observation, interviews, econometric analysis. Other students opted for survey research,[11] and still others for elite interviewing. In common was the fact that students got their hands dirty, that they went out and collected new data, analyzed it, confronted a policy problem, and spoke wisely about it.

My enthusiasm for coupling internships and seminars ought to be obvious. The former gave students unparalleled weekly exposure to matters that were central to the seminar. Where the literature was consistent with their experiences, the hypotheses of this literature were internalized in a way not possible in standard courses. And when experiences conflicted with the literature, no presumption as to which should trump prevailed. After all, many assertions about police behavior are somewhat dated,[12] and there seemed to me to be no a priori reason to accept someone else's contentions over those of my students. Matters were, of course, not settled; the proverbial "more data are needed" are needed. But by coupling existing descriptive and theoretical literature with an internship, the class was able to analyze a current policy proposal in sophisticated and fruitful ways. And though I remain unsure about the necessary and/or sufficient variables that led to this happy result, I do know that the experience — for students and faculty alike — was more than profitable; it was uniquely productive, uniquely stimulating. In short, it was genuinely unique.

Notes

1. The grant was to be used to expand into new areas of service-learning. Research and design for both new curricula and service placements focused on four key areas, one of which was Criminal Justice: Public Law and Safety.

2. Title XX of the crime bill, the "Police Corps and Law Enforcement Training and Education" Act, provided for scholarships in the amount of $7,500 per academic year, or $10,000 per calendar year for students attending classes year-round, with total expenditures not to exceed $30,000. In addition to the four-year service requirement, the Police Corps cadets are to participate in two 8-week training sessions while in col-

lege, after the sophomore and junior years. During these training sessions, cadets would receive a stipend of $250 per week. Public Law 103-322, 108 stat. At 2049 (Sept. 13, 1994).

3. The President's Commission on Law Enforcement and the Administration of Justice concluded that "[t]he quality of police service will not significantly improve until higher educational requirements are established for its personnel." The task force's goal was "that all personnel with general enforcement powers have baccalaureate degrees." President's Commission on Law Enforcement and the Administration of Justice, *Task Force Report: The Police* (Jersey City, NJ: 1967), p. 126.

In 1973, the National Advisory Commission on Criminal Justice Standards and Goals also emphasized the need to attract college-educated candidates to policing. National Advisory Commission on Criminal Justice Standards and Goals, *Police* (Washington, DC: U.S. Government Printing Office, 1993).

4. The popularity — despite not much empirical support — of linking desirable police performance to college education is summarized in William Jordan, "College Education and Police Officer Performance — A Summation of the Research," a paper presented at the annual meeting of the American Society of Criminology, Miami, November 1994.

5. The graduate student, Judithanne Scourfield, was a splendid coworker. Her work in all aspects of the course and in subsequent essays about our work has been invaluable, and I, along with the students, are very much in debt to her for the wisdom and enthusiasm she brought to the seminar. I am also grateful to Ms. Scourfield and another of our graduate students, Jennet Kirpatrick, for their excellent comments on this paper.

6. The internship was part of Rutgers's path-breaking CASE program (Citizenship and Service Education). CASE has been at the forefront of service-learning, and indeed was a major reason President Clinton chose Rutgers as the site to launch his AmeriCorps program.

7. We are currently preparing a bound volume of these papers. Until this is available, copies of specific papers are available at the Political Science Department at Rutgers.

8. Other papers examined specific attributes of the present Police Corps proposal (e.g., community policing; four years service requirement), while some explored the links between greater education for the police and various aspects of police performance (e.g., courtroom testimony).

9. Again, see Jordan's "College Education" paper for a useful summary of much of the empirical work on this relationship. His conclusion is that despite many claims for the importance of college education, on most performance measures the evidence does not support the hypothesis that college education makes a significant difference.

10. For an informative collection on how service-learning can affect subsequent citizenship, see Benjamin R. Barber and Richard M. Battistoni, eds. *Education for Democracy* (Dubuque, IA: Kendall/Hunt, 1993).

11. With the cooperation of the agency in which he was interning, one student mailed a survey to a nationwide sample of 1,000 police executives. (His return rate was a little higher than 30%.)

12. "The police field is rich with studies about its basic functions, goals, and institu-

tional arrangements. . . . Much of the research is dated, however, and does not encompass the changes policing has seen over the past decade or the variety of police or the variety of police organizations." National Institute of Justice, "Solicitation — NIJ Invites Proposals for Policing Research and Evaluation," May 1995, p. 5.

Police Corps Pilot:
Criminal Justice, Citizenship, and Democracy
790:410
Fall 1994

Professor Milton Heumann
Office Hours: Tuesday 2:00-4:00, and by appointment
Phone: 932-9265

The seminar will examine President Clinton's proposal for a police corps, a
police corps modeled in part after the ROTC program. The proposal
envisions a cadre of liberal arts students working in police departments
for four years in return for tuition payments during their college years.
At its most idealistic level, proponents anticipate that the infusion of
college-educated officers will substantially improve police behavior.
     The seminar has three tasks. First, we will carefully examine the
literature on the police corps, and reflect on the assumptions upon which
it lies and which. it makes. Second, we will look at the police literature
itself and attempt to develop a model of the variables which explain police
behavior. A police corpstype irmovation will then be considered in the
context of this model. Third, the seminar will consider the readings and
experiences to which future police corps participants should be exposed.
     An important component to this seminar is the related internship
experience. In addition to providing the opportunity for students to spend
time with police officers, each student will select an internship for one
day a week in a criminal justice agency (e.g., police department, public
defender's office, prosecutor's office, court, prison). These internships
will not only provide invaluable insights into the real world of policing,
but also will provide a realistic appreciation of the criminal justice
world in which the police are embedded.

Required Reading:

     These books will be placed on reserve in Douglass Library and have
been ordered at the Douglass bookstore. The coursepack will be distributed
to. students on the first day of class.

- Benjamin Barber and Richard Battistoni, eds. *Education for Democracy*.
  Dubuque, IA: Kendall/Hunt Publishing Company, 1993.

- James Q. Wilson. *Thinking about Crime*. New York: Vintage Books, 1985
  (first published by Basic Books in 1975).

- Malcom Feeley. *Court Reform on Trial: Why Simple Solutions Fail*. New
  York: Basic Books, Inc., 1983.

- Thomas Church and Milton Heumann. *Speedy Disposition: Monetary
  Incentives and Policy Reform in Criminal Courts*. Albany: The State
  Universitv of New York Press, 1992.

- Elliott Currie. *Confronting Crime: An American Challenge*. New York:
  Pantheon, 1986.

- James Q. Wilson. *Varieties of Police Behavior*. Cambridge, MA:
  Harvard University Press, 1968.

- William Muir. *Police: Streetcorner Politicians*. Chicago: University of Chicago Press, 1977.

- Jerome McElroy, Colleen Cosgrove, and Susan Sadd. *Community Policing: The CPOP Program in New York*. Newbury Park, CA: Sage Publications, 1993.

- Herman Goldstein. *Problem-Oriented Policing*. Philadelphia: Temple University Press, 1990.

- And the coursepack, hereafter designated "CP."

Requirements:

Students are expected to come to class prepared and to participate actively in discussions. Failure to do so will no doubt contribute negatively to the assessment we necessarily make of each student's contribution to the study of the Police Corps.

Each student is also expected to write a major research paper on an aspect of the police corps proposal. Students can work in groups on some of these projects, but they must prepare individual papers. Topics we hope are covered in student papers for our overall assessment of the police corps include the following:

- the relationship between college education and subsequent police behavior
- the design of police corps courses and its relationship to the values candidates bring to police courses
- the economics of the police corps
- the relationship between the police corps and community policing
- a critical assessment of the police corps in light of the voluminous literature on police behavior
- the design of performance measures to eventually evaluate the efficacy of the police corps
- the relationship between the police corps, minority recruitment, and the role of minorities in police forces
- assessing the police corps in light of the structure of innovation in the criminal justice system

One additional requirement will be a trip to New York City to visit a center for alternative sentencing, a jail, and various police officials involved in the New York City "police cadet program." The costs of transportation will be covered by the seminar.

Also, as noted under the requirements for the internship course (which is required of students in the police corps seminar), all students will be expected (unless they object for whatever reason) to ride (or walk) on a complete shift with two different police departments.

Week I: The Crime Problem in America: Intractable Problem, Exhaustible Resources, Plentiful Proposals, and No Easy Answers

Crime has once again moved to the top of the public's agenda as a matter of concern and as a problem in need of attention. In this week, we will take our first, albeit preliminary, foray into the crime literature. We will focus on how we each would divide the public crime funds--which are necessarily limited--to. grapple with this problem. Among other things, we

will have the opportunity during the first part of the seminar to view a
video on precisely this resource allocation issue.

Readings:
- Selected articles on crime and the 1994 crime bill. (CP)
- James Q. Wilson, *Thinking about Crime*, pp. 13-60.

**Week II: Criminal Justice Reform: Plus ca Change Plus Ca La Meme Chose, Old
Wine in New Bottles and New Directives for Institutionalizing Policy
Reforms**
    The lessons learned from attempts to reform the criminal justice
system-whether these have taken the forms of changing the purposes of the
system, the, programs offered in prisons, or the nature of policing--have
been generally rather bleak. Typically, a flurry of reform seems to lead to
very little "real" change; often the instant proposal is nothing more than
a re-worked version of a long-ago rejected policy prescription. More
recently, scholars have built into their policy suggestions experimental
designs, and at least some of these have also included market-driven,
rather than imposed from "above," features.

Readings:
- Malcom Feeley, *Court Reform on Trial*
- Thomas Church and Milton Heumann, *Speedy Disposition*

**Week III: Confronting Thinking About Crime: The Liberal and Conservative
Approaches to the Problem of Crime in the Criminal Justice System**
    These books put into stark contrast two very different- -and very
important-approaches to the causes of crime, the treatment of crime, and
the shape of our criminal justice system. Class discussion will explicitly
adopt a debate between these approaches.

Readings:
- James Q. Wilson, *Thinking About Crime*, pp. 61-260.
- Elliott Currie, *Confronting Crime: An American Challenge*

**Week IV: The Police Corps: Our First Look at a Centerpiece of President
Clinton's Crime Package**
    The readings constitute most of the extant literature on the police
corps proposal. By looking at these political, academic, and popular
writings we should be able to recreate the model(s) of the police corps
which are currently being considered.

Readings:
- Legislative history of the police corps proposal. (CP)
- Selections of academic and popular articles on the police corps. (CP)
- Benjamin Barber and Richard Battistoni, *Education for Democracy*, Part
  1: "Citizenship and Service," pp. 179-222.

**Week V: Police Behavior: The Variables Which Shape the Police and Police
Departments**
    In this week we will develop models which explain police behavior.
The variables which affect, or putatively affect, are many and rather
complicated. Our purpose will be, at a minimum, to sharpen our sense of
the conditions under which one variable, or a combination of variables, are

more or less likely to have differing effects on the police or police behavior.

Readings:
* James Q. Wilson, *Varieties of Police Behavior*
  (This book is for students who have not taken Political Science 404, the Politics of Crime and Criminal Justice.

or
* William Muir, *Police: Streetcomer Politicians*
  (This book should be read by students who have already studied Wilson's book in Political Science 404.)
  In addition to a reserve copy, copies of this book will be on reserve in the 5th floor mailroom in Hickman Hall.

Weeks VI and VI: Community Policing: Panacea or Yet Another Innovation Parading as a "New' Solution?
Cormmunity policing is the "hottest" reform proposal currently being considered by police departments across the country. Definitions of exactly what is meant by cormnunity policing vary, though typically proposals include, inter alia, returning patrol officers to the beat. Readings range from the VERA evaluation of the New York City experience in community policing to a series of both laudatory and critical essays. Though community policing is not a necessary component of a police corps scheme, generally it is included as part and parcel of any of the police corps proposals currently being designed. We will want to. explore the relationships between community policing and the police corps, and assess the linkages between the two.

Readings:
* Barber and Battistoni, *Education for Democracy*, Part 1: "Citizenship and the Psychology of Belonging," Dostoyevsky, *The Grand Inquisitor*, pp. 67-82; William James, *The Moral Equivalent of War*, pp. 89-98 - Robert Bellah, *Habits of the Heart*, pp. 99-117 and Part 1: "Citizenship, Morals and Responsibility," Aristotle, *The Politics*, pp. 135-138; Thucydides, *The Peloponesian War*, pp. 139-146; Abraham Lincoln, *Springfield Boys' Lyceum, First Inaugural, Second Inaugural, Gettysburg Address*, pp. 147-160; Benjamin Barber, *Neither Leaders Nor Followers*, pp. 161-170
* Jerome McElroy, Colleen Cosgrove, and Susan Sadd. 1993. *Community Policing: The CPOP in New York.*
* Robert Friedman. 1992. *Community Policing: Comparative Perspectives and Prospects*, pp. 1-94. (CP)
* Roy Roberg and Jack Kendal. "Prospects for the Future of Policing," included in *Police and Society*. Belmont, CA: Wadsworth Publishing CO., 1993. (CP)
* David Bayley. 1988. "Community Policing: A Report from the Devil's Advocate," later included in Jack Greene and Stephen Mastrofski, *Community Policing: Rhetoric or Reality?* (CP)
* "Community Policing in Seattle: A Model Partnership between Citizens and Police." National Institute *of Justice Research Brief*, August 1992. (CP)
* Mark Moore and Robert Trojanowicz. "Policing and the Fear of Crime." *Perspectives on Policing*. National Institute of Justice, June 1988. (CP)
* Mark Moore, Robert Trojanowicz, and George Kelling. "Crime and Policing." *Perspectives on Policing*. June 1988. (CP)

- George James. "Bratton Puts Focus on Beat for Shake-Up." The New York Times. 24 January 1994. (CP)
- Ralph Blumenthal. "Community Policing, A Case Study: In a Precinct in Queens, a Mixture of Praise and Opposition." *The New York* Times. 31 January 1994. (CP)

Week VIII: Problem-Oriented Policing: A Close Cousin to Community Policing
Problem-oriented policing is another current policy prescription for a reallocation of police resources. Like community policing, problem-oriented policing is easily merged with the police corps proposal.

Readings:
- Herman Goldstein. *Problem Oriented Policing.*
- Kirby, Clark, and Wall. "Needed: A Community Experiment in Problem Oriented Justice." 20 (Spring 1993) *Fordham Urban Law Journal* 43 I- 8. (CP)

Week IX: Adam Walinsky
Adam Walinsky and Gerald Lynch are among the originators of the police corps proposal. We are hoping to have one of them attend our seminar, or in the alternative, to visit with him in New York City. Negotiations for this class are underway at the time this syllabus is being prepared.

Readings:

- Adam Walisnsky, et at. "The New Police Corps." (CP)
- Gerald Lynch. "Cops and College." *America*, 4 April 1987. (CP)
- Gerald Lynch. "College-Educated Police Officers are Better Prepared for the Street." *Atlanta Constitution*, 29 November 1986. (CP)
- Gerald Lynch. "The Contributions of Higher Education to Ethical Behavior in Law Enforcement." *Journal of Criminal Justice*, Vol. 4, No. 4; Winter, 1976. (CP)
- Additional readings at the speaker's suggestion will also be assigned.

Week X: Roundtable on the Police Corps
Our plan is to invite several police chiefs (e.g., Captain Anthony Murphy of Rutgers, Chief Michael Beltranena of New Brunswick, and Chief Nick Pastore of New Haven) along with several leading scholars (e.g., Mark Moore of the Kennedy School at Harvard, John Dilulio, Jr. of the Woodrow Wilson School at Princeton, and John Eck of the Police Executive Resource Forum) for a discussion of the desirability and design of a police corps program.

Week XI: College Educated Police: Infusion of Desirable Values or Irresponsible Promotion of Naivete?
In addition to the week's readings, a representative of ROTC will be invited to class to discuss how the ROTC program may or may not introduce "good" variables into the military.

Readings:
- Excerpts from the 1967 Presidential Commission on Law Enforcement and the 1973 National Advisory Council on Crime and Criminal Justice. (CP)

- Bernard Cohen and Jan Chaiken. *Police Background Characteristics and Performance*. Lexington, MA: Lexington Books, 1973) pp. 57-61 and pp. 101128. (CP)
- John J. Dilulio. *No Escape: The Future of American Corrections*. Selected excerpts. (CP)
- Barber and Battistoni. *Education for Democracy*. Part III: "The School and the University," pp. 449-526.

Week XII: Reflections on the Future: Student Designs of Future Police Corps Courses
Seminar participants will be expected to come to class prepared with a list of readings and activities they think ought to be included in "real" police corps training. Students should be prepared to defend their choices and to explain the relationships between the items they wish to include and positive reform within the police department.

It is also during this session that we will systematically discuss the relationship between student internships and police corps preparation. The paper on this theme, which is one of the requirements for the internships, will be due on this date.

Weeks XIII and XIV: Student Research Projects
During these two concluding weeks, each student will discuss his or her semester's research on the police corps proposal. Details of these presentations will be discussed during the semester. Suffice it to say here, the presentations will be formal and a rigorous question-and-answer session will follow each.

Bringing Service and Politics Together:
A Community College Perspective

by Mona Field

As a community college political science instructor, I have many goals for my students. I hope to convey to them the relationship between their private lives and the larger civic arena. I hope to share with them my excitement about the possibilities for social change through political action. I hope to inform them about the fundamentals of "how our system works" without dragging them down with details and facts they can easily discover through their own research. I want them to learn to analyze the multiple forms of information that bombard them and to apply their personal values to that analysis and to their political actions.

This is an ambitious set of goals and one that is rarely fully achieved. Like my colleagues, I count myself fortunate if I have "gotten through" to a handful of students each semester. Of course, "getting through" is a subjective concept that test scores and grades may or may not validate. Sometimes the B student is the one who tells me, "I learned a lot and decided to vote for the first time."

Meanwhile, how does service-learning fit into this smorgasbord of teaching goals? Very carefully, in my opinion. Because of the nature of the subject, which is fraught with values and personal opinions (unlike, for example, chemistry), I have always felt a deep commitment to teaching students how to develop their own views and political perspectives. Given this commitment, I have developed certain criteria for service-learning activities. In this essay, I want to share those criteria and the reasons for them in order to open a dialogue with others who share the same goals and are experimenting with ways to achieve them.

Before getting into the specifics of how I have used service-learning in community college political science courses, it is important to note the general bias of the college-level service-learning movement in favor of four-year colleges and universities. In terms of research, grants, workshops, and conferences, those of us at community colleges are often reminded of how invisible we are. Since we are struggling to be identified as legitimate members of the higher education service-learning community and since there exist major differences between our student populations and those of four-year institutions, we need to explain ourselves a bit for those unfamiliar with our missions and our student demographics.

At Glendale Community College, an urban college in the greater Los Angeles area, our student population has changed dramatically over the past 15 years. What was once an upper-middle- and middle-class suburb has become yet another California symbol of the multicultural 1990s. An influx of immigrants and the continuing decline in California's underfunded public education sector have resulted in a community college population that is 50 percent noncitizen and about 50 percent English-as-a-second-language (ESL). In addition, the native-born American students who attend the college are remarkable for their lack of basic skills (average reading scores at an eighth-grade level), study skills, and commitment to academics. Students who might be eligible for a University of California campus or California State University are now rare because they can usually find the money to matriculate directly into those four-year institutions. In short, the average California community college teacher (and perhaps his or her counterpart in other states) now teaches an academically underprepared population.

This means that our instructional challenges are enormous: teach college-level courses but use texts written at high school level; demand test-taking skills and writing skills appropriate to college for students who got through high school without ever writing a paper; maintain academic standards and integrity while not "scaring off" the underprepared students who come to us.

With all these challenges, I would love to say that service-learning is a panacea that bridges all the gaps. However, I cannot say that because there are many limitations regarding what service-learning can do. Unfortunately, it cannot raise student reading levels. On the other hand, it might make students more motivated to find out how to participate in our political process. Service-learning can play a useful role in a community college political science course, but the course has to be very carefully structured so that it genuinely ties into the academic goals of the class. It should not merely give students a chance to do community service that may or may not enhance their understanding of our political system.

A Teacher's Criteria for Service-Learning

Based on my experience of 15 years in this profession, I believe that service-learning in community college political science courses must fulfill the following four criteria: (1) It must be realistically accessible to all students in the class; (2) it must be for extra credit (as opposed to required); (3) it must involve nonpartisan or multipartisan options; and (4) it must be a genuine political science learning experience involving some sort of written reflection/analysis of the experience. In addition to these general criteria, because Glendale Community College is a recipient of a Learn and Serve America Higher Education grant, the Corporation for National Service imposes detailed restrictions on kinds of student activity (more on that later). Since, moreover, my criteria began evolving well before I had ever heard of service-learning, it is perhaps worth mentioning a bit of that history.

In the mid-1980s, long before I had heard the term "service-learning," I knew intuitively that students learn by doing, and I knew that the point of teaching political science was not merely to understand the system but to change it. By serendipity, I hooked up with the nonpartisan Southwest Voter Registration and Education Project (SVREP). This nonprofit project was essentially an arm of the Mexican-American political community and generally targeted Latino communities for voter registration drives. I thought this was a worthwhile activity that reinforced my teaching, so I proposed it to students as an extra-credit activity. Although I did not save the papers they wrote, I remember vividly some of their comments. Demographic changes had not yet swept Glendale, and my upper-middle-class white students wrote openly of their feelings about first-time visits to the barrio of East Los Angeles. For many, it was an eye-opening experience into the lives of an ethnic community soon to become the numerical majority in our state. One student wrote, "I've never seen so many poor people, and they are not that far from where I live." Another commented on how strange it felt to hear nearly everyone speaking Spanish. Without realizing it, I was having my students do precisely the kind of service-learning that our current Learn and Serve America grant requires — nonpartisan, nonideological, yet extremely important political service activity that bridges barriers between communities.

Having no guidance as to how to do this project, I gave students a one-page information sheet that required them to get a signature to verify their six-hour commitment and to write a one-page essay on how the experience affected them. Successful completion of the six hours and a thoughtful written comment were worth 20 points of extra credit (out of 1,000 total points for the course). Somehow I knew that I couldn't require this type of project — it had to be an option. I knew the limitations of my students regarding time and transportation, and I also realized some of their emotional and intellectual limitations. (Many were unwilling to go into unfamiliar neighborhoods, and I felt it was not my role to require such activity.) In retrospect, I feel quite pleased at my primitive service-learning activities. I incorporated the concepts of voluntarism and reflection without even knowing I was doing so, and I required verification of the service by a supervisor on site in order to maintain the integrity of the project. Although I have no proof, I strongly believe that, if I could find those extra-credit students today, they would have forgotten virtually all of the "facts" learned in my class, but they would remember their day in East Los Angeles.

Restrictions and Restraints on Service Activities

Flash forward to the mid-1990s at Glendale College. First of all, we gratefully operate our service-learning program with the financial support of the federal government. Under Learn and Serve America guidelines, students doing any form of service-learning for any academic course or for personal growth are subject to severe restrictions on their activities. Most important from the standpoint of political science classes, they cannot be involved in political advocacy, such as efforts to influence legislation; organizing protests, petitions, boycotts, or strikes; or engaging in partisan political activities or other activities designed to influence the outcome of an election to any public office. While none of these restrictions is intended to prevent participants from engaging in advocacy activities undertaken at their own initiative, they cannot do so as part of a course supported with grant funds.[1]

As any political scientist can see, there must have been quite a lot of lobbying and debate leading to these rigorous restrictions. However, some loopholes might include the possibility of working for a nonprofit political action group in some capacity other than in an "effort to influence legislation" or in an election dealing with a ballot measure rather than a "public office." Of course, service activities may not include any fundraising in any context, so much of what passes for "political activity" in today's world simply winds up prohibited.

For those institutions funded through this grant, these limitations severely constrain options — particularly in political science classes that teach about those very things the grant proscribes. What is left after one eliminates all the prohibited activities? Voter registration is okay, but one must find nonpartisan projects that are accessible. This year I had students do voter registration, after explaining California's multiple-party options and the usefulness of the "decline to state" category for people unsure of their views but interested in voting. Students wrote reflective essays reporting that their primary learning experience was the realization that few people responded positively when solicited to register. They also found out how many noncitizens live in this area, and they expressed concern about noncitizens' lack of access to or lack of interest in electoral politics. (Some of my students doing the project were not citizens themselves, but most were in the lengthy process of obtaining citizenship.)

Another "neutral" project was having my students assist other students, through our Citizenship Center, to fill out the forms to become citizens. However, it turned out that most applicants for citizenship felt competent to do their own paperwork. Thus, my students were trained by the Citizenship Center staff but then had no "customers." I accepted short papers about the meaning of citizenship in lieu of the actual service I had hoped they would perform.

These two projects met my four criteria somewhat, since they required no transportation (both were done on campus) and did not require much political background. However, the one caveat is that many immigrant students shy away from voter registration as a project because of their political socialization in their native countries. Many of our newer immigrant students come from the former Soviet Union, Iran, South Korea, Central America, or Mexico — places where political cultures do not necessarily encourage mass participation and where elections are often corrupt. Their political socialization taught them that political activity was not for everyone and, in some nations, could actually be dangerous to their personal safety. Their life experiences tell them to stay away from politics, including, perhaps, this type of extra-credit project. Of course, part of their political acculturation to our system is to overcome those fears and try something new. I am proud of those who did just that.

Another experiment in service-learning was a project that was really more research than service, and it was a disaster from my point of view. It resulted in precisely the kind of problem I had feared. After interviewing a very charming state legislator (who was transitioning into becoming a congressional candidate) during his "sidewalk office hours," my students' lack of political sophistication led most of them to write glowing reports on the politician even while they clearly disagreed with most of his policy positions! As a political scientist, it is truly painful to know that I have probably contributed to their misinformation by having them meet a delightful gentleman without preparing them with in-depth analytical tools that would help them distinguish between personality and political views. If community college political science courses were sequential and if there were enough student interest to take more advanced courses, I believe we could offer more service-learning in a second-semester course. Students need adequate background to learn from their service experience and to interpret it coherently. This level of knowledge seldom develops until late in a full-semester course, and many of our students do not have the luxury of including more than one political science course in their studies for the associate of arts degree.

As community college political scientists grapple with solutions to these dilemmas, some of my colleagues have tried to redefine "political science service-learning" to include activities that I would classify as social services. They give extra credit for serving food to the homeless, working at an AIDS hospice, doing child care with low-income kids, and the like. Personally, I doubt that our students have adequate understanding of the political economy to translate that kind of service into political analysis. They might well learn something about homelessness, AIDS, child care, or poverty, but can they make the connections between these social problems and our policymakers? Unless the instructor requires lengthy, detailed journal entries and guides students very carefully, I doubt most students will come away with the necessary political understanding. As a teacher of political science, I can find acceptable only service that I know serves to develop such skills. [A syllabus follows on pp. 190-192.]

Between federal restrictions and our students' limitations, there are some enormous constraints on community college political science service-learning options. The results are inevitable: It is very hard to find a political science service-learning activity appropriate to the students' level of political sophistication, accessible to immigrants as well as native-born, within a reasonable distance, nonpartisan, and providing some kind of genuine benefit both to students and to the larger community. In spite of these constraints, when I contemplate not offering a service-learning option, I say to myself: "Give up? Never!"

Service-learning is a critical component of learning about the real world, whether in political science or any other field. Getting out to register voters will create much more enduring views and feelings than just reading about voter participation. Helping applicants for citizenship to fill out their paperwork will increase appreciation of the rights and responsibilities of citizenship as no text or lecture can. When our federal grant ends, and our options for service-learning expand (even as our program must fight for scarce college resources to survive), I hope to involve students in campaigns of their choice — constituent services, lobbying, and other self-directed activities that permit all of them to find tasks that fit their personal values and beliefs. These will be extra-credit options and will require students to engage in basic real-world activities such as seeking information over the telephone, preparing for interviews, and other tasks that are actually new to the immigrant or underprepared community college student.

In my constant search for appropriate service-learning projects, I realized this past election season that many students would happily do campaign work for candidates or ballot propositions if given the extra-credit option. This seems pedagogically defensible, as long as we offer them the chance to work for any candidate of any party or on either side of any ballot measure. Meanwhile, although some community college students do not have the skills needed for long-term internships in elected officials' offices, there are short-term activities that would enhance their understanding of the system and even recruit them into considering majors or careers in political science. Although I believe that service-learning in a community college political science class is a difficult activity to develop, I believe it can and should be done. It will be up to those of us who believe in this tool to experiment with it, to devote the time needed to make it apply to our particular students, and to share the results of our work with others.

Note

1. Learn and Serve America: Higher Education Provisions, Corporation for National Service, Washington, DC, September 29, 1995, Section 7, Prohibited Program Activities, pp. 7-8.

Political Science 105 Mona Field ext 5473 office:SR355
Office hours: MW 12-1 TTh 11-12

The purpose of this 2-unit course is to give you an introduction
to the American Political system and its basic philosophy. In
this class, you will read two complete texts, one of which
requires a lot of active learning and group activities. You will
be exposed to a traditional view and a very anti-traditional view
of America's political and economic system. You must be prepared
to think, question, evaluate ideas, discuss your ideas, and
develop your own political philosophy. If you do not read at
college level, do not attempt this class. Come back when ready.

REQUIRED TEXTS MUST BE PURCHASED AND READ IMMEDIATELY. STAY ON
SCHEDULE WITH READING OR YOUR PARTICIPATION GRADE WILL DROP.

Janda, Berry, Goldman: The Challenge of Democracy, Brief Ed.
Field: Money, Power and You

Week 1: Janda, Field: chapter one
Week 2: Janda: chap 2; Field: chap 4
Week 3: Janda, Field: chap 3
Week 4: Janda: chap 12; Field: chap 2
Week 5: exam
Week 6: Janda: chap 4; Field: chap 6
Week 7: Janda: chap 5
Week 8: Janda: chap 6
Week 9: Janda: chap 7; Field: chap 7
Week 10: Janda: chap 8
Week 11: exam
Week 12: Janda: chap 9
Week 13: Janda: chap 10
Week 14: Janda: chap 11
Week 15: Field: chap 5
Week 16: Field: chap 8
Week 17: final exams

Exams will generally cover 3-4 chapters from each text. You will
be told which chapters are included on the test. It is your
responsibility to read and understand the material; if you need a
dictionary, use one. If you still don't understand, ask.

Grading will be based on a 1,000 point total as follows:

Attendance: 100

Participation (including small groups): 150
Multiple Choice Exams: 200 - 200 - 150
Paper: 200

Participation grading will be discussed at the first class
meeting. Exams will be announced at least two weeks in advance.
No makeups are permitted. Do not miss an exam. Paper
instructions will be given in plenty of time for the due date.
Late papers will lose points. After 3 days, NO late papers will
be accepted. YOU CANNOT PASS THE CLASS WITHOUT TURNING IN A
PAPER.→

Political Science 105 - Extra Credit Option

For extra credit in this class, you may choose one of several
projects. Each one must be done according to deadlines given.
Maximum extra credit points = 30 possible (NOT GUARANTEED).

Choice 1: Book review. See book review instruction sheet for
information. First deadline: Choose appropriate book and get
teacher approval by _____. Book review due by
_____. You must follow the instructions and format
for book reviews given by your instructor for this class. No
other book review style or approach is acceptable.

Choice 2: Newspaper/magazine article journal. This assignment
requires you to read major newspapers and/or magazines regularly.
(Ex: L.A. Times, N.Y. Times, Wall St. Journal, Time, Newsweek,
U.S. News and World Report). You must clip out articles of
importance to this class. You must write a brief comment on each
article explaining why it is important to you and important to
the nation/the world. Your comments will "grow" as your
knowledge of politics increases through the semester. You should
include your questions, concerns, views, and opinions in your
comments. Your journal must include at least 6 articles; they
must be from a time period no less than six weeks long and must
be spread out to indicate a fairly constant reading process. The
comments must be typed, double-spaced and using your best writing
and spelling skills. You need my approval to begin this project.
Deadline to get my approval and begin is _____.
Deadline for turning in complete newspaper/magazine journals is

_____.

Choice 3: You may do a service learning activity as extra credit for this class. This requires a minimum of 6 hours of service on a project approved by your instructor. Your instructor will announce any opportunities that come up. You must have my approval before beginning your project. You will write a short paper on your six (or more) hours of volunteer work. The paper will be typed, double-spaced and include a summary of the tasks accomplished, the agency and persons served, your personal thoughts on the value of the work you performed, and your political science reflections on the reasons that American society needs volunteers for such tasks. Project must be selected and approved by _____. Short paper on project must be turned in by _____.→

Experiencing Government:
Political Science Internships

by Stephen Frantzich and Sheilah Mann

The founding of the American Political Science Association (APSA) in 1903 marked the evolution of political science as a distinct academic discipline in colleges and universities. At that time, two educational objectives were claimed for the emerging discipline: citizenship and training for careers in public service. From the beginning, these objectives were related: Contact with elected and appointed public officials and observation of how government works, even government work experiences, were advocated by political scientists. Students would be encouraged to learn about how government works and how to work in government. For the student, direct experience was recommended to supplement formal instruction in government and politics. The benefit for government differed depending on the professional expertise of the participant. It was asserted that graduate students and more senior academics could make government better by providing an influx of expertise and new experiences. The benefit to government of opening its doors to undergraduates was more indirect. In the long run, some would be better prepared to work in government, and all would be better citizens because of the experience. A short history of the profession's rationale and activities reveals support for experiential education and internships.

The earliest records of professional discourse advise political science teachers to expose students directly to government and politics. The first official APSA education committee, the Committee of Five of the American Political Science Association on Instruction in American Government in Secondary Schools, recommended that students be informed about the "workings of government" by observation, in addition to reading newspapers and hearing presentations from public officials (Haines 1910: 206).

The belief that education for citizenship and for serving in government required direct contact with government continued to be an emphasis of committees and subcommittees of the APSA from 1905 until World War II:

> [C]olleges and universities have other responsibilities than the training of
> doctors, lawyers, preachers, and teachers or the older type of cultured gen-
> tleman. These responsibilities are summed up in duties to the community
> and the nation at large; duties which make it incumbent upon every insti-
> tution deserving the name college to aid progressively in the development
> of a more effective type of citizenship supported and strengthened not only
> by a knowledge of government in its historical evolution and present form

of organization but also by an intimate acquaintance with the practical operation of modern political institutions. (209)

The Committee of Seven's report in 1916 advised that college instruction include observation and *practice:* the "establishment of reference libraries and research laboratories for study and for the purpose of rendering aid to government officials and interested citizens" (APSA Committee on Instruction 1916: 148).

The APSA's official Committee on Policy, led by Thomas Reed (1934, 1936), issued reports during the 1930s describing successful conferences all over the country between political scientists and state/local political officials. These conferences were designed to inform faculty about how government works and to enable political scientists and public officials to work together on public policy issues and processes. A Subcommittee on Personnel planned projects devoted to training students who would pursue public service careers. While not using the specific terms of "experiential education" or "internship," these formats were acknowledged as components of the career training provided by political science education. Access to all levels and branches of government continued to be recommended as contributing to citizenship education.

The emphasis Reed's reports placed on practical politics and applied careers met some opposition from Charles Merriam and other political scientists who argued that the profession should focus on scientific research and inquiry into politics and political entities (Somit and Tannenhaus 1967: 98-99). Nonetheless, the connection of political scientists with government and public policies grew as the Depression continued, and increased even more during World War II (83-142). Consequently, while scientific inquiry became more important in political science scholarship, practical applications and civic contributions continued to be important professional activities, particularly in wartime.

In his 1943 APSA presidential address, William Anderson (1943: 6-11) claimed that political scientists were obligated to preserve democracy and serve governments. As professionals, they were to do so with analysis and criticism as warranted to improve policies and their implementation. At that time, an Association Committee recommended that candidates for faculty positions be selected not only on the basis of their training but also on their interest and aptitude for contacts with government officials (Somit and Tannenhaus 1967: 140).

After World War II, association reports continued to advocate that students be exposed directly to the work of government and the political process. The APSA's major report of the post-war decade, the 1951 "Report of the Committee for the Advancement of Teaching," stated:

[A]ll efforts to improve the practicality and effectiveness of citizenship education . . . should be a balance between reading and discussion and first-hand observation. ("Goals for Political Science" 1951: x)

The experiential education formats recommended in the 1951 report as innovations in teaching included fieldwork and internships (xxiii). The report drew, in part, upon a survey of political science departments and found that 50 (of the 252 departments responding) did offer experience education to their students. Examples were given of specific programs at specific colleges (281). But, the report concluded that too little was being done systematically to foster experiential learning (282).

It is arguable as to whether the growth in experiential education programs that followed, beginning with internship programs in the nation's capital, can be attributed to this report. It is more likely that the professional association and political science faculty around the country realized the importance of giving their undergraduates an opportunity to study and work in governmental agencies and political organizations.

The Growth of Formal Undergraduate Programs

The nature, location, and oversight of internship programs defy easy categorization. For many students, internships were based on ad hoc independent study arrangements made between a faculty member and a student. Thrust into the "real world," students were often asked to keep a journal or write a paper summarizing their experiences in order to receive academic credit. Washington, DC, became the mecca for students interested in national politics. Congressional offices, and later executive branch agencies and private interest groups, welcomed the free help with open arms. Increasingly, the informal arrangements were formalized, often making internships one component in a more comprehensive Washington program of seminars and speakers. Some colleges and universities found it possible to go it on their own, while others joined together to capitalize on efficiencies of scale.

Individual College Programs

Beginning in the 1960s and 1970s, a significant number of individual colleges developed Washington programs for their students. Most early programs were developed by selective private colleges, with state college and university programs following somewhat later. The first formal program in Washington, DC, was created by Colgate University in 1935. Other early programs could be found at Wellesley, Ohio Wesleyan, Barnard, and the University of Louisville ("Goals for Political Science" 1951: 281).

By 1995, more than 40 colleges and universities had their own Washington programs, most of which either offer or require an internship experience.[1] Many of these programs send full-time faculty to Washington for the semester in which the program is offered. Most programs enhance the internship experience with required seminars, a speakers series, and/or graded research.

Cooperative Programs

Many colleges and universities lacked the expertise, financial backing, and/or critical mass of students to develop their own programs. At the same time that individual campus programs were developing, other institutions joined forces to create consortia to offer internship experiences in Washington, DC.

In 1947, American University established the Washington Semester, the first formal cooperative undergraduate experiential education program for national government based in the capital city. A formal internship in government and political institutions was added to the program in 1969. Originally a consortium of five colleges, the Washington Semester now has 210 institutional affiliates from around the world. While the original focus on American government and politics continues, the Washington Semester currently offers students internships in other fields, including justice and law, international organizations, journalism, economic policy, international business, and museum study (Brown 1995).

The Washington Center, established in 1975, expanded opportunities for undergraduate internships. The center is a nonprofit facility that offers internship placements enhanced by seminars. Students receive academic credit from their own colleges and universities for participation in the center's programs. In 20 years, the Washington Center has hosted 20,000 students from 750 public and private colleges. The center's brochure states purposes that echo those of the earlier APSA reports: namely, that experiential education should "link together for the students their substantive learning, professional development, and sense of civic responsibilities."

During the 1980s, two smaller and more focused consortia, the Christian College Coalition and the Lutheran College Washington Consortium, were developed to serve the needs of students from these specific colleges.

Strengthening the Academic Component

Political scientists with experience managing internship programs have taken a professional interest in understanding the nature of learning facilitated by internship and in codifying lessons for managing high-quality internship experiences. The fear of imposing unprepared and unguided interns on unsuspecting and diverse intern sponsors has led to a concern for intern training, scrutiny of placement procedures, and the strengthening of evaluation techniques. Convention panels at professional meetings and a growing body of literature allowed intern program administrators to share their success and failures (Balutis and Honan 1984).

The Changing Foci of Undergraduate Programs

Over the last three decades, the breadth of internship opportunities has increased and the motivations of interns have expanded.

Broadening Internship Settings and Opportunities

Early undergraduate internship programs focused on formal governmental institutions. Internship opportunities were expanded in the last decade from a concentration on government and politics to encompass organizations in specific policy areas; notably, the environment and criminal justice. Specific programs were created to serve the needs of identifiable constituencies such as women and minorities. Purely political or governmental internship settings were expanded to include cultural institutions, particularly museums.

Washington is now only one of many political science internship sites. Extensive programs in government are operated throughout the country, and an emerging set of international opportunities has developed (Baker 1973).

Cost to the student continues to be a hurdle, especially for programs in Washington, DC, but an increasing number of schools have found ways to cover costs through financial aid procedures. Creative faculty have shown college administrators how internship programs can produce revenue through lower faculty costs and guaranteed blocks of students to fill empty dormitory rooms on their return. Groups such as the Congressional Black Caucus and the TELACU Education Foundation have developed special internship scholarships for minority students. Some internship sponsors, most notably Congress, have found ways to compensate interns for part of their costs. In a recent paper, William D. Pederson and Norman W. Provizer trace this development and conclude that "now with some planning, virtually *every* student has the same opportunity to participate in a Washington semester" (1995: 3-6).

Expanding Internship Goals

Internship programs were developed with a number of goals in mind. Ronald Hedlund's 1973 essay "Reflections on Political Internships" provides references to a substantial literature on the objectives and components of internship programs by political scientists and to the existence of some 1,000 political internship programs in the United States. He proposes that the primary goals are education (as a complement to formal in-class instruction), research (especially for graduate students and more-advanced students), and public service to the host institution or organization.

In recent years, the goals for students considering internships have expanded also. The ability to use real-world experiences to illuminate academic learning remains, but an increasing percentage of students use internships as low-risk vehicles for trying various career options. As the job market gets tighter, internships often serve as an entree to paid positions. For the organizational sponsor, accepting a student as an intern provides a low-cost technique of on-the-job evaluation. An increasing percentage of government and political workers have one or more internships on their resume.

Internships for Graduate Students and Professionals

The experience and the considerable responsibility held by many political scientists in national government during World War II led to internships and programs for graduate students as well.

Post–World War II internship programs represented both the public-regarding objectives of contributing to public service and the career preparation of the programs' participants. Reference to job-placement advantages and career enhancement was even more focused for graduate-level internship programs.

The first post-war program was the Citizenship Clearing House–National Center for Education in Politics (CCH-NCEP) founded in 1946, whose objective was to help political science majors — undergraduates and graduates — get practical political and governmental experience. The CCH-NCEP was an independent entity supported by grants that closed in 1961, when it could no longer secure funding. CCH-NCEP established regional affiliates (thereby recruiting a considerable grass-roots network of political scientists), maintained experiential and citizenship education projects, and distributed information about public affairs (Somit and Tannenhaus 1967: 170).

In 1953, the APSA established the Congressional Fellowship Program (CFP) to place political scientists, journalists, and federal agency executives on the staffs of senators, congressmen, and congressional committees for a nine-month period. This professional-level internship program was to provide Congress with the added expertise of political scientists and other professionals, and these congressional fellows would emerge with a broader perspective on the political process. The political science fellows would also be better research scholars and teachers as a result of their work in

Congress.

The CFP is the oldest and most prominent professional internship program in Congress. There have been some 1,400 congressional fellows, and many of these alumni have distinguished careers as scholars, educators, and journalists and in government service. The Congressional Fellowship Program has succeeded in providing skilled staff assistance to Congress and congressional committees and in enhancing scholarship and media coverage of Congress as well as the careers of CFP alumni.

The success of the CFP led the APSA to initiate an internship program for political science graduate students in state and local governments in 1966. The program was funded by the Ford Foundation, and universities competed for grants from the APSA to support graduate student placements in state and local legislative bodies and executive agencies. Grants were awarded annually from 1967 through 1972; 67 graduate departments and 186 graduate student interns were supported by the program, which culminated with a conference publication, *Political Science and State and Local Government* (1969, 1970, 1971, 1973).

Professional internships were not confined to the formal institutions of government. In the 1960s and early 1970s, the APSA coordinated the National Committee Fellowship Program, which placed a political scientist with the Democratic and Republican national committees for a year. This program enabled political scientists to participate in party governance and operations, thereby enhancing opportunities for observation and research and providing the national committees with the assistance of professional political scientists.

Promoting Internships and Experiential Education

Rather than running its own internship program, the American Political Science Association has largely taken a supporting role, providing information and mechanisms for communications. In 1973, it underwrote the publication of *Storming Washington: An Intern's Guide to National Government* (see Frantzich), a comprehensive guide to internship programs in Washington, DC, and a handbook for students seeking internship programs. Now in its fourth edition, it has sold more than 25,000 copies.

The Experiential Education section of the APSA was created during the 1980s to "promote the quality and use of experienced-based techniques of teaching in political science." It offers panels at professional meetings and maintains a mailing list of individuals interested in experiential education.

At all levels of education, internships and the experience of observing and/or working in government and politics share the objectives of allowing students to better understand how government works, facilitating intern contributions to public/community service, and preparing students for careers in the public sector. Over the years, the emphasis on using internships to directly improve government has been deemphasized in relation to an increased emphasis on the immediate benefits to the intern. For undergraduates, career training and orientation have grown in importance. For graduate students and established scholars, internships are primarily justified for providing the expanded understanding and access with the potential for improving research. The long-term objective of developing knowledge and skills important to the citizens of a democracy remains an important one for high school students and undergraduates.

Political scientists continue to be prominent leaders of internship and experiential education efforts. Their contributions are varied: as innovators, administrators, curriculum developers, and educational theorists. In recent years, political theorists have explored the meaning and functions of citizenship in democracies, broadly and in American democracy specifically. Several of these studies address the connection between civic involvement through experiential education and civic learning.

Allowing students to experience politics and government firsthand has proven fruitful both for students' personal development and for their academic performance. Students generally gain a new appreciation of formal academic learning and a more realistic appreciation for the demands on political practitioners. The practitioners who serve as intern sponsors often develop a new respect for academic endeavors and appreciate the dialogue with those who study what they do. In building a bridge between the academic and practical worlds, political scientists have found a way to enhance both and denigrate neither.

Some Lessons for the Future

The experience of political science with internships provides suggestions for the future of service-learning. First of all, it is important to remember that "one size does not fit all." The type of program desirable for a graduate student may well not be appropriate for an undergraduate. In a similar vein, there is considerable room — in fact, almost a requirement — for local institutional innovation and initiative. Like internships, service-learning programs must be tailored to the needs of the students involved, the sponsoring institution, and the agencies in which students are placed. It is also necessary to recognize that the objectives and characteristics of a program may well change over time. Good experiential education programs are almost constantly in a mode of self-assessment and potential change.

Second, in the process of creating and fine-tuning service-leaning programs, networking among program managers will facilitate the exchange of information on topics such as procedures and standards. Third, but crucial, the programs must constantly work to establish and maintain their academic integrity as well as practical utility. If the substantive and experiential components are connected, service-learning as well as internship programs are likely to result in educational, developmental, and practical benefits for students and to make contributions to the communities being served.

Note

1. Internship programs run by individual colleges and universities fall into two general categories: those open only to on-campus students and those accepting students from other colleges. The following colleges and universities currently have Washington semester programs, most of which include an internship component.

Open to on-campus students only: Brigham Young University, Brown University, UC-Berkeley, UC-Davis, UCLA, Carleton College, Claremont-McKenna College, Cornell University, Dartmouth College, Duke University, George Washington University, Holy Cross College, University of Kansas, Lewis and Clark College, Metropolitan State College (Denver), University of Maine, University of Michigan, University of Michigan-Dearborn, Mount Holyoke College, University of Pennsylvania, Pepperdine University, Smith College, Stanford University, Union College, Washington State University, Wellesley College.

Open to students from other colleges: Ball State University, Baylor University, Boston University, Drew University, Frostburg State College, Georgetown University, Goucher College, Hamilton College, Louisiana State University at Shreveport, Mount Vernon College, State University of New York, Trinity College, University of Southern California.

References

Anderson, William. (1943). "The Role of Political Science." *The American Political Science Review* 37:1-17.

APSA Committee on Instruction. (1916). *The Teaching of Government.* New York: Macmillan.

Baker, Earl M. (1973). "University In-Service Education and Public Service: The Intergovernmental Personnel Act of 1970 and Political Science." In *Political Science and State and Local Government.* Washington, DC: American Political Science Association.

Balutis, Alan, and Joseph Honan. (1984). *Public Affairs Internships: Theory and Practice.* Cambridge, MA: Schenckman Publishers.

Brown, David. (September 29, 1995). "Statement on the Washington Semester and World Capitals Program at American University." Unpublished manuscript.

Frantzich, Stephen. (1973). *Storming Washington: An Intern's Guide to National Government*. 4th ed. Washington, DC: American Political Science Association.

"Goals for Political Science: Report of the Committee for the Advancement of Teaching." (1951). New York: William Sloane.

Haines, Charles G. (1910). "Is Sufficient Time Devoted to the Study of Government in Our Colleges?" *Proceedings of the American Political Science Association* 7:202-209.

Hedlund, Ronald D. (1973). "Reflections on Political Internships." PS: *Political Science & Politics* 6:19-25.

Pederson, William D., and Norman W. Provizer. (1995). "Washington Semesters at Private Colleges and Universities: The Liberal Arts Contributions to Civic and Cultural Education." Paper presented at the Annual Meeting of the American Political Science Association, Chicago.

"Political Science and State and Local Government." (Summer 1969, Summer 1970, 1971, 1973). PS: *Political Science & Politics* 2:497-498, 3:553-554, 4:385-387, 6:293-295.

Reed, Thomas H. (1934). "Report of the Committee on Policy of the American Political Science Association for the Year 1933." *American Political Science Review* 28:124-133.

—————— . (1936). "Report of the Committee on Policy of the American Political Science Association for the Year 1935." *American Political Science Review* 30:142-165.

Somit, Albert, and Joseph Tannenhaus. (1967). *The Development of American Political Science*. Boston: Allyn and Bacon.

Service-Learning and Empowerment

by Ed Schwerin

Advocates of service-learning, including many of the authors in this volume, cite important advantages for service-learning such as its value as successful "civic leadership pedagogy" (Couto), its ability to promote the idea of "citizenship as public work" (Boyte and Farr), its ability to provide "practice in the democratic political arts" (Markus), and its ability to help students develop their capacities as "citizen policy analysts" (Hudson). Many of these proponents imply, or explicitly argue, that service-learning can be empowering for students as well as for community participants involved in service-learning projects. In this regard, Hudson states that "the most important contribution of service-learning to student learning in my course was through the way it seemed to empower students" (see p. 91).

How does service-learning empower students, and why is this an important outcome for students, community participants, and the future of service-learning? How is student empowerment relevant to the development of citizenship, leadership, democratic participation, and perhaps sociopolitical transformation?

The purpose of this essay is to explicitly consider the potential of service-learning for personal empowerment, and the relevance of empowerment for service-learning pedagogy as well as for citizenship and democracy. To begin, I define empowerment and discuss the importance of empowerment theory for education, personal growth, social movements, and transformational politics. I then consider the ways in which specific models of service-learning and types of empowerment might be linked. I conclude with some suggestions for research on the empowering potential of service-learning.

Empowerment Theory

What is empowerment theory? Why is empowerment theory important? What are the implications of empowerment theory for individual change and structural transformation?

In recent years, the term "empowerment" has appeared with increasing frequency in the popular media as well as the literature of many different fields and disciplines. Julian Rappaport, a leading proponent of empowerment in community psychology, argues that "empowerment is a pervasive, positive value in American culture" (1987: 127). Indeed, the positive value of empowerment seems to be so widely accepted that it is embraced by people with quite different values and ideologies. For example, Republican conservatives such as Jack Kemp have organized a group based in the Heritage Foundation called Empower America, while the present Democratic administration of Clinton and Gore is sponsoring "community empowerment zones" to facilitate urban development.

Empowerment is considered a core concept in many fields, movements, and disciplines such as education (Kindervatter 1979), political and economic development (Friedmann 1992), democratic theory (Boyte and Reissman 1986), African-American politics (Hanks 1987), feminist politics (Deutchman 1991), mental health (Rose and Black 1985), community psychology (Rappaport 1985), business (Block 1987), communitarianism (Etzioni 1993), and transformational politics (Schwerin 1995).

Despite or perhaps due to its widespread use, "empowerment" has taken on many meanings. It is used as if it were synonymous with a variety of other related concepts, such as self-esteem, self-reliance, self-actualization, self-transformation, personal competence, power, coping skills, citizen participation, community building, and social or political transformation. Empowerment can be viewed from many different perspectives. First, it may be viewed as a state or condition of possessing empowerment. Second, empowerment may be considered as a way of being in the world. Third, it may appear as a vision for personal or political transformation or as self-transcendence. Fourth, it may be conceived as a lifelong, often arduous, individual process of becoming. Fifth, empowerment may be seen as the collective human evolution toward optimal functioning, and the actualization of each individual's potential.

Empowerment is a multidimensional concept with many forms, and a multilevel concept with relevance for individuals, groups, organizations, communities, and larger systems. For example, at the individual level, empowering processes might include organizational or community involvement, and empowering outcomes might include perceived control, skills, and proactive behaviors. At the organizational level, empowering processes might include shared leadership and decision making, and outcomes might include organizational networks, effective resource acquisition, and policy leverage. Finally, at the community level, empowering processes might include accessible government, media, and other resources, and outcomes might include evidence of pluralism, the existence of organizational coalitions, and accessible community resources.

The multidimensionality and complexity of the empowerment concept present many opportunities as well as conceptual challenges. For example, with regard to the question of service-learning and empowerment, we might ask how service-learning might empower individuals such as students, community participants, and even faculty members. Or we might inquire about the empowerment impact of service-learning on community groups and organizations and on the culture or structure of universities that promote service-learning programs. We might also examine the impact of service-learning on the development of community resources, on the degree of social conflict or collaboration.

With regard to conceptual challenges, Julian Rappaport (1985) has indicated the difficulties in clarifying this concept:

> It is a very complex idea to define because it has components that are both psychological and political. The word is used by psychologists and social workers, and by sociologists and political scientists, as well as by theologians. It suggests a sense of control over one's life in personality, cognition, and motivation. It expresses itself at the level of feelings, at the level of ideas about self-worth, at the level of being able to make a difference in the world around us, and even at the level of something more akin to the spiritual. (17)

For the purposes of this paper, I will focus primarily on the potential impact of service-learning on students; therefore, I will emphasize the conceptual clarification of individual empowerment, and refer to organizational and community empowerment only peripherally.

In a recent book (Schwerin 1995), I have developed a conceptual analysis of empowerment delineating key characteristics from the leading scholars in the social sciences, education, and other disciplines. The following discussions on conceptual clarity and theory development draw substantially from that research. I define personal empowerment most simply as "the process of gaining mastery over one's self and one's environment in order to fulfill human needs" (81). This statement captures essential qualities of personal empowerment. An empowered individual strives to achieve some degree of control or mastery of the self, as well as perceived control over the social, political, and physical environments. As discussed below, it is useful to distinguish between three types of personal empowerment: psychological, social, and political empowerment.

It is also useful to distinguish the primary characteristics of personal empowerment, from empowerment processes and empowerment outcomes. Empowering processes are ones in which attempts to gain control, obtain needed resources, and critically understand one's social and political environment are fundamental. Empowerment outcomes refer to operationalization of empowerment so we can study the consequences of citizen attempts to gain greater control in their community, or the effects of interventions designed to empower participants.

I have suggested that "the empowerment process links individual attitudes (i.e., self-esteem and self-efficacy) and *capabilities* (i.e., knowledge and skills and political awareness) to enable efficacious individual *and collabora-tive* actions (i.e., social and political participation) in order to attain person-al and collective social political goals (i.e., political rights and responsibili-ties, and material, psychological, and sociopolitical resources)" (81). This def-inition suggests the development of an empowerment theory framework in which the individual's attitudes and capabilities enable the individual to participate in various social and political processes, which may produce empowering outcomes such as increased resources and rights for the indi-vidual and group.

Attitudes and capabilities are the key attributes of individual empower-ment. The self-esteem and self-efficacy components define a positive self-concept that is basic to an individual's psychological empowerment. Knowledge and skills and political awareness are the capabilities or person-al competencies required for social and political empowerment that enable an individual to participate effectively in a variety of social and political activities and accomplish their empowerment goals. Those individuals who have developed higher levels of self-esteem and self-efficacy as well as high-ly developed knowledge and skills are more likely to be socially and politi-cally active.

Possessing social skills as well as knowledge about community needs and the availability of resources changes the individual's possibilities and probabilities for participation in community events and organizations. Developing increased political awareness might facilitate involvement in community organizing activities, or in conducting environmental campaigns to close nuclear plants or save the whales. Individuals with highly developed political awareness may be expected to participate in more political activi-ties than other less politically sophisticated individuals, who may be equal-ly active in the community but are involved in some type of social participation.

Human needs represented in the theory framework by political rights, responsibilities, and resources are a powerful source of explanation for human behavior at all levels, from interpersonal to international relations. Individuals striving to fulfill their needs interact with other individuals attempting to do the same. In the spheres of social and political participa-tion, opportunities exist for conflict or collaboration. To obtain the empow-erment outcomes — political rights and responsibilities, and psychological, social, and material resources — individuals will often collaborate in various social and political settings. This social and political participation may in turn empower individuals by making them feel more confident and compe-tent, thus enhancing their self-esteem and self-efficacy. There may be an increase in individuals' level of knowledge about themselves and their envi-ronment, and increase in social and political skills, and perhaps the development of "critical consciousness." As participation brings the individuals more opportunity to exercise their political rights and responsibilities, and to access their community resources, their level of activity and commitment to groups and community associations may further increase. Gaining increased access to rights, responsibilities, and resources may correspondingly increase self-esteem and self-efficacy. As this causal reciprocity between various empowerment components develops, a synergistic empowerment process is set in motion for individuals involved in it.

Thus, empowerment has important implications for enhancing citizen participation and democratization. Empowered citizens are essential to the successful functioning of a democratic system. A viable and vibrant democratic society presumes the existence of an educated electorate and relatively high levels of citizen participation. Citizens must have the basic skills and knowledge and political awareness that are vital elements of political competence. Citizens must possess sufficient levels of self-esteem and self-efficacy to participate in the political system and to believe that they are capable of political actions that will influence the political system and bring about transformational changes to improve functioning of the system. They must be willing to take responsibility and to act individually, as well as collaboratively with others, in order to achieve democratic values, such as freedom, equality, and social justice.

In addition to its relevance to individual empowerment, citizenship, and democracy, I would suggest that empowerment theory as described here provides a theoretical foundation for empowering pedagogy as well as a guide to teaching practice. While empowering processes and empowering outcomes are relevant to service-learning, my focus in this paper is on the key components of individual empowerment most relevant to empowering approaches to teaching, including self-esteem, self-efficacy, knowledge and skills, and political awareness.

Self-esteem. Self-esteem is the evaluative function of the self-concept. High self-esteem indicates a positive attitude toward oneself and one's behavior. Self-esteem is considered to be essential to one's mental health, and research has linked high self-esteem to increased democratic political participation (Sniderman 1975).

Self-efficacy. Perhaps even more important for personal empowerment is the related concept of self-efficacy, which refers to the experience of oneself as a cause agent. High self-efficacy involves a positive attitude toward one's control over the environment. Albert Bandura contends that both self-esteem and self-efficacy "contribute in their own way to the quality of human life" (1986: 410). In addition, both self-esteem and self-efficacy contribute significantly to the formation of an individual's psychological empowerment.

Knowledge and skills. The inculcation of general and specialized forms of knowledge and skills is a fundamental objective of most forms of pedagogy. The most important type of general *knowledge* relevant to personal empowerment is basic literacy (see Freire 1970). Also important are the kinds of practical knowledge that enable individuals to survive in a recalcitrant environment and facilitate the development of personal competence, such as knowledge about conflict dynamics and conflict-resolution processes. In addition, self-knowledge of one's goals, values, limitations, and strengths is fundamental to increasing and maintaining self-empowerment. Other relevant kinds of specialized political knowledge are discussed in the section on political awareness below.

Skills are defined as a coordinated series of actions that help to attain goals or accomplish tasks. The list of empowering skills might include stress management, coping, communication, negotiation, problem-solving, and conflict-resolution skills. In addition, political activists might include skills such as community organizing, developing grass-roots transforming leadership, and other political activists skills. More recently, Internet and other computer skills are becoming essential for those who desire to be effective citizens, scholars, and political activists.

Political awareness. The development of political awareness is essential for those concerned with personal empowerment and political transformation. The questions linked to political awareness are integral to empowering teaching. One aspect of political awareness is "critical consciousness," a special type of empowering knowledge that enables people to develop their own concepts of social justice and provides conceptual tools to realize those goals. The notion of critical consciousness is associated with Paulo Freire (1970) and his ideas about "liberation education."

Underlying my conception of political awareness are four key interrelated questions: What is (or, where are we now)? Where are we headed? Where should we be headed? And how do we get there from here? These are complex questions with no easy answers, but they might provide four vital foci for empowering teachers.

The first type of political analysis requires development of the necessary theories, data, analysis skills, political experience, and political intuition to determine *what is*. In other words, what is the political game being played? Who has the power? Who pays most and who benefits most from the system? Understanding how the political game is played is essential for all citizens. This is true for mainstream politicians who wish to be effective; conflict resolvers who believe that it is vital to get at the root (structural) causes of deep-rooted social conflict; and other reformers and transformationalists who seek to understand and to critique the status quo in order to improve, or fundamentally transform, the existing system. This is the area of political and economic policy analysis. For example, an empowering teacher might decide to focus on problems such as the causes and consequences of the growing economic disparities in the United States and other areas on the world.

The second type of political analysis asks *where are we headed,* or *what will be?* In other words, given our understanding of existing political systems and the apparent trends and transformations, changes, and continuities, what will the future look like? Anticipating the future is perhaps even more difficult than understanding the present, but it is essential for future planning and developing effective policies. Anticipating *"what will be"* is crucial, especially if one believes that the consequences of present policies and trends will be disastrous in the long run, and that consequently there is a need for major preventive efforts to avoid the possible environmental and political disasters looming in the third millennium.

The third aspect of political awareness, which follows directly from a critical analysis of the existing socioeconomic-political trends and structures, is prescriptive analysis, or the ability to decide *what should be.* This normative "vision" of a better future may be based on a clearly articulated theory, or an ideology based on core values such as human survival and quality of life.

The fourth aspect of political awareness is the ability to develop viable transition strategies, or to determine *how to get there from here.* If one is convinced that the existing political-economic system is relatively fair, and that the future indicators for a continuation of the status quo are salutary, then all that may be required are routine system maintenance activities or minor piecemeal reforms. On the other hand, if one believes either that the present economic-political structures are oppressive, dysfunctional, and disempowering or that these structures are basically satisfactory but may be seriously deteriorating, then the task of achieving major structural transformation is somewhat more daunting. Under these circumstances, the ability *"to get there from here"* involves a combination of capabilities, such as the critical analysis of root causes of alienation and the barriers to transformation, as well as planning and transforming leadership skills to strategize and implement the individual and collective actions essential to the transformation of individuals and structures.

Political awareness as I have described it here is the core component of developing political competencies or of political empowerment, and is therefore a key component especially of empowering political science education. In combination with the self-esteem and self-efficacy attitudes, and the knowledge and skills components, political awareness enables a citizen to function effectively in different types of political activities.

In short, empowering teaching goals and objectives should be specifically designed to enhance self-esteem and self-efficacy, to develop the kind of knowledge and skills discussed above, to teach students how to learn so that they can teach themselves and others, and to develop the kind of critical political awareness essential for democratic citizenship.

Service-Learning Models and Types of Empowerment

How is service-learning potentially empowering? What aspects of service-learning are empowering? How can we design more empowering models? What types or models of service-learning are empowering?

All forms of education are designed to be empowering, at least in the sense that education provides new knowledge, and knowledge and skills are major components of personal empowerment. However, education might in some cases also be disempowering. For example, critics of traditional educational practices argue that such practices foster dysfunctional competition and discourage cooperation, are authoritarian, promote student passivity, and support the economic and political objectives of the dominant elites (Becker and Couto 1996; Freire 1970). As the influential Brazilian educator Paulo Freire has pointed out, education can either domesticate or liberate. The traditional teacher-centered classroom is hierarchically structured, and students are taught in an unquestioning way to digest information offered to them in a lecture format. Traditional educators acting as authoritarian experts often behave as if they were the sole possessors of "truth." In teacher-centered classrooms, the teacher's function is to impart knowledge to students whose minds are like blank slates. This type of teaching, called "banking education" by Freire, involves a one-way exchange between teachers and students in which information and skills are deposited in a student's brain to be used at some later time. Students in traditional classes become authority dependent, and often unlikely to value their own insights. According to the critics, schools are not merely instructional sites, they are also cultural and political sites, and powerful agencies of social, economic, and cultural reproduction. Therefore, traditional education is seen as a political instrument that perpetuates the privileges of the power elite and justifies a conservative continuation of the economic and political status quo.

To the extent that service-learning classrooms are teacher-centered, hierarchically organized, and apolitical or even uncritically support the political status quo, they might be vulnerable to this same kind of criticism leveled at traditional models of education. However, most well-intentioned service-learning programs seek to provide a more democratic and empowering experience for students.

Service-learning proponents argue that not only does it have unique educational benefits for students, it can also benefit the community in many ways, and it has great potential for personal empowerment and social and political transformation. Some argue that service-learning can revitalize civic education and promote "strong" democracy (see Barber 1992; Couto 1993). Barber and Battistoni (1993) point out that "this spirit of citizenship revitalized and the idea of service recoupled to democracy have guided the pioneering experiment in civic education and community service" (235).

The label "service-learning" can be applied to a broad variety of models and activities. One approach to community service in school settings views service to the community as a strictly voluntary and extracurricular activity. The assumption of this model is that service by itself can contribute to education without the need for any additional classroom instruction. This approach emphasizes the value of the service to the community and takes for granted that there will be pedagogical benefits to the students who volunteer to serve their community. As Barber and Battistoni point out, "this approach was associated with voluntarism and philanthropy, and is only weakly linked (if at all) to civic responsibility and citizen education" (236). They argue that the "civic" and "philanthropic" motives offer "two distinctive justifications for service-learning which, while they may be mutually reinforcing in certain ways, nevertheless pose contradictory choices and yield different pedagogical strategies" (237).

The philanthropic orientation emphasizes service as altruism and is associated with notions such as noblesse oblige and the obligations of better-educated or well-off citizens to help others who are disadvantaged. In contrast, the civic view, according to Barber and Battistoni, "emphasizes mutual responsibility and interdependence of rights and responsibilities, and it focuses not on altruism but on enlightened self-interest. The idea is not that the well-off 'owe' something to the less fortunate, but that free democratic communities depend on mutual responsibility and that rights without obligations are ultimately not sustainable. Here the focus is on the nurturing of citizenship and the understanding of the interdependence of communities. The civic approach also encourages an educational partnership between college and community, with the community actively involved in defining its own needs as well as the role service will play in the education of students" (237).

All models of service-learning are potentially empowering for students, but they will be empowering in different ways. The approach that views service to the community as a strictly voluntary and extracurricular activity may empower students by increasing their self-esteem and self-efficacy as a result of providing assistance to the homeless and other vulnerable individuals in the community. Making a difference in the community may increase students' feelings of self-efficacy. By doing volunteer work, students may also develop new knowledge about community problems and learn useful new skills such as advocacy and grant writing. But these kind of programs may be apolitical, and students may view service as an alternative to politics. In these cases, students may focus on the plight of individuals but be unaware of the root causes of these problems and the political power structures that give rise to social and economic inequities. In these programs, it is doubtful that students would be substantially empowered with regard to increasing their levels of political awareness.

Therefore, while all forms of service-learning have value and may provide benefits for the students and the community, it is the models that are based primarily on civic justifications, that attempt to specifically link political theory with reflective practice, and that are fully integrated with the core academic curriculum, that are of primary relevance to the goals and objectives of empowering education. In addition to the Rutgers program, there are many other service-learning programs and educational experiments that are similarly attempting to revitalize civic education, educate democratic citizens, build more democratic communities, increase political awareness, and facilitate more democratic structural transformation. For example, service-learning courses have been designed to provide a critical education for citizenship by using Televote polling experiments as a form of experiential education in modern democracy (Becker and Couto 1996). At the University of Richmond, the Learning in Community Settings (LINCS) program offers several credit-bearing service-learning models including community service, school-based instruction, a community problem-solving seminar, and action research (see Couto in this volume).

Conclusions

Service-learning appears to have a great deal of potential for empowering students and other participants. However, there has been little empirical research to confirm these suppositions. Therefore, future research on service-learning might usefully focus on determining the empowering impact of various types and models of service-learning on the participants, including not only students but also the community participants and faculty involved with service-learning programs. A variety of approaches could be used to determine levels and types of individual empowerment, including interviews, surveys, and existing psychological scales to measure gains in self-esteem and self-efficacy. For example, researchers might ask, Do service-learning students develop greater political self-efficacy as a result of their experiences? Do they increase their participation in community and political organizations and activities after involvement in service-learning? Do they begin to seek leadership roles in these organizations or consider running for office?

Other studies might look at the empowering impact of service-learning at the group or community level, looking, for example, at changes in the organizational culture, the processes and outcomes of organizations and groups as well as the institutions of higher education associated with service-learning programs. Are there changes in leadership style, increases in use of democratic management processes, or changes in the type and amount of resources available? At the community level, are there discernible improvements in the quality of life? Is there an increased capacity for community conflict resolution and problem solving? Is there increased access to government services, media, and other community resources? Is there evidence of the development of more effective organizational coalitions and increased pluralism?

There may be at least two important benefits derived from research on the empowering impacts of service-learning. First, learning more about the empowering impact of service-learning on individual participants, as well as the impacts on organizations and communities, will enable the design of more effective service-learning models that might maximally empower service-learning participants and the community.

Second, empirical evidence for the empowering impact of service-learning on participants, affiliated organizations, and communities might provide persuasive arguments for the continued development and further dissemination of service-learning programs. This evidence may help to persuade those faculty and institutions considering service-learning to move ahead and overcome any personal, professional, or institutional barriers to implementation. This is especially true for those who recognize the need for increased personal empowerment and widespread political transformation, and who attempt to promote significant empowerment in their personal and professional activities and relationships.

References

Bandura, A. (1986). *Social Foundations of Thought and Action: A Social Cognitive Theory.* Englewood Cliffs, NJ: Prentice-Hall.

Barber, Benjamin R. (1992). *An Aristocracy of Everyone: The Politics of Education and the Future of America.* New York: Ballantine.

————— , and Richard Battistoni. (June 1993). "A Season of Service: Introducing Service Learning Into the Liberal Arts Curriculum." *PS: Political Science & Politics* 26:235-240, 262.

Becker, Theodore L., and Richard A. Couto, eds. (1996). *Teaching Democracy by Being Democratic.* Westport, CT: Praeger.

Block, P. (1987). *The Empowered Manager.* San Francisco: Jossey-Bass.

Boyte, Harry C., and F. Reissman, eds. (1986). *The New Populism: The Politics of Empowerment.* Philadelphia: Temple University Press.

Couto, Richard A. (1993). "Service-Learning in Leadership Development." In *Rethinking Tradition: Integrating Service With Academic Study on College Campuses.* Edited by Tamar Y. Kupiec, pp. 67-71. Providence, RI: Campus Compact.

Deutchman, I.E. (1991). "The Politics of Empowerment." *Women and Politics* 11:1-17.

Etzioni, A. (1993). *The Spirit of Community.* New York: Crown.

Freire, P. (1970). *Pedagogy of the Oppressed.* New York: Continuum.

Friedmann, J. (1992). *Empowerment: The Politics of Alternative Development.* Cambridge, MA: MIT Press.

Hanks, L.J. (1987). *The Struggle for Black Political Empowerment in Three Georgia Counties.* Knoxville: University of Tennessee Press.

Kindervatter, S. (1979). *Nonformal Education as an Empowering Process.* Amherst, MA: University of Massachusetts.

Rappaport, J. (1985). "The Power of Empowerment Language." *Social Policy* 16:15-21.

——————. (1987). "Terms of Empowerment/Exemplars of Prevention: Toward a Theory of Community Psychology." *American Journal of Community Psychology* 15(2): 127-148.

Rose, S., and B. Black. (1985). *Advocacy and Empowerment: Mental Health Care in the Community.* London: Routledge and Kegan Paul.

Schwerin, Edward W. (1995). *Mediation, Citizen Empowerment, and Transformational Politics.* Westport, CT: Praeger.

Sniderman, P.M. (1975). *Personality and Democratic Politics.* Berkeley: University of California Press.

Civic Leadership

by Richard A. Couto

Service-learning, more than political science, has been central to my professional career as a political scientist. Since 1975, I have not been in a political science department. Rather than teaching about politics, my teaching has centered on giving students political roles, in a broad sense of civic participation in social problem solving. Since 1991, I have been on the faculty of the Jepson School of Leadership Studies, which is the first and only interdisciplinary undergraduate degree program on leadership. I brought to my current work 16 years of experience with service-learning in various settings and under different names.

In 1975, when I went to Vanderbilt University to direct the Center for Health Services, I thought of my work as a remnant of the preceding decade's efforts at social change on college campuses. Student projects of the center, such as the Appalachian Student Health Coalition, conducted community services as a tool to support local leaders in their organizing and development efforts. By 1980, the various projects had assisted local leaders in the development of more than 20 community-directed primary-care centers in rural areas without health services and in the establishment of citizens groups, such as Save Our Cumberland Mountains, which is still going strong after 25 years. Students, with few but important faculty allies and modest university support, were making change.

I learned many valuable lessons in the first few years at Vanderbilt (see Couto 1982). Our work seldom started organizing and much more often continued the labor union or civil rights organizing that had preceded it. Our work also renewed free spaces in the community and got nowhere without them. I learned those prospects for and problems of running a program of social change and democratic development from a university base that Ted Becker and I have spelled out elsewhere (see Becker and Couto 1996). Fundamental to the topic at hand, I learned that the more students felt that they were working for positive social change effectively, the more they reported outcomes associated with liberal arts education and personal development. Ancillary lessons included the importance of orientation, how to distinguish a good community learning context from a poor one, and the importance of reflection.

By the mid-1980s, I was interested in integrating community service into the curriculum. This interest coincided with reports on higher education in the early 1980s that articulated the need to reintegrate democratic values and civic participation into the curriculum. In contrast to the concern over student activism a decade before, the problem now seemed student apathy (Levine 1980). Major new initiatives on community service in higher education, Campus Compact and COOL (Campus Outreach Opportunity League), began with a decided emphasis on two separate tracks, the curriculum and community service, and only slowly began to integrate them. The late Ernest Boyer found in the discussion of the "new American college" another opportunity to urge colleges and universities to address the social problems of their surrounding communities and to use their resources, including the curriculum, to address those problems.

The Jepson School of Leadership Studies offered me the unusual opportunity to help shape a curriculum with service-learning at the center of it. I have recounted the experience of establishing a curriculum and a place for service-learning within it elsewhere (see Couto 1993; Couto et al. 1994). That atypical experience occurs once in a lifetime, perhaps. More pertinent to the purposes of this monograph are the efforts to integrate community service into other course offerings at the University of Richmond. These efforts suggest how a political science department may lend assistance to other departments in a pedagogy of civic leadership.

Before I share that experience, it may be useful to be explicit about my assumptions about politics and pedagogy. I assume the broadest possible function for politics. Politics shapes who we are as a people; what we fear and hope for; and what we love and hate. It extends far beyond government and specific policy choices to include cultural symbols and social values. Politics extends beyond how followers select and influence leaders, as well. It entails how followers relate to one another; the degree of trust among them; and the sense of responsibility they have for one another. Placing students in opportunities to address social and individual problems is an avenue to reflect on this element of *their* politics, *their* civic virtue. This pedagogy, according to Paulo Freire (1970), should make problems as well as address problems. Freire has stirred the imaginations of educators around the world, especially those who combine education with a concern for social justice and democratic practice. Freire insists that learners reclaim an essential political role: agents, not objects, of history who have a part in shaping, not merely conforming to, the future. That political role touches the essential nature of human beings:

> The future is essentially problematic. We have different possibilities for the future, not just one. I understand history as a time of possibilities, not a time for determined things but a time of possibilities.
>
> Liberals today speak about capitalism as the future which we already have and the future as the finishing of history. The capitalist system has reached such a level that it exhausted history, you see. I don't believe that.
>
> I believe that we are engaged permanently in changing or preserving

the present. *The future depends on what we change or what we preserve. This is the future: to fight in favor of change or to fight in favor of keeping the present.*

The moment in which we no longer have amazement in the sense of espertado [awe] we are dead. Human beings are beings ontologically amazed. We are epistemologically curious which gives us the ability to know. (as quoted in Couto and Shepherd 1995: 2-3)

Freire offers an unusual bridge from political science to other disciplines, many of which claim him. He also provides common ground on some pedagogical principles for political scientists and other members of academe. His work suggests various ways in which service-learning can transcend disciplinary boundaries and permit a political science department to foster civil leadership pedagogy across the curriculum. I now turn to the experience of one political scientist's effort to do this.

LINCS: A Model of Civic Leadership Pedagogy

The Jepson School of Leadership Studies seemed a place where the integration of community service and the curriculum could happen. After the construction of the initial curriculum and testing out some methods in coursework, students and I disseminated and nurtured service-learning in other schools and departments of the university. Specifically, the Learning in Community Settings (LINCS) program at the University of Richmond offers faculty and students several models for course-related or credit-bearing service-learning: (1) community service, (2) school-based instruction, (3) action research, and (4) a community problem solving (COMPS) seminar. The program thereby offers distinct models of service-learning that can be incorporated into different courses in different ways. Equally important, this approach implies that political science departments and teachers can disseminate service-learning and the teaching of democracy throughout the curriculum beyond classes in one department (Bozeman 1996).

Community Service

Some instructors require a limited amount of community service, 10 to 15 hours ordinarily, to fulfill the requirements for a class, or offer students the option of community service in place of another assignment. Russian language students, for example, were assigned Russian émigrés by the Refugee Resettlement Program in Richmond and were expected to meet and talk with those individuals and families and to help them conduct normal chores, such as recreation or shopping. In this model, students learned conversational Russian and the émigrés acquired more knowledge of English.

Students in special-topic courses in political science — e.g., AIDS and Public Policy, Women and Politics, or Environmental Politics — might be required to work with an agency for 20 hours during the course of the semester.

Though limited, these kinds of experiences can be powerful teaching tools, especially among traditional-aged college students from privileged backgrounds. James MacGregor Burns (1978) argues that this group most likely has the least preparation for political leadership in "a pluralized, complex, and open society." Adolescents "in a child-centered affluent suburban community" are likely to have, according to Burns, "linear, monistic, and overwhelmingly cumulative" role demands that lessen their ability "to cope with diversity of persons or roles" (99).

Service-learning has the potential to impact such students immediately and profoundly by illuminating the nature of class and inequality in American life. In one instance, for example, a University of Richmond student visited a homeless shelter for men, and on her first visit reported through her journal, "I was never so aware of my race, my gender, and my socioeconomic class as I was that evening." It was disconcerting for her, if not a little frightening. Her second evening there was "awesome." After her third visit, she volunteered to serve on the board of the agency representing student volunteers. Her journal entries went on for pages, with deep personal reflection about the site, the men she visited, past and present parental advice, and herself. She now works for a national fraternity, coordinating the community service component of their program reform.

Getting students into situations in which differences of class and degrees of human need are evident may be a small step in teaching democracy, but surely it is a step in the right direction. Civic leadership surely begins with the insight that social problems involve both the haves and the have-nots and that members of both groups are human, with their foibles and their strengths.

Service-learning differs from field trips, another means of getting students into new settings, in a significantly political way: Students belong in the battered women's shelter, the AIDS project's office, or the public defender's office because they are doing something about the problem. They are there to learn, but they pay a portion of their debt for their instruction through service. Students who share the common experience of community service will sometimes build a special and unique camaraderie. Sharing rides to and from the service site brings students together in rudimentary teams. Teamwork and group sharing are welcomed antidotes to the ordinary message of individual effort and competition that is a central feature of most curriculums.

School-Based Service-Learning: Community Service and Teaching

The difficulty of finding an adequate site for service-learning, one hospitable to a structured opportunity to meet the needs of different constituencies, provides an incentive for school-based service-learning. Some instructors offer their students the chance to organize modules of instruction, tutoring, and other forms of teaching. Political socialization classes can take a lively twist with a trip to a nearby high school with the expectation that students will present a module on an upcoming election or local, national, or regional current events. School-based service-learning can be supported by an independent study, a special-topics or fieldwork course, or within an existing course as a group assignment.

This form of service-learning has several advantages. It is far more predictable and reliable than working with several different community organizations, nonprofit agencies, or offices of local government. It provides students a service experience within a structure with which they are familiar. It can meet a very real need in terms of creating new instructional resources — especially in public schools. It requires students to master a topic in order to teach it to others. It also provides students the opportunity to apply what they are learning, test out their ideas, and assess and analyze their theories after applying them. Moreover, school-based service-learning requires students to collaborate more extensively and thus offers more opportunity for students to work in teams.

The advantages of this form of service-learning can deter working for its deeper, political significance. The satisfaction of students and teachers may be high enough that there is little incentive to probe into the roles and purposes of public education; the racial makeup of different schools; the race and gender of administrators and teachers; the differences among schools in facilities, equipment, repair, and cleanliness; the professionalism and dedication of teachers; the educational future of the students of different schools; and the tax base that determines many of these factors. However, it is precisely in reflection on these issues about the social provisions for the education of children of different classes and races that we begin to teach democracy.

Action Research

Action research coordinates the information needs of social services, public agencies, and public interest organizations with requirements of courses. It provides a specific orientation to internships with community organizations and agencies such as the city manager's office, the Catholic Worker, the United Way, or member groups of "the backyard revolution" (Boyte 1980). Such groups can always use talented researchers to assist in fundraising, lobbying, direct action, or advocacy work.

Students can also participate in action research in an independent study project, a term project in a class, or lengthy student research assignments in capstone or honors courses or thesis seminars. For example, one American studies student did her senior seminar thesis on landownership in an inner-city neighborhood. In addition to reading about the development of the inner city in the past three decades, she went to city hall and researched ownership of every lot in a three-block square. She did this work at the request of a community center run by the local Catholic parish. The work was needed for the larger goal of neighborhood redevelopment that was part of the vision of the leaders of the community center. So far, her report has been part of neighborhood-wide discussions of two development plans.

This example also illustrates central and distinguishing features of successful action research as service-learning. First, it involves independent research by students. Second, that research is requested by a community group or agency and conducted under its supervision. Third, the community agency has a use for the research that it can specify clearly. Fourth, the research is turned over to the community agency for its use (Couto 1987; Park 1992).

As noted above, action research may also fit into course requirements for a class. For example, students in a social movement class may work with leaders in a gay and lesbian organization, a domestic violence hot line, an organization of mental health consumers or the physically handicapped, or some similar organization to research an issue or to conduct some other information-gathering action related to its work. Students then satisfy term paper or other research requirements in those classes by addressing the information needs of the agency. For example, the director of the Virginia Coalition for the Homeless has identified her organization's need to continue the annual census of the homeless in the state and to monitor the hearings of state legislative committees on poverty in Virginia. Students in a state and local government course could couple their classroom work with assignments to monitor, report, and analyze the hearings and recommendations of legislative committees.

Given the size of most action research assignments and the limited time that students have to fulfill one assignment in one class during a single semester, it is useful to organize class members into teams and for team members to break the action research into smaller, discrete parts that can be accomplished in a semester. In this manner, one team in a community leadership course worked with the Richmond AIDS Ministry Program to research care programs during the day for persons with HIV. Members of that team traveled to other cities to learn about programs there. Other members researched federal funding sources for such programs. Together, team members prepared a proposal with information on funding sources. Another team in that class worked with an international agency for children to devise methods of evaluation. Reports of local projects from national offices around the world varied widely. Students examined them and made suggestions about the current methods of reporting that provide information on the 10 goals of children's well-being that the international office had established. They also recommended changes in reporting that would be useful to acquire additional information to track the progress of each project in achieving the 10 goals of the agency. Finally, the action research potential afforded by online databases via the Internet is boundless.

Community Problem Solving Seminar: Putting It All Together

Service-learning can also combine classroom work, experiential education, and community service in major new ways. In the Community Problem Solving (COMPS) seminar, students review social problems of the nation, inquire into a particular city's social problems, discuss them and possible solutions with local leaders, and address one of those problems through service with a community agency or advocacy group. The seminar combines class work, reading, visiting lecturers, field trips, and a 20- to 30-hour weekly internship. This program encourages students to think globally, to act locally, and to combine democratic theory and action. In this way, COMPS extends action research. Students have 20 or more hours a week over a semester to devote to a research issue. This permits them to take on a larger issue and to do more work on it (Schott 1994). Some examples of COMPS projects include establishing a computer spreadsheet program for the office of Habitat for Humanity to track mortgage payments of participants; assisting the state Planned Parenthood office to develop a program of school-based sex education; and assisting a statewide health agency to establish a program to recognize innovative community-based health programs.

By themselves, none of these tasks will bring on a new democratic America, but each of them helps construct improved democratic practice, including democratic teaching. When students undertake these tasks, they enter an off-campus classroom of Freirean education on housing policy and class structure; on the influence of race, class, and gender roles on teen pregnancy; and on power within the health care system. They also learn specific concrete steps to address these problems through individual courage and collective action. These lessons of Freirean education, in the hands of a skillful teacher-facilitator, complement classroom texts to explain social problems, their origins and causes, and specific steps to deal with them. COMPS combines lessons of democratic critique and improved democratic practice about which we spoke in the Introduction.

Gleanings from student essays at the conclusion of the 1994 COMPS seminar at the University of Richmond suggest its democratic, pedagogical outcomes. Although derived from a very small sample, the responses are representative of other students' comments extending over almost 20 years and more than a thousand students.

Students reported personal development. They became aware of and grappled with "white guilt" in working with other racial groups; socioeconomic class differences; the benefits and costs of careers they contemplated; different styles of relating to people in various positions of authority and situations (e.g., welcoming new staff members into an organization, volunteering and meeting commitments, etc.). This personal development included learning skills that extend beyond the classroom. Students reported understanding better that formal education was related to acquiring skills to be applied in real life rather than for merely passing tests. Others were faced with the social consequence of their habits of procrastination and their need to exercise more self-direction, initiative, and self-assertion in order to work more effectively with people.

Students reported social and political development. This included lessons about personal trust: How and why is it given? How and why is it acquired? Their reports included lessons they acquired from their work and from observing others with whom they worked about the capacity to affect the lives of people in need. They also learned the cost of time and commitment to exercise this capacity. One student confessed frankly that he was probably not ready to make the commitment that he saw his coworkers and supervisor make. Students acquired a sharper awareness of their differences from other people as individuals and as members of groups; for example, their attitudes toward education or pregnancy as a teenager. On the other hand, they also became more aware of the common bonds they had with people they took to be different from them — such as the formerly homeless man who conducted a walking tour of homelessness for the group through the streets of Richmond one bright and hot May morning. They became aware of the importance and usefulness of networks in bringing about change, and left with hope that change is possible.

Perhaps the greatest implications of COMPS for democratic teaching related even more to the teacher-facilitators than to the students. **Democratic teaching requires the redistribution of classroom resources,** no less than improved democratic practice in other fields. Service-learning, as democratic teaching, redistributes some university resources to people and agencies in the community who would have no benefit from those resources otherwise. If done well, extensive service-learning formats such as action research and COMPS may provide groups with necessary but otherwise unavailable information and powerful allies for political action. This may provide academic institutions with a new or more formal role in the community of response. It is altogether possible and fitting that this new role spark faculty and student deliberation and action about the allocation of resources for its role in the community of response.

The COMPS seminar required a full-time student assistant during the summer semester when we conducted it. LINCS now has a staff of two full-time persons, but began with one part-time student coordinator. Programs such as LINCS and COMPS require resources. Faculty and students have adopted service-learning at the University of Richmond because the LINCS staff has assisted them. Acquiring staff for a program such as LINCS requires the allocation of new resources or a reallocation of existing ones. In either event, developing resources to improve democratic teaching may, as in this case, require a school to rearrange its priorities and redistribute its resources.

Service-learning requires the redistribution of power and authority within the classroom as well. The successful integration of service-learning into class work requires turning over significant amounts of class time to the students for planning and reporting. Coordinating team members' efforts requires time spent together, and often class members see one another only in class. Likewise, accountability in service-learning requires some form of reporting mechanism, such as oral reports to the class. Use of class time in this fashion turns that time over to the students for their use. This contrasts sharply with traditional methods, especially lecture and class discussion. More generally, service-learning requires teachers to redistribute time and attention from themselves, assigned readings, and lectures to the students, their experience, and the distillation of lessons from discussion.

Delegating control over class time is not an abdication of teaching responsibility but a deliberate pedagogy to foster the community required for problem solving and civic leadership. The different forms of service-learning we have described require varying amounts of class time. The service-learning of 15 hours requires perhaps a special class session or limited but regular reference and incorporation in class. COMPS, on the other hand, devotes the largest portion of class time to service-learning and reflection upon it. These two forms of service-learning have inverse ratios of traditional class and service-learning time.

COMPS provides students a very intense and extensive service-learning experience, and their evaluative comments reflect that. Yet, every form of service-learning can provide similar outcomes to some degree. These results, ultimately, are the justification of service-learning in the curriculum. They serve the purposes of the curriculum, which are to educate students and to assist in their personal development. To these we have added the component, which many argue has been too long ignored on American campuses, of preparing students to participate effectively in democratic processes of public problem solving.

Service-Learning and Civic Competence

Political science has a central role to play in preparing college students for work and citizenship in a democratic society. Service-learning offers political scientists one central means to carry out that role. Others have recognized this, even if as a group political scientists have yet to do so. John Dewey, for example, offered clear, precise, and reasonable principles for democratic sharing and interaction:

- mutual respect and attention;
- creative thinking;
- arriving at creative solutions to mutual problems; and
- working to implement those solutions (Barber 1992).

Service-learning in its various forms can assist political scientists to develop the theory and practice of these principles with their students. Action research, for example, imparts several democratic lessons. It instructs students on the limits and possibilities of addressing political problems efficaciously. If done in the manner of participatory research, this form of service-learning — as well as the other forms — also requires students to listen to one another, to deliberate critically about common problems and issues, to arrive at solutions to mutual problems creatively in community settings, and, perhaps, to work together to implement solutions. Obviously, some of these outcomes will be better met than others in the course of a single semester and depending on the form of service-learning. Their combination, however, is the democratic constellation of which Dewey wrote.

Recent work on leadership development reflects the premises of Dewey and reinforces the findings of the COMPS program. Helen Astin and Alexander Astin (1996) devised a model of leadership development premised on the assumption that all students have the potential for leadership and that service "provides a powerful vehicle for developing student capacities" provided that reflection helps them make meaning of the service experience (18). The Astins assume also that social change, assisting our institutions and society to function more effectively and humanely (19), is the "ultimate goal of the creative process of leadership" (21). As the hub of leadership development, social change efforts hold together the "seven Cs" of their model: Service-learning helps students to develop the individual values of consciousness of self; congruence of actions and beliefs; and commitment to act on opportunities for change. Service-learning also assists students to develop group-process values of collaboration, common purpose, and controversy with civility. Finally, in the Astin model, service-learning develops the societal and community values of citizenship.

Political scientists are not solely responsible for developing the civic competence and leadership of college students. Civic leadership, however, fits uniquely well with politics and its study. Service-learning is one avenue to develop that fit within political science and to uniquely express the discipline's responsibility, within higher education, for the development of the civic competence and leadership potential of students.

References

Astin, Helen S., and Alexander W. Astin. (1996). *A Social Change Model of Leadership Development*. Los Angeles: University of California, Higher Education Research Institute.

Barber, Benjamin R. (Fall 1992). "Going to the Community." *The Civic Arts Review* 5(4): 10-12.

Becker, Theodore L., and Richard A. Couto. (1996). *Teaching Democracy by Being Democratic*. New York: Praeger.

Boyte, Harry C. (1980). *The Backyard Revolution*. Philadelphia: Temple University Press.

Bozeman, Marci. (1996). *Service-Learning Guide for Faculty*. Richmond, VA: Learning in Community Settings (LINCS) Program, University of Richmond.

Burns, James MacGregor. (1978). *Leadership*. New York: Harper & Row.

Couto, Richard A. (1982). *Streams of Idealism and Health Care Innovations: An Assessment of Service-Learning and Community Mobilization*. New York: College Teachers Press.

————. (1987). "Participatory Research: Methodology and Critique." *The Clinical Sociology Review* 5:83-90.

————. (1993). "Service-Learning in Leadership Development." In *Rethinking Tradition: Integrating Service With Academic Studies on College Campuses*. Edited by Tamar Kupiec, pp. 67-71. Providence, RI: Campus Compact.

————, Marc E. Swatez, and Anne W. Perkins. (Winter 1994). "The Fruits of Our Labor: Experiential Education in a Leadership Curriculum." *National Society for Experiential Education Newsletter* 21(2): 7ff.

Couto, Richard A., and Anne Shepherd. (Winter 1995). "A Conversation With Paulo Freire." *National Society for Experiential Education Newsletter*, 2ff.

Freire, Paulo. (1970). *Pedagogy of the Oppressed*. New York: Continuum.

Levine, Arthur. (1980). *When Dreams and Heroes Died*. San Francisco: Jossey-Bass.

Park, Peter. (Winter 1992). "The Discovery of Participatory Research as a New Scientific Paradigm: Personal and Intellectual Accounts." *The American Sociologist*, 29-42.

Schott, Cheryl. (1994). *COMPS: Community Problem Solving Seminar Handbook*. Richmond, VA: Learning in Community Settings (LINCS) Program, University of Richmond.

Afterword

by Benjamin R. Barber

This is a very practical book about a very controversial theory: education-based community service, or, more simply, service-learning. The service-learning movement is now nearly a decade old and has moved well beyond abstract debates into the world of higher education curricula and civic pedagogy. President Reagan's Points of Light program and President Bush's Commission on National and Community Service have metamorphosized into President Clinton's Corporation for National Service, which, despite political controversy, has put tens of thousands of AmeriCorps volunteers into the field and given the idea of national service a popular currency that it has not had since the early days of the Peace Corps — or perhaps, some would say, since the heady years of the WPA during the New Deal.

Two Questions

As the contributions to this volume suggest, the question is no longer "Is service-learning a viable curricular strategy?" but "How can we make service-learning work? How various are its ways? What are the challenges of institutionalizing it in a curriculum?" The answers that emerge here are these: Its ways are many, its strategies various, its justifications multiple, but — and this is perhaps the crucial point — it does work. At institutions as different as Stanford, Providence College, the University of Minnesota, Hobart and William Smith Colleges, the University of Richmond, and Rutgers University, service-learning is no longer just a provocative idea: It has become an institutionalized reality.

Yet beyond the concrete challenges of a viable practice, two fundamental questions remain open — no more settled perhaps today than they were a decade ago when they were first systematically raised: What is service-learning in its essence, voluntarism or citizenship? And, if it is about citizenship, can it really make better citizens? The first question concerns the aims of service-learning, and raises the kinds of questions that Harry Boyte and James Farr, Meta Mendel-Reyes, and Richard Couto raise in their essays: Is service-learning about voluntarism, character building, and philanthropy, or is it about citizenship, social responsibility, and politics in the broadest sense? The second question asks whether service-learning actually makes

©1997 Benjamin R. Barber

good on its promise and enhances civic behavior and civic affect in concrete and measurable ways. Here, there are some remarkably promising results from an evaluation instrument that has been developed at the Walt Whitman Center for the Culture and Politics of Democracy, at Rutgers University. As a kind of afterword to this splendid volume of essays on the subject, let me comment briefly on the political question, and then turn to the results of the Measuring Citizenship project.

Social Work Voluntarism or Citizen Education?

In a 1996 op ed essay in *The New York Times,* Scott G. Bullock charges President Clinton with "distorting the concept of volunteering" by calling for mandatory high school community service.[1] Like many other critics, Bullock thereby commits himself to the view that service is about volunteering and about building altruistic character rather than about fostering civic identity and cultivating a sense of the relationship between rights and responsibilities. This dispute is of more than academic interest precisely because it has powerful academic entailments. If service-learning is about *voluntary* service, it does not belong in the curriculum, should not be mandatory, and, indeed, when it is mandatory may violate the Constitution. If service-learning is about *learning,* however, then it needs to be directly folded into curricula, it can be made mandatory just as English or biology can be made mandatory (for pedagogical, not social welfare reasons), and it no more violates the Constitution than does a requirement for freshman math or swimming.

What the essays here affirm is that service-learning works best when it is viewed as service *education;* when schools and universities are taken as pedagogical rather than social welfare institutions that include service because it offers an important experiment in experiential education. Understood in this fashion, it makes little sense to evaluate service-learning by the number of homeless meals service-givers offer or the number of park cleanups they participate in. For young service-givers cannot one by one remedy the social problems that have been created over decades by the failings of social policy or the inequities of entrenched social structures. To expect them to do so is to invite burnout and cynicism among those serving and to transfer to individuals the responsibilities of communities — of local, state, and federal governments.

Service education is not tantamount to the claim that service is education, but represents the belief that service *plus* education can help create contributing, responsible citizens. This is a task schools and colleges can be expected to undertake, for it reflects nothing more than a recognition of and recommitment to the traditional ideal of education as preparation of young people for civic life in a free society. There is no school or college mission statement I have seen from the 18th or 19th century that does not include a direct appeal to the need to educate men and women for citizenship. Service-learning is best understood, and the challenges to it best met, when it is seen in this perspective.

Thomas Jefferson celebrated his founding of the University of Virginia above his presidency (the former but not the latter is inscribed on his tombstone) because he believed that American democracy could only work when citizens were educated in public virtue and social responsibility. From Benjamin Rush to John Dewey, democrats have insisted that without formal attention to what Alexis de Tocqueville had called that "most arduous" of all apprenticeships, the apprenticeship of liberty, schools would fail to do their job and democracy would fail to secure the responsible citizens it needs to flourish.

Can Service-Learning Make Better Citizens?

The second critical question is whether service education can actually enhance the qualities and capacities we associate with responsible citizenship. If we argue that it is the *educational* mission of service education that is to count, then we need to be able to demonstrate some concrete pedagogical payoff that can be measured across curricula and programs.[2] To develop such a measure is exactly the purpose of a three-year norming study of the impact of education- and noneducation-based community volunteer work on civic skills, activities, and beliefs currently being undertaken by the Whitman Center at Rutgers, with support from the Surdna, the Markle, and the Ford foundations.[3]

One can view community service programs as requiring three sorts of evaluation: an assessment of the program's impact on the community itself, an assessment of its administrative efficiency, and an assessment of the impact of service on volunteers and service workers. It is this third and, for citizenship, crucial evaluation need that the Measuring Citizenship project addresses. The project has developed a test that allows us to understand basic components of citizenship and civic activity, while striving for sensitivity to cultural differences.[4] The resulting instrument measures important civic skills, activities, and beliefs — and differs from ordinary citizenship tests by asking *why* respondents answer key questions as they do. Over the past two years, the project expanded to a national norming study, testing volunteers and nonvolunteers at 19 high school, college, and nonprofit community service programs at a total of 23 sites (including a group of historically black colleges developing new and innovative service-learning programs), allowing for a comparative evaluation of many different kinds of service-learning programs as well as for a control (the nonvolunteers).[5] The study has already developed interim findings based on data from nearly 1,700 pretests and posttests from 12 college, high school, and nonprofit volunteer and control groups at 14 different sites.

These preliminary findings not only demonstrate that service education can have a measurable effect on citizenship but challenge the implications (if not the actual data) of recent press reports about politically apathetic and uninformed college students. The long-term University of California at Los Angeles survey that annually draws an increasingly dismal portrait of the civic knowledge and attitudes of college freshmen is, by the measure of the Whitman Center test, misleading with respect to overall student civic involvement and civic capacities. While "typical" freshmen may enter college as politically inactive and underinformed citizens, they are also entering academic institutions where student activism, including service-learning, is growing rapidly. At Rutgers in 1995-96, some 2,000 students performed community service work through 68 service-learning courses, under the Citizenship and Service Education Program. Nationally, service-learning programs connect student volunteers to community needs at more than 600 campuses.

The Whitman Center results provide evidence that students who engage in service-learning show a measurable, statistically significant increase in their civic capacities, most notably in two areas: in estimating their leadership skills and in racial tolerance. Furthermore, those participants who are predominantly college educated and working through the full-time, 10-month, nonprofit Public Allies program reported statistically significant decreases in their alienation from government, and statistically significant increases on a voting-participation scale and on a scale measuring their sense of civic obligation. Public Allies is partly funded through AmeriCorps, President Clinton's national service program, and engages young people in an intense, year-round program of service that features an emphasis on ongoing reflection and education.

The Measuring Citizenship test itself uses a dozen scales that focus on tolerance, leadership and issue activity, voting and other forms of civic participation, civic obligation, civic efficacy, and civic leadership skills. The most dramatic results have come from the scales measuring civic leadership, where the percentage of student volunteers scoring "high" increased from 27 percent on the pretest to 43 percent on the posttest, part of an overall change that was highly significant statistically. In comparison, the percentage of student nonvolunteers (a control group) scoring "high" on this scale was 28 percent on the pretest and 31 percent on the posttest, a change that was not statistically significant. Moreover, improvements from pretest to posttest in the college volunteer group's average (mean) score were statistically significant on 20 of 23 civic skill items, while changes in the college nonvolunteer group's mean scores were significant on only two items and in a negative direction. As part of the project's citizenship test, participants were asked twice, before and at the end of their service, to compare their performance on a list of 23 civic skills and activities with those of most people. This list includes important civic capacities, such as the sense of effectiveness in achieving goals, the ability to speak in public, listening skills, knowing where to find information, knowing whom to contact in order to get things done, and the ability to compromise.

The project's preliminary analysis also shows that the college volunteer group recorded a statistically significant increase on a scale measuring racial tolerance, suggesting that service has a positive impact on the willingness of young people to tolerate those with views on race radically different from their own. The percentage of college volunteers scoring "high" in racial tolerance increased from 19 percent on the pretest to 30 percent on the posttest, while the percentage of college nonvolunteers in the "high" category went from 22 percent to 26 percent; the changes from pretest to posttest in nonvolunteers percentages on this scale were not statistically significant.

For this question, test participants were asked whether they thought someone with extreme racial views should or should not be allowed to speak at a local library, teach at a local high school, teach at a nearby university or college, host a weekly TV cable access show about the cause, run for local office, and organize demonstrations to change federal policy. Overall, the college volunteer group began service as less racially tolerant than the nonvolunteer group, but ended service with a statistically significant improvement on the racial tolerance scale, and with an average (mean) tolerance score close to that of the college nonvolunteer group.[6] [See tables on pp. 232-233.]

Without going into greater detail, and acknowledging that these findings are still preliminary, we can nonetheless conclude that there is significant evidence that points toward the success of service-learning in molding civic values and instilling civic attitudes and capacities. Moreover, there is some preliminary evidence that the impact increases with the intensity and duration of the service (the Public Allies results). More generally, test results corroborate liberal pedagogical assumptions about how we "learn" liberty and acquire the skills to exercise rights and responsibilities in a coherent and effective fashion. From Benjamin Rush to John Dewey, democratic theorists have insisted that citizenship depends on particular forms of civic education. The service education movement that this book describes and evaluates is but the latest installment in this long-term story of democracy's dependence on pedagogy. It is more than satisfying that empirical surveys are now confirming the theory behind the practice of service-learning:

Preliminary Data From the Measuring Citizenship Test

Civic Leadership Skills

College Volunteers			
	Skill Level		
	Low	Medium	High
Pretest (N=379)	5%	68%	27%
Posttest (N=227)	2%	55%	43%

The phi correlation for this table is statistically significant at the .00005 level.
Pretest mean = 62.70;   Posttest mean = 67.18
The F test for group mean variance is statistically significant at the .0001 level.

College Non-Volunteers			
	Skill Level		
	Low	Medium	High
Pretest (N=310)	5%	67%	28%
Posttest (N=187)	5%	64%	31%

The phi coefficient is not statistically significant for this cross tabulation.
Pretest mean = 63.62;   Posttest mean = 63.53
The F test for group mean variance is not statistically significant.

Racial Tolerance

College Volunteers			
	Tolerance Level		
	Low	Medium	High
Pretest (N=389)	47%	34%	19%
Posttest (N=230)	38%	30%	30%

The phi coefficient is statistically significant at the .05 level for this cross tabulation.
Pretest mean = 9.71;   Posttest mean = 9.25
The F test for group mean variance is statistically significant at the .05 level.
(Because of test formatting, a lower mean indicates higher tolerance.)

College Non-Volunteers			
	Tolerance Level		
	Low	Medium	High
Pretest (N=326)	34%	43%	22%
Posttest (N=197)	29%	45%	26%

The phi coefficient is not statistically significant for this cross tabulation.
Pretest mean = 9.29;   Posttest mean = 9.12
The F test for group mean variance is not statistically significant.
(Because of test formatting, a lower mean indicates higher tolerance.)

Service-learning not only intends to enhance civility in the root sense, it succeeds in doing so!

In an America that sometimes seems to have lost its democratic moorings, where alienation, cynicism, and incivility have become the norm in a politics of resentment and disgust that does more to repel than to involve citizens, the existence of the service-learning movement and the apparent success of its pedagogy are most welcome. Not only does it suggest that, for all our problems, our democracy remains viable: It also suggests that those who have devoted scholarly and teaching time to the development of education-based service programs of the kinds described and assessed in this volume are making a major contribution to the securing of a free American society into the next millennium.

Notes

1. President Clinton made his plea for mandatory service at the May 1996 Penn State graduation ceremony. Bullock responded with "Public Service, or Else," *The New York Times,* May 16, 1996.

2. For a full discussion of this philosophy, see Benjamin R. Barber, *An Aristocracy of Everyone* (New York: Oxford University Press, 1993).

3. A project team headed I headed in my capacity as director of the Whitman Center has developed and appraised several versions of the test. Other development team members include Jeffrey Smith, a nationally known expert on educational testing and acting associate dean of the Graduate School of Education; Janice Ballou, director of the Eagleton Center for Public Interest Polling; Robert Higgins, current project director; John Dedrick, former project director and a program officer at the Kettering Foundation; and Kim Downing, research faculty at the University of Cincinnati School of Policy Research.

4. The project commenced with conferences in the fall of 1992 and 1993 at which the development team, other scholars, community activists, and representatives from foundations and government agencies discussed the possibilities, limits, and means of measuring citizenship. The development team conducted initial rounds of testing, revision, and appraisal in 1993 and 1994 through the Rutgers University Citizenship and Service Education program (RU/CASE).

5. The norming portion of our study confirms that the test questions and scales produce the expected differences in results for groups with different educational levels and lengths of service. Specifically, while we see improvements in overall test results for all volunteers, high school students show less improvement than do college students, and volunteers in Public Allies full-time, year-long, nonprofit program show the largest overall improvement.

6. A much smaller group of participants in Public Allies, a full-time, 10-month, nonprofit program that is partly funded through AmeriCorps, recorded statistically significant decreases in their average (mean) alienation score on questions pertaining both

to the federal government and to local government. This is despite the fact that this volunteer group began the study more alienated from both levels of government than either the college volunteer group or the college nonvolunteer group. These results are especially noteworthy given high levels of public cynicism about government. Slightly older on average than the college-organized groups (23 years vs. 21), most (87%) of the Public Allies participants had some college education.

The Public Allies participants also showed statistically significant increases in their average (mean) voting participation and civic obligation scores. The voting participation scale asked about voting in national, local, and primary elections and about learning about candidates and understanding local referenda issues. The civic obligation scale asked participants to rate, on a scale of importance, 14 civic activities ranging from registering to vote and reporting for jury duty to donating blood and recycling.

Appendix
Annotated Bibliography

Barber, Benjamin R. (1992). *An Aristocracy of Everyone: The Politics of Education and the Future of America*. New York: Ballantine Books.

This book thoroughly examines the connections between education and democracy in the late-20th century in light of controversies over the "crisis" in education over what should be taught and how. After exploring issues concerning "the canon" and "multiculturalism" in higher education, the book concludes with a provocative proposal tying a revitalization of community service to the future of citizen education in America.

——————— , and Richard M. Battistoni, eds. (1993). *Education for Democracy: Citizenship, Community, Service*. Dubuque, IA: Kendall/Hunt.

This edited volume of more than 60 essays, short stories, poems, and speeches provides an interdisciplinary text for courses connecting community service with the curriculum. While its emphasis is on the connection between service and democratic citizenship, therefore making it ideally suited to service-learning courses in political science, the text has been used in service-learning courses in other disciplines.

——————— . (June 1993). "A Season of Service: Introducing Service-Learning Into the Liberal Arts Curriculum," *PS: Political Science & Politics* 16(2): 235-240, 262.

This essay explores the central questions posed to any faculty member wishing to develop service-learning courses or programs, ranging from whether service should be mandatory or voluntary to whether or not faculty ought to participate in community service alongside students, giving arguments on all sides of each question in light of the civic mission of a liberal arts curriculum.

Becker, Theodore L., and Richard A. Couto, eds. (1996). *Teaching Democracy by Being Democratic*. New York: Praeger.

This edited volume focuses on how to "teach democracy" in an experiential and egalitarian fashion. After an introduction of the theoretical and analytical framework of democracy and democratic pedagogy, six chapters written by prominent political scientists explore issues such as structuring a democratic classroom; democratic practices that empower students; problem solving and community service that make the classroom a laboratory for democracy; and university-based programs of democratic alternatives that serve the community.

Boyte, Harry C., and Nancy N. Kari. (1996). *Building America: The Democratic Promise of Public Work*. Philadelphia: Temple University Press.

Using a variety of case studies, including the Civilian Conservation Corps, as the foundation, Boyte and Kari explore the concept of "public work" in democratic theory and practice, in ways that have deep implications for community service and service-learning.

Lappé, Frances Moore, and Paul Martin DuBois. (1994). *The Quickening of America: Rebuilding Our Nation, Remaking Our Lives*. San Francisco: Jossey-Bass.

A resource book for those interested in revitalizing democratic theory and practice in America. The authors draw on a number of examples at the local level where everyday citizens have acted in their communities to empower people and contribute to a contemporary understanding of democracy and public life. Includes a listing of resources and organizations for "building a living democracy."

Lempert, David. (1995). *Escape From the Ivory Tower: Student Adventures in Democratic Experiential Education*. San Francisco: Jossey-Bass.

The author presents a model of democratic experiential education based on his experiences as both a student and a teacher in various settings, from American urban communities to Ecuador. Lempert has worked with students from several elite American universities in a variety of experiential projects. He draws from this experience a new vision of democratic education that goes "beyond internships, service-learning, independent study, and seminars."

Markus, Gregory B., Jeffrey P.F. Howard, and David C. King. (1993). "Integrating Community Service With Classroom Instruction Enhances Learning: Results From an Experiment," *Educational Evaluation and Policy Analysis* 15:410-419.

Using a quasi-experimental design, the authors present the results from an experiment with different sections of an introductory American government class, where some students performed community service and others did not. The questions raised and answered range from the contribution of community service to knowledge of American politics to changes in attitudes about citizenship and civic responsibilities.

Putnam, Robert D. (January 1995). "Bowling Alone: America's Declining Social Capital," *Journal of Democracy* 9:65-78.

A now legendary article that claims to document a decline in civic engagement among Americans. Putnam reviews statistics on people's participation in a wide variety of organizations, from bowling leagues to PTAs, and finds a decline in participation over time. The article has generated substantial discussion and substantial critiques. A variety of excellent follow-on articles have appeared in *The American Prospect*.

Waldman, Steven. (1995). *The Bill: How the Adventures of Clinton's National Service Bill Reveal What Is Corrupt, Comic, Cynical — and Noble — About Washington*. New York: Viking.

Another version of "how a bill becomes a law" — this time using the AmeriCorps legislation as the case study. The book will introduce students to how Congress operates and the politics of the legislative process while providing solid background on the debate on national service.

Appendix

Additional Service-Learning Courses in Political Science

Bates College
Internships in Community Service seeks to provide students with experiential learning opportunities through placements in a variety of community service agencies. Students combine community service with readings and reflection on (1) the purpose, satisfactions, hazards, and learning potential of community service and (2) the populations served (e.g., the homeless, the poor more generally, battered women). Much of the course takes place in the community service agency. But, throughout the short term, students will meet as a group with the instructor. The course is designed to encourage maximum student participation, so that all learn from one another's experience.

Contact: Mark Kessler, Associate Professor and Chair, Department of Political Science, Bates College, 45 Campus Avenue, Lewiston, ME 04240

Central College
Citizen Politics examines the forms of citizen participation in politics, including such topics as political parties, interest groups, public opinion, voting, mass demonstrations, violence, and revolution. This class on how to be a good citizen is an ideal place to adopt a service-learning approach. Students are required to spend at least 15 hours during the semester working for a nonprofit group, political party, or interest group. Daily journals document service experience and are compiled in a final composite report on the entire service experience.

Contact: Don Racheter, Professor of Political Science, Central College, 812 University, Pella, IA 50219

College of the Atlantic
In *Community Decision Making on Mount Desert Island, Maine,* students are offered an introduction to current issues facing Mount Desert Island, home to Acadia National Park and destination for up to five million seasonal visitors annually. The course provides an overview of how local governments function, the interface between local towns and state government, and how citizens are involved. Using interviews with town officials and volunteers, stories from the local newspapers, and the experience of the instructors, students construct a list of current issues, gather background, and select one or more for development of an "issue book," after the model developed by the National Issues Forum and the Study Circle

Center, based on research by Daniel Yankelovich. Student issue books and community meetings have been used to help the local communities understand and move toward public judgment on issues such as affordable housing, protection of fresh drinking water supplies, and conflicts among user groups of Acadia National Park's carriage roads.

Contacts: Ron Beard, Extension Educator, University of Maine, and Town Councilor, Bar Harbor; and Jill Goldthwait, Maine State Senator, College of the Atlantic, 105 Eden Street, Bar Harbor, ME 04609, rbeard@umce.umext.maine.edu

College of Charleston

The Civic Community: Problems, Policy, and Practice is designed as an exploration of our conceptions of community, what it means to be a part of a community, and what we as individuals and groups are capable of contributing to our communities. It seeks to put what we discuss and explore into practice by identifying needs inherent in our communities, following these efforts up with action outside the classroom to address those needs, and evaluating those efforts in a way that enhances our intellectual exploration. The ultimate goal of this course is to encourage discussion of what constitutes responsible citizenship in communities and to promote the skills and competencies that form the basis for an informed, active citizenry. The course requires two to three hours of community service per week. Each student selects a service site with the assistance of course instructors.

Contacts: Lynne Ford and John Creed, Department of Political Science, College of Charleston, 114 Wentworth Street, Charleston, SC 29424, FORDL@cofc.edu or CREEDJ@cofc.edu

Miami-Dade Community College

The Social Environment, an introductory general-education course, is designed to present the political, geographic, sociological, economic, and historical factors that shape the contemporary local, national, and international social environment in which students intend to learn, earn, contribute, and co-benefit as individuals, family members, career seekers, and civic persons. A combination of academic, experiential, and service-learning strategies are implemented to engage the multiple student learning styles with varied faculty teaching styles for content comprehension, conceptual applications, and related technical mastery of principal materials presented through lectures, audiovisual programs, in-class simulations, service-learning, substantive and reflective writing, and oral communication pertinent to personal, professional, and citizen applications and appreciation of course outcomes. Students are encouraged and facilitated to take advantage of the "competitive edge" offered by Miami, the multicultural microcosm of the world. Service-learning projects of 40 to 60 hours' duration are optional for up to one-third of the final grade.

Contact: Michael J. Lonaghan, Chairperson, History/Political Science Department, Miami-Dade Community College, North Campus, 11380 NW 27 Avenue, Miami, FL 33167

Occidental College

Diplomacy and World Affairs 390, Proseminar in International Relations, is required of sophomore or junior majors or minors. It requires a service-learning component of some 20 hours in cooperation with area high schools and/or the Pasadena/Foothills chapter of the United Nations Association (UNA). Recent topics have been (1) cooperation with the UNA in organizing and implementing the Global Policy Project and International Women's Day — efforts to secure greater participation of underrepresented urban community groups in multicultural Los Angeles and the San Gabriel Valley — and preparation of background material and short presentations of issues by the students themselves in project meetings; and (2) working with teachers and students in local high schools to discuss international issues and to encourage participation in the annual UNA high school essay contest. The former has been intrinsically easier to organize because of the structure and continuing activities of the UNA, but the latter is especially valuable because it brings the ivory tower of the selective liberal arts college into direct and personal interaction with the community reality of urban Los Angeles/Pasadena and because the college students may act as role models and achievement examples for high school students.

Contact: Brice Harris, History Department, Occidental College, Los Angeles, CA 90041, *bharris@cheshire.oxy.edu*

Pitzer College

PS112: Labor Internship provides an intensive, workshop-based orientation in the first three weeks of the semester, followed by a 13-week internship with a labor union or labor advocacy group. The internship may have an organizing focus or a research focus, or it may involve working on video or Internet projects with the host organization. The pedagogy underpinning the course is that of service-learning: education through active participation. In the first part of the course, students are expected to acquire three kinds of knowledge: (1) A basic, introductory knowledge of "labor studies": an interdisciplinary field covering history, law, politics, economics, video, art, and gender and ethnic studies. This will be accomplished via a series of seminars/workshops. (2) Hands-on campaigning and organizing skills: principles of organizing, role of the organizer, one-on-one communication, tactics, and strategy. This is accomplished through a state-of-the-art two-day training provided by the AFL-CIO Organizing Institute. This class is the first ever to have a dedicated training by AFL-CIO professionals. (3) Applied research and communication skills: skills such as interviewing, searching public records, Lexis-Nexis, email, webpage construction, video-conferences, etc. These skills are taught in a series of tutorials. Internships are at local and greater-Los Angeles sites. Students are required to be in the field for the equivalent of one full day per week. Each intern has a designated mentor in the host organization.

Contact: Nigel Boyle, Assistant Professor of Political Studies, Pitzer College, Claremont, CA 91711, *NBOYLE@bernard.PITZER.EDU,* webpage: *www.pitzer.edu/~nboyle/Political_Studies_112/*

Appendix

Contributors to This Volume

Benjamin R. Barber is the Whitman Professor of Political Science and director of the Walt Whitman Center for the Culture and Politics of Democracy at Rutgers University.

Richard M. Battistoni is currently professor of political science at Providence College, where he also directs the Feinstein Institute for Public Service.

Harry C. Boyte is codirector of the Center for Democracy and Citizenship at the Humphrey Institute for Public Affairs at the University of Minnesota.

Richard A. Couto is professor of leadership studies at the Jepson School of the University of Richmond.

Cynthia R. Daniels is associate professor of political science at Rutgers University.

Jean Bethke Elshtain is the Laura Spelman Rockefeller Professor of Ethics at the University of Chicago.

James Farr is professor of political science at the University of Minnesota, where he also works with the Center for Democracy and Citizenship.

Mona Field is currently associate professor of political science and sociology at Glendale Community College (CA).

Stephen Frantzich is professor of political science at the U.S. Naval Academy.

Richard Guarasci was recently named provost and professor of political science at Wagner College. Previously, he was dean of Hobart College at Hobart and William Smith Colleges.

Milton Heumann is professor of political science at Rutgers University.

William E. Hudson is professor of political science at Providence College.

Sheilah Mann serves as director of education programs at the American Political Science Association.

Gregory B. Markus is professor of political science and research scientist at the Center for Political Studies at the University of Michigan.

Meta Mendel-Reyes is currently assistant professor of political science, and the director of the Democracy Project, at Swarthmore College.

Daniel J. Palazzolo is currently associate professor of political science at the University of Richmond.

Ed Schwerin is associate professor of political science at Florida Atlantic University.

Bill Swinford is assistant professor of political science at the University of Richmond.

Robert H. Trudeau is professor of political science at Providence College.

Karen D. Zivi is a Ph.D. candidate in political science at Rutgers University. Her dissertation explores the intersection of liberal political theory and feminist practice in AIDS policy debates.

Edward Zlotkowski is professor of English at Bentley College. Founding director of the Bentley Service-Learning Project, he has published and spoken on a wide variety of service-learning topics. Currently, he is also a senior associate at the American Association for Higher Education.

About AAHE's Series on Service-Learning in the Disciplines

Consisting of 18 monographs to be released over 1997-98, the Series goes beyond simple "how to" to provide a rigorous intellectual forum. Each volume in the Series details why and how service-learning can be implemented within a specific discipline. *Theoretical essays* illuminate issues of general importance to educators interested in using a service-learning pedagogy. *Pedagogical essays* discuss the design, implementation, conceptual content, outcomes, advantages, and disadvantages of specific service-learning programs, courses, and projects. All essays are authored by scholars in the discipline for educators in the discipline.

Representative of a wide range of individual interests and approaches, the Series provides substantive discussions supported by research, course models in a rich conceptual context, annotated bibliographies, and program descriptions.

See the order form on the reverse for the list of disciplines covered in the Series, pricing, and ordering information.